Retaking the Philippines

RETAKING
THE
PHILIPPINES

America's Return to
Corregidor and Bataan,
October 1944–March 1945

William B. Breuer

ST. MARTIN'S PRESS   *NEW YORK*

Dedicated to
John Duncan Bulkeley
Rear Admiral, United States Navy,
a living legend in American
history. Had it not been for
his breaking through the
Corregidor blockade in PT-41 to carry
out General MacArthur,
the epic events in these pages
might never have happened.

Intrinsically, Corregidor is but a barren, war-worn rock, hallowed, as so many places, by death and disaster. Yet it symbolizes within itself that priceless, deathless thing, the honor of a nation. Until we lift our flag from its dust, *we stand unredeemed before mankind.*

Until we claim again the ghastly remnants of its last gaunt garrison, we can but stand humble supplicants before Almighty God. There lies our Holy Grail.

—General Douglas MacArthur
Australia, 1942

The Philippines

Contents

Maps

Acknowledgments

Creating this book would have been impossible without the dedicated assistance of scores of persons. Appreciation is expressed to those who took time from heavy schedules to read and critique drafts of this work: Brigadier General George M. Jones (Ret.), Lieutenant General John J. Tolson III (Ret.), Major General William E. Blake (Ret.), and Colonel Robert M. Atkins (Ret.), the Corregidor operation chapters; Major General George N. Pearson (Ret.), Colonel Henry A. Burgess (Ret.), and Colonel Kenneth Murphy (Ret.), the chapters concerning operations around Manila Bay and also the Japanese paratroop drop on the American airfields on Leyte; and Rear Admiral John Harllee (Ret.), naval operations and battles.

Thanks is also given to Dr. John Slonaker of the U.S. Army Military History Institute and to Rear Admiral John D. H. Kane, Jr., U.S. Navy Historical Foundation, and their staffs for their invaluable research assistance. Likewise to Mrs. Linda P. Donnelly, of Woodbridge, Virginia, for data and other information regarding the 24th Infantry Division battalion commanded in the Corregidor operation by her late father, Colonel Edward Postlethwait. Appreciation is expressed to former Red

Cross Field Director Harold Templeman for permission (granted by 503rd Parachute Regiment Association officers) to draw on his booklet, *Back to Corregidor*. And to Lieutenant General Edward M. Flanagan (Ret.).

Adding immeasurably to the vitality of this book are information, drawings, and other materials furnished by dedicated and highly knowledgeable history buffs Lou Varrone, Harry Pearlmutter, Laurence Maxton, and Keith Rose. Going above and beyond the call of duty in helping the author track down participants in the Philippines epic were Dr. Ralph Llewellyn, Major Rocco Narcise (Ret.), Harry Bailey, and Richard Hoyt, among others.

The author was fortunate to have working with him in the production of this book Senior Editor Jared Kieling and Assistant Editor Shari Jee, and their associates at St. Martin's Press.

—William B. Breuer
Willowbrook, Illinois
January 1986

Prologue

Seated at his desk in Tokyo, Japanese Premier Hideki Tojo sifted through reports from commanders of the rampaging Imperial Army. It was January 3, 1942. Tojo, the supreme warlord, was elated. Not only were his victorious armies fanning out over vast portions of the Pacific, scoring one stunning triumph after another, but the entire force of Americans and Filipinos defending the island of Luzon in the Philippine chain was trapped on the tiny peninsula of Bataan.

Nicknamed "The Razor," Tojo was barely five feet four inches tall. His unkempt mustache and round, oversized horn-rimmed glasses gave him an owlish appearance. For ten years General Tojo, the strong man of the army, had been the principal architect of a strategic master plan designed to unleash a devastating series of invasions throughout the Pacific.

A man of enormous ambition, drive, and dedication, Tojo had gained a reputation in the Imperial Army as a brilliant organizer and administrator, a skilled and daring strategist. He had a particular hatred for the United States. His master plan had called for launching the blitzkrieg with a bold sneak attack aimed at destroying or severely crippling the American fleet at Pearl Harbor.

The commander of the Imperial Navy, Admiral Isoroku Yamamoto, had been outspokenly opposed to going to war with the United States. "America is militarily weak, but is a sleeping giant," Yamamoto had argued. Tojo had quickly silenced the navy chief and other hesitant military officers and statesmen, and on Sunday, December 7, 1941, swarms of Japanese naval carrier planes had virtually destroyed the United States fleet at Pearl Harbor and brought an ill-prepared America into global conflict.

Three days later, on December 10, Japanese troops had stormed ashore on Luzon, the largest and most important island in the Philippine chain, five thousand miles west of Hawaii. Twin-engined Mitsubishi bombers had destroyed nearly half of America's warplanes in the Philippines in a one-hour attack on Clark Field near Manila. At the same time, Japanese heavy bombers had wiped out the Cavite Navy Yard, the United States fleet's only Asian base.

In the Philippines, General Douglas MacArthur's resources were meager. His force of 15,000 American and 64,000 Filipino soldiers was poorly equipped and inadequately armed; most of the Filipinos were inadequately trained. MacArthur's men fought desperately, but out-moded weapons refused to fire, equipment wouldn't work, four out of five grenades failed to explode, and two-thirds of the mortar shells were duds. MacArthur's exhausted men were pushed back steadily toward Bataan, a desolate peninsula that formed the western shore of Manila Bay. Bataan was a montage of tangled jungles and rocky hills, a green wilderness infested by crocodiles, snakes, and huge pythons.

All the while, MacArthur had been sending Washington frantic calls for help from Corregidor, a tiny fortress island perched in the mouth of Manila Bay two miles off Bataan. "Just three airplanes so I can see," he pleaded. "You can't fight them if you can't see them."[1]

Army Chief of Staff General George Marshall cabled MacArthur: "A stream of four-engine bombers is en route. . . . Another stream of similar bombers started today from Hawaii. . . . Two bomber groups leave next week."[2] And President Franklin D. Roosevelt signaled Philippine President Manuel L. Quezon: "I can assure you that every vessel available is bearing the strength that will eventually crush the enemy and liberate your native land."[3]

Buoyed by the encouraging words from Washington, MacArthur issued a statement on January 15 and ordered company commanders to read it to all troops on Bataan: "Help is on the way from the United States. Thousands of troops and hundreds of airplanes are being dispatched...." Spirits soared among the men, who now called themselves the "Battling Bastards of Bataan." But not a single American soldier, airplane, or ship ever reached the beleaguered Philippines.

Unknown to MacArthur, Roosevelt and his high command had already decided to give first priority to the defeat of Nazi Germany, after which America's full strength would be sent against the Japanese. Based on a recommendation by Brigadier General Dwight D. Eisenhower, a planner in the War Department, an agonizing decision had been reached. The force trapped on Bataan and Corregidor would be written off, and Australia, twenty-five hundred miles to the south, would be developed as a base for assembling troops and aircraft to eventually strike back at the Japanese. MacArthur, who had taken a vow to die with his men on Corregidor, received a cable from Roosevelt on February 23 ordering him to Australia to "assume command of all U.S. troops [there]."

MacArthur was plunged into gloom. He told staff officers that he had been placed on the horns of a dilemma. If he disobeyed Roosevelt's direct order—an option he was considering—he could be court-martialed. If he followed the order, he would be deserting his men. He saw only one way out of his predicament: he would resign his commission and volunteer to fight on Bataan as a private. (That night he would dictate his resignation, but confidants would prevail on him not to submit it to Washington.)

MacArthur's staff pleaded for MacArthur to go to Australia, pointing out that Roosevelt's order was the best hope for salvaging the situation in the Philippines. Clearly, they stressed, MacArthur was being sent to Australia to lead an army back to the Philippines.

Still the general could not bring himself to withdraw. On March 6 he received a prodding from Roosevelt: "The situation in Australia indicates desirability of your early arrival there." Three days later MacArthur reached an anguished decision: he would shift his command post to Australia, take charge of the army there, and return quickly to the Philippines—hopefully by July 1 and in time to rescue the Battling Bastards of Bataan.

Four decrepit PT boats, barely running after numerous transfusions of cannibalized parts, would carry MacArthur and his party on the first six-hundred-mile leg to the large, southernmost island of Mindanao. The seventy-eight-foot-long boats, operating in total blackness through largely uncharted waters, would have to penetrate a Japanese naval and air blockade and slip past enemy-held islands to reach their destination, where aircraft dispatched from Australia were to pick up their special cargo. Few expected MacArthur and his escorts to survive the dash. On Corregidor, Navy officers were predicting that MacArthur faced five-to-one odds—at best—of reaching Mindanao.

The day after MacArthur made his decision to leave, he summoned Major General Jonathan M. "Skinny" Wainwright from Bataan and told him the news. Wainwright, a gaunt, leathery old cavalryman, would be placed in command on Luzon. As Wainwright prepared to depart, MacArthur put an arm around his old friend's shoulder and, in a voice choked with emotion, said, "If I get through to Australia, you know I'll come back as soon as I can with as much as I can."

There were a few moments of silence. Off toward Bataan could be heard the muffled thunder of guns. Wainwright replied softly, "You'll get through, Douglas."

MacArthur quickly added, "And *back!*"[4]

Two days later, at dusk, MacArthur, his wife Jean and four-year-old son Arthur, fourteen other generals, and a key sergeant climbed aboard Navy Lieutenant John D. "Buck" Bulkeley's four battered PT boats and headed for Mindanao.

The escapees and crewmen were literally sitting on powder kegs. Every boat had on its deck twenty steel drums, each filled with fifty gallons of high-octane gasoline. A single bullet could turn the little craft into fireballs. There were many close calls. Several times the silhouettes of Japanese warships were seen on the horizon. The engine of one PT boat conked out, and its passengers had to crowd into the remaining three.[5] On reaching Mindanao, the group had to wait at Del Monte airfield for three tense days as Japanese forces launched repeated attacks in an attempt to overrun the base.

Just as MacArthur landed at an Australian airfield near Darwin, he received the most shocking news of his career. The "army" that he was to lead in a swift return to rescue Wainwright and his troops did not exist. Counting Australians, there were only 32,000 Allied troops in the entire country, and most of them were noncombat soldiers. In addition, there were fewer than a hundred serviceable aircraft, and not a single tank in all of Australia. In a rare moment of despair, a grim-faced MacArthur muttered to an aide, "God have mercy on us!"[6]

Traveling by rail from Darwin to Melbourne, a trek of one thousand miles, General MacArthur paced the aisle of the decrepit, dusty, stiflingly hot and fly-infested wooden coach. His mounting fury was directed at "Washington," meaning President Roosevelt, who, the general was convinced, had betrayed him by implying that significant help was on the way to the Philippines. This had led MacArthur, in turn, to unknowingly deceive his beseiged men on Bataan and Corregidor. Never again would MacArthur trust Roosevelt.

Arriving at a Melbourne station, a cheering crowd of thousands buoyed the general's spirits. In a wrinkled, ribbonless, khaki bush jacket, he told the throng, "The President of the United States ordered me to break through Japanese lines . . . for the purpose, as I understand it, of organizing an offensive against Japan, a primary object of which is the relief of the Philippines. I came through and I shall return."

The last three words captivated the American public and electrified the hard-pressed people of the Philippines, burning into them an invincible determination to bitterly resist the Japanese invaders. "I shall return!" became the battlecry of the Filipinos. It would sustain them during the blackest hours and eventually become the motto of victory.

All the while, a bitter dispute had been raging in Washington between Army and Navy brass: Who would be the supreme commander in the Pacific? MacArthur, who had spent many years in the Pacific, seemed to many to be the logical choice and was supported for the post by most Army officers. But the admirals and their staffs had been feuding with MacArthur for years, and most of them hated him intensely. "Over my dead body will MacArthur be named," said an incensed Admiral Ernest J. King, the brusque Chief of Naval Operations.

King declared that the Pacific war would be largely a naval operation, so why should an Army officer be appointed to command it? King's candidate for commander of Pacific operations was the able and steady Admiral Chester L. Nimitz, an old friend. But Nimitz was junior in rank to MacArthur. It was not until April 18, 1942, more than four months after America went to war with Japan, that the bitter command controversy was resolved—by compromise.

Violating military doctrine, the U.S. Joint Chiefs of Staff—ground, sea, and air—created *two* theaters of operations. MacArthur, based in Australia, was appointed Supreme Commander of the Southwest Pacific Area, and Nimitz, whose headquarters were in Hawaii, five thousand miles east of the Philippines, was designated commander of the Pacific Ocean Area.

In the meantime, a bloody curtain was being lowered on the drama in the Philippines. Weakened by disease—mainly malaria, dysentery, beriberi, and scurvy—and suffering hunger, Wainwright's men were losing their capacity to resist. To supplement meager rations—less than a cup of rice daily per man—they ate mule, dog, cat, lizard, monkey, and iguana meat, and gnawed on roots, bark, and leaves. On April 10, knowing that his exhausted men were nearly out of food and ammunition, General Wainwright surrendered.

Corregidor's trapped garrison of 15,000 Americans, only 1,300 of whom were trained for combat, braced for the inevitable thunderclap. It struck on May 4, when Japanese artillery saturated the tiny island with 16,000 shells and an amphibious force stormed ashore. Heavy fighting ensued, but the American situation was hopeless. On May 6, a white flag was raised over the bastion known to Americans as "The Rock."

There began what came to be known in America as the "Death March." The captives, all of them in abominable physical condition, were taken from Mariveles on Bataan fifty-five miles to the railhead at San Fernando under inhumane conditions. The 76,000 prisoners were a pitiful lot. Their clothes hung on them like tattered rags. Many had no shoes; long bedraggled hair framed gaunt ashen faces. Some wore fixed grins—the ghastly, skeleton-like rictus of the dying. During the march, 2,300 Americans and from 8,000 to 10,000 Filipinos perished.

By the spring of 1942, Japan had conquered the Philippines, Singapore, Hong Kong, the Dutch East Indies, Malaya, Borneo, the Bismarck Islands, Siam, Sumatra, the Gilberts, the Celebes, Timor, Wake, Guam, most of the Solomons, and half of New Guinea. Japanese bombers had pulverized the key Australian port of Darwin, and citizens of Brisbane, Melbourne, and Sydney feared an imminent invasion. The Japanese empire now radiated for five thousands miles from Tokyo in nearly every direction, and Emperor Hirohito, the diminutive and mild-mannered father of six, reigned over one-seventh of the globe.

In Washington, gloom contended with chaos. Generals and admirals were stunned by the power, speed, and skill of the Japanese advance, and reached a grim conclusion: with full mobilization of manpower and resources, and at a frightful cost in casualties, it would require at least ten years to reconquer the Pacific.

When two partially trained U.S. divisions reached Australia in June 1942, filling in what had been a paper force, General MacArthur vowed to take the offensive. On July 20, only four months after his hair-raising escape from Corregidor, he moved his headquarters fifteen hundred miles forward to Port Moresby, New Guinea.

Despite meager manpower and resources, General MacArthur launched what he called a "hit-'em-where-they-ain't" campaign of speed and surprise aimed at "leapfrogging" the enemy. During the next two years, in some of the most stunning campaigns in history, MacArthur conducted eighty-seven amphibious landings—all of them successful, and all of them stepping stones to the Philippines. By late July 1944, MacArthur's troops had landed on Vogelkop Peninsula, the northwestern tip of New Guinea. Bataan, Corregidor, and Manila, by Pacific distances, were just over the horizon.

Always Douglas MacArthur's thoughts had been on the Philippines. From there he could get his hands around the throat of the enemy and begin to throttle him; liberate seventeen million loyal Filipinos; restore tarnished American prestige in the Pacific; and avenge Bataan and Corregidor.

All the while MacArthur's American and Australian troops had been leapfrogging northward, United States Marines and Army infantry under Admiral Chester Nimitz had been slugging it out with the Japanese in a bloody, brutal, island-hopping campaign westward across the

Pacific. Supported mainly by U.S. Navy carrier-based aircraft and naval guns, Nimitz's troops conquered such previously unheard-of islands as Guadalcanal, Tulagi, Makin, Tarawa, Kwajalein, Eniwetok, and Saipan.

By July 1944, the Western Allies, having forged an iron ring around the Japanese Empire, were ready to screw it tight.

Retaking
the
Philippines

1
Confrontation With "Mr. Big"

General Douglas MacArthur's four-engined Flying Fortress, the *Bataan*, was winging through the clear blue Pacific skies, bound from Brisbane, Australia, to Hickham Field, Hawaii, twenty-six hours and four time zones away. It was July 25, 1944. Four-star General MacArthur, supreme Allied commander in the Southwest Pacific, had been in a foul mood during much of the lengthy flight, pacing the aisle and grumbling about the indignation being inflicted on him by the powers in Washington. "They" had forced him to leave his command headquarters, where he was preparing the assault on the Philippines, to fly to Honolulu for "a political picture-taking session."[1] Never before in his long career had anyone succeeded in "dragooning" him away from his command in wartime, the sixty-four-year-old MacArthur fumed. Even when wounded and gassed in World War I, he had remained with his division.

The main target of his wrath was the commander-in-chief himself, President Franklin D. Roosevelt, whom MacArthur felt had betrayed him and his men on Bataan more than two years before, by writing off the Philippines and concentrating the nation's military might on the

European theater instead. Only five days earlier, on July 20, 1944, the Democratic convention in Chicago had nominated Roosevelt for an unprecedented fourth term. The next day the president had left San Diego aboard the new heavy cruiser *Baltimore* to sail to Honolulu for a meeting with his two commanders in the Pacific, MacArthur and Admiral Chester Nimitz. MacArthur felt that Roosevelt's long journey was contrived to let the president, who had an election approaching, bask in his reflected limelight, and indeed the victorious general had become a popular national hero. But MacArthur had also concluded that the Honolulu conference would be a showdown to settle a high-level dispute that had been developing for weeks: what was the best strategy for administering the knockout blow to Japan?

For weeks, Pacific strategy sessions in the sprawling Pentagon had been intense and acrimonious. Officers who held to the views of Admiral Ernest J. King, Chief of Naval Operations, had been lobbying to bypass the Philippines and strike directly at Formosa (later Taiwan), a mountainous island rising from the South China Sea a hundred miles off the China mainland and three hundred miles north of the Philippines. At one meeting, Secretary of War Henry L. Stimson, whom some regarded as having the keenest mind in wartime Washington, had pounded vigorously on the table while a red-faced Admiral King was in the middle of a diatribe against MacArthur. "There will be no personal attacks at these sessions," Stimson sternly reminded the participants.

President Roosevelt, a patient man, had finally grown weary of the ongoing dispute over strategy, and shortly before the Democratic convention had told Stimson and Navy Secretary Frank Knox, "I know what everyone's opinion is in the Pentagon. Now I am determined to meet face-to-face with MacArthur and Nimitz, get their views, and settle this thing once and for all."

Much to the annoyance of the Joint Chiefs of Staff, Roosevelt would do some bypassing of his own, leaving his senior ground, sea, and air commanders behind in the Pentagon and going to Honolulu with only two aides, presidential speech writer Sam I. Rosenman and Elmer Davis, the astute, bow-tie-wearing head of the Office of War Information (OWI), America's propaganda arm.

Typically, MacArthur considered the looming showdown a case of "me against them." For a decade or more, the general had been feuding with the Navy, and most admirals and their staffs loathed him. For his part, MacArthur had been convinced for months that the Navy intended—once his forces had leapfrogged up the forbidding fifteen-hundred-mile spine of New Guinea—to take over the war in the Pacific and administer the *coup de grace* to Japan. MacArthur's suspicions had been intensified when the commander of his Eighth Army, Lieutenant General Robert L. Eichelberger, had returned from a short trip to Honolulu with the current gossip from the Army circles there: the U.S. Navy wanted the final defeat of Japan to be "their show and no one else's."[2]

MacArthur felt that he could not count on the support of his own boss, Chief of Staff George Marshall. Relations had been strained between the two iron-willed men since their days at West Point and from the time they were both young lieutenants in the Philippines. While the swashbuckling Douglas MacArthur had been winning decorations and fame as a thirty-seven-year-old brigadier general in the front lines in France during World War I, George Marshall had been a colonel on the staff of General John J. Pershing, where he had gained an Army-wide reputation as a brilliant administrator and organizer. Since that time, MacArthur had disdainfully viewed Marshall as a desk general and military politician. His loathing for Marshall, the man he had once outranked and from whom he now had to take orders, had intensified during the catastrophe on Bataan and Corregidor, when, MacArthur was convinced, Marshall had conspired with President Roosevelt to give false hope to the beleaguered forces there.

In recent weeks, the Army chief of staff's position on where to strike next in the Pacific had become clear to MacArthur. Marshall had cabled him: "Bypassing the Philippines is not synonymous with abandonment." A few days later MacArthur's blood had boiled when Marshall chastised the supreme commander in the Southwest Pacific in another cable: "With regard to the reconquest of the Philippines, we must be careful not to allow our personal feeling and Philippine political considerations to overrule our great objective [winning the war against Japan]."[3]

The third member of the Joint Chiefs of Staff, General Henry H.

"Hap" Arnold, the smiling, capable head of the Air Corps, was leaning toward next striking at Formosa, which he wanted as a base for his new B-29 bombers. From Formosa, the massive B-29s could be launched against Tokyo and other cities and installations on the Japanese mainland. MacArthur would not have a strategy ally in Hap Arnold, either.

As the *Bataan* neared Hawaii, MacArthur's irritation grew. The entire affair had been cloaked in mystery. A coded message from General Marshall had said merely that MacArthur was to proceed to Honolulu to "meet with Mr. Big." MacArthur knew that had to be the President of the United States. But he had been told nothing else. He had radioed Washington to inquire about the purpose of the conference and to ask which staff officers he should bring. The reply had been terse and evasive: "The meeting is top-secret and no information can be given." So MacArthur had left Australia without maps, charts, statistical data, or other materials that might help him plead his case.

Meanwhile, the president was relaxing on the *Baltimore*—a one-year veteran of fifteen Pacific engagements—as she plowed toward Hawaii. The crippled, sixty-two-year-old president was tanned and cheerful, no doubt happy to be six thousand miles from Washington's oppressive heat and equally stifling political climate. Just before the *Baltimore* churned into sight of Hawaii's majestic Diamond Head, she was greeted by several squadrons of fighter planes and a score of swift PT boats. Franklin Roosevelt, a master showman and politician, had made certain that he would receive a tumultuous welcome at the Honolulu docks. The populace had been alerted to the arrival of the President of the United States, and when the *Baltimore* berthed at 2:55 P.M. on July 26, thousands of cheering Hawaiians lined the docks.

Admiral Nimitz, Lieutenant General Robert C. Richardson, his ground force commander, and fifty-four other officers in crisply pressed uniforms were waiting at the dock. They immediately boarded the *Baltimore* to pay their respects to the president. But General Douglas MacArthur was nowhere to be seen, nor did anyone know of his whereabouts.

MacArthur's Flying Fortress had landed at Hickham Field, outside Honolulu, more than an hour before the *Baltimore* berthed, and in plenty of time for the general to be on hand with the other brass to greet the president. Instead, MacArthur had ordered his driver to take him directly to the house where he would be staying. There, he had leisurely unpacked his bag and taken an unhurried bath.

On the *Baltimore*, Roosevelt noticed that his famous general was not present, and some thirty minutes later he asked Admiral Nimitz if he knew where MacArthur was. Before the soft-spoken, white-haired admiral could reply, an ear-splitting siren pierced the air and a formation of snappily dressed military policemen on shiny motorcycles escorted an open limousine onto the dock. With a raucous screeching of tires, the limousine lurched to a halt in front of the *Baltimore*'s gangplank. Perched regally on the back seat was an imposing figure wearing a leather jacket, outsized sunglasses, and a jaunty, gold-embroidered Philippine field marshal's cap. Not surprisingly, MacArthur was puffing on a long corncob pipe.

A thunderous cheer erupted as the Hawaiians recognized the new arrival. There were loud cries from the throng of "Mac-artur! Mackartur!" The general, with four silver stars on each shoulder glistening in the bright sunlight, stoop up in the limousine and acknowledged the adoring crowds with waves in each direction.

As the ovation subsided, MacArthur strode briskly up the gangplank. Halfway to the top another enormous cheer broke out, and MacArthur turned to wave once again. Reaching the deck, the general walked rapidly to where President Roosevelt, all but overlooked in the excitement, was seated, and the two men, who had not seen each other in seven years, shook hands warmly. If the president resented having been upstaged by one of his generals, he gave no indication of it. Flashing his famous lop-sided smile, Roosevelt said, "It's good to see you, Doug."

"Thank you, Mr. President," MacArthur replied. "It's good to see you, too."[4]

When it was time for Roosevelt to leave the *Baltimore*, two husky assistants carried the president down the gangplank and into a waiting car. Photographers lowered their cameras as he went past: there had been an unwritten rule among American newsmen that Roosevelt not be photographed when he was being physically aided. Once in the vehicle, Roosevelt let out a sigh of relief as he eased the straps holding the fifteen-pound metal braces to each leg.

The president was driven to the palatial home owned by Christian R. Holmes overlooking the surf at famed Waikiki Beach. The road to the mansion was blocked to traffic, and the grounds were surrounded with barbed wire and guarded by platoons of Marines. Until recently, the cream-colored stucco house had been a rest home for Navy pilots. Even the president, born to wealth, was awed by the splendor and magnitude of the structure and its furnishings. His spacious guest bedroom was fifty feet long, causing Roosevelt to remark gleefully to a visitor, "On a clear day, I can see the other end of my bedroom." Even the two presidential aides, Sam Rosenman and Elmer Davis, found themselves in the midst of opulent luxury—their bathrooms had sunken tile tubs "big enough to swim in."

For two days, President Roosevelt toured the region in an open Packard, his wrinkled seersucker suit and Panama hat conspicuous among the gold braid and glittering stars of the gathered admirals and generals. He visited marine and naval air stations near Honolulu, a jungle training center, ammunition dumps, supply bases, hospitals, Hickham Field, and Pearl Harbor. It was an exhausting forty-eight hours of almost continuous inspections, and the president looked drawn and tired when he went to bed on the evening of the second day.

But the next morning, Roosevelt was chipper as the showdown on Pacific strategy got underway at 10:30 A.M. in the spacious, book-lined living room of the Holmes mansion. Present in addition to Nimitz and MacArthur were the president's military adviser and confidant, Admiral William D. Leahy, and General Robert "Nellie" Richardson, Nimitz's army commander.

Roosevelt opened the session by saying that alternative plans for the ongoing drive toward Tokyo had been narrowed to two: one was to hit Formosa and bypass the Philippines; the other was to attack the Philippines and bypass Formosa. Acting as moderator, the president turned the floor over to Admiral Nimitz, who argued for an invasion of Formosa. As he spoke, both Roosevelt and MacArthur listened intently.

It soon became evident to the sagacious William Leahy that the quiet Admiral Nimitz, though sincere in his arguments, was laboring under three handicaps: he was far from eloquent; he was presenting not his own case but that of his boss (Admiral Ernest King); and he was either unprepared or unwilling to discuss the political and moral aspects of bypassing the Philippines.[5] Roosevelt, periodically abandoning his role as referee, put some penetrating questions to Nimitz. The admiral admitted that Manila Bay would be of considerable benefit to the Navy, and he conceded that an invasion of Formosa would be successful only if airfields and deep-water anchorages for ships were available in the Philippines.

As Admiral Nimitz concluded his argument, MacArthur set his pipe in an ash tray, rose, took up a pointer, and walked to a huge wall map of the western Pacific. He paused dramatically and glanced about at the small gathering. Silence hung over the room; from outside came the faint rustle of the cooling tropical breezes that swept over Waikiki. Then MacArthur, who long had had a gift for mesmerizing an audience, began to present his case.

He spoke of his "high esteem and extraordinary admiration" for Admiral Nimitz and his naval associates. But, he stressed, the Navy's strategic thinking was wrong. As President Roosevelt listened impassively, MacArthur declared that it had been a major blunder—by implication, Roosevelt and Marshall's—to have abandoned the Battling Bastards of Bataan in 1942. Had America had the will to do so, he said, it could have opened a way to reinforce Bataan and Corregidor and probably not only have saved the Philippines but also stopped the Japanese advance toward Australia. "To sacrifice the Philippines a second time would be neither condoned nor forgiven," MacArthur emphasized.[6]

Roosevelt continued to puff on his cigarette in its extra-long holder. If the President of the United States and commander-in-chief of its armed forces was stung over being rebuked by one of his generals, there was no outward sign of it now.

Along with what he considered sound military logic, MacArthur stressed repeatedly the moral implications of bypassing the Philippines. "Japanese troops would steal the food and subject the population to starvation and misery," he declared. "The Filipinos look on the United States as their mother country, and consigning them to the bayonets of an enraged army of occupation would be a blot on American honor." MacArthur was at his eloquent best, spellbinding his sophisticated and tough-minded listeners with phrases such as "morally wrong," "grossly unethical," and "shameful."

At one point, Roosevelt interrupted to exclaim, "But, Douglas, taking Luzon would demand heavier losses than we can stand."

MacArthur knew that this had been the pet argument of his rival in the Pentagon, Admiral Ernest King. "Mr. President," he replied, "my losses would not be heavy, no more than they have been in the past." (In his "hit-'em-where-they-ain't" strategy of the past two years, MacArthur's casualties had been relatively moderate.)[7]

As his presentation progressed, MacArthur appeared to be winning over his audience—even Nimitz. At one point the general emphasized that Admiral King's plan to put a naval blockade around the main Philippine island of Luzon after it had been bypassed wouldn't work. "Luzon is far too big," MacArthur said. Admiral Bill Leahy cast a furtive glance at Chester Nimitz and thought he detected a slight nod of agreement with MacArthur's view on the blockade.

His arguments completed, MacArthur placed the pointer on the rack below the map and walked to his chair. There was a moment of silence as the realization came over those present that one of the major councils of the war had just been concluded. It had lasted ninety-two minutes. President Roosevelt adjourned the meeting, and indicated he would sleep on the matter before reaching his decision.

Before retiring for the night, Roosevelt summoned his personal physician to his spacious bedroom. It had been a long day and the president was extremely tired. "Give me an aspirin," he told the doctor. "In fact, give me another aspirin to take in the morning. In all my life *nobody* has ever talked to me the way MacArthur did."[8]

The next morning, Roosevelt, seated on the immaculately groomed lawn of the Holmes house, under a palm tree from which all the coconuts had been cut lest one drop on the unprotected presidential head, met with a clutch of newspaper reporters and photographers to give them a rundown on his Hawaiian visit. The president, apparently relieved to have reached a decision on a thorny question of Pacific strategy, was in high spirits. Seated next to him was MacArthur, and the president noticed that the general's fly was open. Gleefully, Roosevelt called out to a photographer in a stage whisper, "Do you see what I see? Quick, get a shot of it!"[9]

MacArthur was not amused. As the photographer was focusing his camera, the general quickly corrected the situation.

Getting down to business, Roosevelt expressed his pleasure at being in Hawaii, then told the reporters, "We have had an extremely interesting and useful conference. We are going to get the Philippines back, and without question General MacArthur will [lead us there] . . ." That night, stateside newspapers gave the president's dramatic announcement second billing: in Europe, the Allies had just broken out of the Normandy beachhead and tank-led columns were driving deep into northwestern France.

The next morning, Franklin Roosevelt's ship weighed anchor. As the *Baltimore* headed homeward through the Pacific fog, the president cast a fishing line overboard. His catch: one halibut, one flounder.

That day, some four thousand five hundred miles from Honolulu, Emperor Hirohito received a distinguished visitor at the Imperial Palace in Tokyo. General Hideki Tojo, in full uniform complete with medals and a ceremonial sword, bowed before the emperor and confessed his failures. Since the glory days of mid-1942 when the empire of the Rising Sun had extended its rays over enormous expanses of the Pacific, Tojo had watched as the Imperial armed forces had suffered one defeat after another. Now the Allies had drawn a noose around the empire. General Tojo, the supreme warlord, therefore resigned.

Stepping into the disgraced Tojo's office was another two-fisted Army man, General Kuniaki Koiso. The sixty-four-year-old Koiso had two nicknames. He preferred "The Singing Frog," which he felt was a tribute to his deep, resonant voice but actually was used derisively behind his back. (He particularly liked to sing old folk tunes when amply fortified with sake.) But General Koiso was better known as "The Korean Tiger" because of the brutalities he had allowed while governor of Korea. Hideki Tojo's departure would not result in a slackening of Japan's war efforts; a militaristic clique was still in power. General Koiso told the emperor, "We will fight to ultimate victory!"

On August 1, Manuel Quezon, first president of the Philippine Commonwealth, was lying in a log house in Saranac Lake, New York, eleven thousand miles from his homeland. The sixty-five-year-old Quezon, who was a symbol of freedom to millions of his countrymen, and had escaped from Corregidor by submarine in March 1942, had long suffered from tuberculosis. His physician was reading aloud from the Sermon on the Mount. But Quezon did not believe he could die while the sun was shining, and the morning had dawned bright and sunny. After the reading, he asked that the radio be turned on and was thrilled by the news: American troops had landed at Sansapor, Dutch New Guinea. Manuel Quezon, who had dreamed of returning to his beloved Manila arm in arm with General MacArthur, exclaimed, "Just six hundred more miles!"

Then he started to cough; he had begun to hemorrhage. Summoned from mass, his wife rushed in to his bedroom, but he waved her away to spare her the sight of his suffering. In a few minutes his labored breathing had stopped.

Manuel Quezon would return to Manila with Douglas MacArthur only in spirit.

2

Guerrillas, Spies, and Saboteurs

Corporal William Becker III was only twenty years old, but months of constant running and hiding from an enemy bent on his destruction had given him a maturity far beyond his years. Becker was one of Douglas MacArthur's guerrillas who were living like hunted animals in the jungles of the Japanese-infested Philippines. There he operated an improvised meteorological station that he had helped erect in order to provide MacArthur's forces with weather conditions in the islands.

Now, on August 6, 1944, an angry Corporal Bill Becker was firing off a radio signal reflecting the endless frustrations with which he was confronted addressed to MacArthur. Becker no doubt thought that his message would get no further than some corporal or sergeant:

> If this weather information is as important as I think it is and you say it is, then it deserves proper handling. It is getting just that at this end. If one radio set and good operators cannot be devoted [in Australia] to appointed frequency at the appointed time, we may as well stop running and hiding. No contact all day August 4, no contact this morning. I volunteered to do a job and am doing

it. Let us have some cooperation. Where the hell is station KAZ? Those operators must be rookies . . . Corporal William Becker III.

Indeed a corporal in Australia did receive Becker's indignant message, but he did not pigeonhole it as Becker had anticipated. It was turned over to Major General Courtney A. Whitney, Sr., who was in charge of guerrilla and espionage operations in the Philippines. Whitney showed the signal to MacArthur, who read it while smoking his corncob pipe.

The general decided to respond personally, and assured the beleaguered corporal that the failure to establish radio contact with him was being investigated by his chief signal officer. "I understand the difficulties of your position, and everything possible will be done to insure prompt reception of your reports, which are of great value. But desire in the future [that you] endeavor to exercise the patience and disciplined restraint expected of us soldiers and without which duty cannot be well done . . . MacArthur."[1]

Corporal Becker was one of the thousands of people involved in the most far-flung espionage, sabotage, and guerrilla operation that history had known. Under the direction of a super-secret cloak-and-dagger agency known as the Allied Intelligence Bureau (AIB), the operation had been put together hastily in Australia during the black days of early 1942 after MacArthur realized he was fighting "blind." (When the Japanese struck at Pearl Harbor, neither the U.S. armed forces nor the nation had an intelligence service worthy of the name.)

The Allied Intelligence Bureau was under the overall supervision of MacArthur's chief intelligence officer (G-2), Major General Charles Willoughby. A hulking figure of a man, Willoughby had been born Karl Weidenback in Germany, and still spoke with a thick Teutonic accent. Known to some as "Sir Charles," Willoughby was regarded as a stern and demanding Prussian taskmaster by those under him, considered a genius by many, and held in high esteem by the Big Boss, Douglas MacArthur.

AIB was divided into several branches. One was known as Special Operations Australia, a benign and misleading designation for a group that specialized in every phase of sabotage and silent killing. Its skilled agents operated throughout the South Pacific, and their targets were factories, power plants, arsenals, military trains and vehicles—and Japanese soldiers and civilian officials. Another branch, mainly run by the British, was headed by a London-born Royal Navy commander and was so secret his name could not be made public. An imaginative and capable intelligence chief, his agents stole and decoded Japanese messages, often under their noses. The third branch of AIB was a propaganda operation under the direction of Australian Commander J. C. R. Proud. Its function was to raise the morale of civilian populations under the Japanese yoke and to demoralize enemy forces in the South Pacific.

There was also an AIB division known as the Coastwatchers, an unorthodox outfit code-named Operation Ferdinand. The Coastwatchers, many of them middle-aged and elderly civilians and nearly all volunteers, numbered only a few hundred men. Daily they risked their lives, and frequently lost them, in order to supply the Allies with accurate and firsthand intelligence on Japanese ship and aircraft movements. Equipped with bulky radios, difficult both to carry and conceal, the Coastwatchers maintained vigils in scores of inhospitable spots, moving from place to place with their cumbersome equipment. Caucasians could not pass themselves off as natives, nor could they exist without help. Coastwatchers had to trust the local people for assistance; often that trust was misplaced and they were betrayed to torture and death.

The cloak-and-dagger activities of the AIB ranged over an enormous area of the South Pacific, covering tens of thousands of square miles of ocean and scores of islands. This far-flung operation—so secret that not even Philippine President Manuel Quezon knew of its existence—had one purpose: to pave the way for Douglas MacArthur's return to the Philippines.

In mid-1943, MacArthur had brought in Colonel (later Major General) Courtney Whitney, Sr., to take over AIB's Philippine section. Whitney had been a pilot in World War I and practiced law in Manila for twenty years. He promptly moved into an office next to MacArthur's, rolled up his sleeves, and plunged into his work.

Almost at once Colonel Whitney and his small staff realized there was a major problem in the Philippines: how to combat the constant flow of Japanese propaganda. Japan controlled all the media—radio, newspapers, magazines, billboards—and anti-American publicity was beginning to erode the morale of Filipino guerrillas and civilians. On August 10, 1943, Whitney submitted a memorandum to MacArthur, outlining a solution to the crucial problem:

> Items scarce in the Philippines, such as cigarettes, matches, chewing gum, candy bars, sewing kits and pencils, would be individually packaged with the American and Philippine flags on one side, and the phrase "I shall return!" over General MacArthur's facsimile signature on the other side. These "victory packages" would be slipped into the Philippines via submarine and distributed throughout the islands.

MacArthur read the memorandum with apparent delight. At the bottom he scrawled: *No objections. I shall return! MacA.*

Eventually, millions of these packages flooded the Philippines, thwarting frantic Japanese efforts to stem the "American propaganda" tide. There were eighty-seven dialects in the Philippines, but no translation of the English was needed. Every Filipino understood "I shall return!"—a phrase that had long been a promise of ultimate deliverance to the hard-working and devout people of the Philippines. It was a sacred personal pledge from Douglas MacArthur rather than from the United States, which had abandoned the Philippines in her worst hour. If *he* said *he* was coming back, the Filipinos believed the pledge would be kept.

During the months since America had been driven out of the Philippines, the flame of armed resistance in the islands had burned brightly. Even while the trapped defenders of Corregidor were firing their final feeble rounds, bands of Filipino resisters were forming in the jungles and rugged hills of northern Luzon. The largest group of guerrillas was known as the "Huks" (short for Hukbalahaps) and was led by Luis Tarluc, a fire-eating Communist, as were some members of his band.

A number of other guerrilla leaders on Luzon were Americans who had escaped from Bataan or from POW enclosures at Santo Tomás University, Los Baños, Bilibad, and Cabanatuan. Lieutenant Colonels Martin Moses and Arthur Noble, who had been with the Philippine 11th

Division, escaped from Bataan and organized a force of over six thousand Filipino guerrillas in northern Luzon. At first the ragtag band was armed mainly with machetes, but they were soon given a formal designation by MacArthur—United States Forces in the Philippines (USFIP)—and their weapons were upgraded. Over the months a steady stream of messages from Colonels Moses and Noble poured into MacArthur's headquarters: "Large group of enemy vehicles destroyed. . . . Bridges blown up . . . Enemy telephone poles torn down. . . . Food dumps burned . . . Much enemy arms and ammunition captured . . . Morale and behavior [of Filipino guerrillas] excellent . . . Need more arms. Thousands eager to fight."

Eventually, the swashbuckling Colonels Noble and Moses took one chance too many; they were captured by the Japanese, tortured, and shot. Lieutenant Colonel R. W. Volckmann, an American officer, immediately took command, and the USFIP on Luzon continued to function without losing stride.

For many months, the Japanese had labored to stamp out or disrupt the Allied sabotage-and-espionage network that had been built throughout the Philippines. These efforts intensified as American forces edged closer to the archipelago. Heavily armed patrols regularly beat the bushes in the remote regions, and in the cities the *Kempei Tai*, the dreaded Japanese secret police, searched, bribed, arrested, and tortured in an effort to expose Filipino and American espionage agents. In this pursuit they were aided by native collaborators whose motives were complex and varied. Some cozied up to the Japanese for personal gain, others because they feared the occupiers. There were those who preferred Oriental masters to Occidental ones, and some thought the best way to serve their country was to cooperate with the invaders. In 1943, more than five thousand Filipinos had joined the *Makapili*, a group sponsored by the Japanese. They were issued rifles and trained to fight American soldiers if MacArthur returned to the islands.

Since his arrival at MacArthur's headquarters, Courtney Whitney had given the highest priority to penetrating Manila, a city of one million and the nerve center of Japan's war effort in the Philippines. By August 1944, Manila was infested with Allied spies, nearly all of them Filipinos. They came from all walks of life, and while going about their legitimate daily routines collected countless pieces of information about the Japanese occupiers and their war machine. Despite their diverse backgrounds, the part-time spies had one common denominator, however: each lived under the constant threat of arrest and public beheading by the *Kempei Tai*.

At the Allied Intelligence Bureau, recently promoted Major General Whitney received a message in August 1944 from a Manila spy revealing that Field Marshal Hisaichi Terauchi, supreme commander of all Japanese forces in the South Pacific and General MacArthur's opposite number, had taken over the Imperial Suite in the ornate Manila Hotel. Whitney showed the message to MacArthur, who smiled faintly. This was the same suite that the general and Mrs. MacArthur had lived in for several years until forced to flee by the Japanese closing in on the capital. Handing the cable back to Whitney, MacArthur remarked dryly, "Well, I'm glad to know who is occupying the apartment. He should like it. It has a pair of vases given by the [Japanese] emperor to my father in 1905."[2]

Employees in the Manila Hotel did not look or act like spies. They were gracious, even deferential, to the Japanese brass and high-level government officials who paraded in and out. Friendly, smiling desk clerks, bellboys, and elevator operators inquired casually how long a guest would be in Manila, and even as to the purpose of his visit. The Filipino staff members usually slipped in off-hand remarks about how deplorable it was that some Filipinos resented the presence of the Japanese in the islands. Hardly had new guests registered than clandestine radios began transmitting detailed reports to MacArthur's headquarters: "Guests, July 24, Commanders Nakajama, Tiro, and Notoura . . . July 27, Count Haisaki Torino . . . July 29, General Ammoto and unidentified woman . . ."

Filipino workers at the railroad yards in Manila reported regularly on trains running to the north and south, particularly Japanese troop trains. A popular Manila radio news broadcaster closed each program with a brief sentence in predesignated code that tipped off the AIB as to the approximate shipping tonnage that had entered and departed Manila Bay during the previous twenty-four hours. The broadcaster received his daily classified data from a veteran Filipino harbor official whose function was to coordinate the arrival and departure of ships and to assign them dock space, and whom the Japanese kept on the job in order to keep Manila Bay operating smoothly. Naturally, he could not intelligently allocate berths unless the Japanese informed him of the tonnage, and sometimes the contents, of each ship.

A Filipino architect, slight of build and with a boyish face, succeeded in renting a studio in one of Manila's finest office buildings, which also happened to be occupied by the *Kempei Tai*. Cheerful, amiable, always smiling, the young man quickly made friends with the Japanese sentries at the building's front door. Bowing and beaming, the architect invariably stopped to chat, and the guards ceased the normal checks and searches. Soon the Filipino began hearing things about underground ammunition and fuel dumps being built secretly at Nichols Field outside of Manila.

Within a few days a Filipino applied for a job as a waterboy on a construction job at Nichols Field and was accepted. Clad in short, ragged pants and a floppy straw hat, he looked much like the other fourteen- and fifteen-year-olds who circulated around the project with fresh water for the work crews. No one noticed that the new boy always managed to serve workers toiling in the off-limits underground storage dumps. The new boy was also industrious, often staying on after the others had left. No one noticed that he was scratching out rough drawings of the new installation. After putting on a suit and returning to his office in the *Kempei Tai* building—for the water boy and the architect were one and the same—he would draw out large, detailed plans on long sheets that had to be rolled up. How to smuggle them out of the guarded building remained the biggest obstacle to the success of his efforts.

Boldness was the best course, he decided. But what if there happened to be new sentries who didn't know him? Or what if the usual sentries decided to check his documents? Those were chances he would have to take. Holding the roll of drawings, the Filipino approached the front door one afternoon and offered up brief thanks to the Virgin Mary: the old sentries were on duty. Grinning and bowing, the architect forced himself to joke and chat with them for several minutes. His legs felt as though they were rubber. Finally taking his leave, he went directly to his Manila contact, who took the priceless drawings to a predesignated rendezvous with a submarine. A few days later officers at the Allied Intelligence Bureau were carefully examining the espionage bonanza.

Later, when American warplanes thundered over Manila, the Japanese high command on Luzon would be perplexed over how the bombadiers had managed to pinpoint top-secret, camouflaged underground ammunition dumps at Nichols Field.[3]

Manila became a magnet that attracted nearly every guerrilla leader from outlying islands bent on establishing espionage posts there. One of those was Jesus Villamor, son of a prominent Manila judge. Young Villamor was a major in the U.S. Army Air Corps who, when the Japanese struck the Philippines, had taken off in an obsolete fighter plane to attack a flight of some sixty Mitsubishi bombers and Zero fighters, and had shot down one bomber before having to withdraw. Since the final tragedy played out on Corregidor and Bataan, Major Villamor had been a guerrilla leader—one of the best and most daring. He was well known to many Filipinos—as well as to the Japanese, who had tried mightily to capture or kill him. With his tattered clothes and long, unkempt hair, it was doubtful that even his distinguished father would recognize him. Villamor had gone by his "cover" name—Ramon Hernandez—and his nickname—Monching—for so long that he almost had forgotten his real name. At Allied Intelligence Bureau headquarters his code designation was simply W-10.

Now, many months after escaping from Bataan, Ramon Hernandez was on a rickety little dock on the island of Panay waving good-bye to the three-man crew of a decrepit thirty-foot boat that, chuffing and burbling, was heading northward to Luzon with a load of vegetables destined for Manila. Returning the wave was an old friend of W-10's named Castenada. The seemingly innocent cargo, if discovered for what it was, would result in the crew's arrest and death. The corn, coconuts, potatoes, beans, and pineapples had been split open and tiny radio parts —hundreds of them—delicately inserted. The method to smuggle a radio into Manila had been conceived by Jesus Villamor.

The leaking little boat passed several Japanese patrol boats and reached southern Luzon, where the vegetables were unloaded into three small carts. The three guerrillas began pushing them along dusty back roads toward Manila. Some hours later, they rounded a bend and stumbled into a Japanese roadblock. Backing away was impossible. The three partisans would have to brazen it out. Castenada and the others felt their hearts thumping furiously. Mental images of the public chopping block in front of Fort Santiago filled their heads. Castenada hastily recited a Hail Mary and hoped his quivering hands would not betray him.

Five Japanese soldiers wearing helmets and with rifles slung over their shoulders systematically searched the ragged peddlers, then picked up vegetables at random and began examining them. Castaneda, worried that he would urinate in his trousers, summoned up the strength to protest indignantly: "Those vegetables are for the dining rooms of the Imperial Japanese Army. If we are late in getting there, you will be to blame!"

The Nipponese glared at Castaneda for a few moments, then waved the three-cart convoy onward. The partisans fought off the powerful urge to cast glances back over their shoulders. Instead, they pushed their carts to a safe house inside the old walled city, where the vegetables were again pried open and the tiny radio parts extracted. The components were then tediously assembled—Castaneda was a skilled radio operator —and the clandestine radio was soon in operation, virtually under the noses of the *Kempei Tai,* which had a post just down the street.[4]

By mid-1944, General Courtney Whitney had gained more than a professional interest in the cloak-and-dagger operations in the Philippines. His eldest son, Courtney, Jr., would soon be deeply involved. Young Courtney had left Yale University for the Army, and had reported for duty in the southwest Pacific. Hearing of his arrival, General MacArthur arranged to have the younger Whitney assigned to his father's organization.

Hearing that a small group was to be formed for the first American guerrilla mission to Luzon, Whitney volunteered. The officer who would approve or deny his request was his father, Courtney Senior. It was an anguishing decision for the general, who was fully aware of the hazards involved. Still, despite the peril, there were many volunteers, so whatever choice he made would be seen by some as tainted by favoritism. Whitney took his dilemma to MacArthur. "Let him go," the supreme commander advised.

"Sonny"—as young Whitney was nicknamed—and his comrades

departed for Luzon by submarine. Shortly after they cast off, Whitney's headquarters received an urgent warning from London: certain sabotage materials manufactured in Great Britain had been found to be in danger of spontaneous combustion and should be destroyed immediately. The cable sent a surge of fear through General Whitney. The defective explosives were at that moment on board the submarine heading toward Luzon with his son. But radio silence was in effect during daylight hours and no signal could be sent. The interminable wait for darkness was an agony for the general.

When the submarine surfaced that night to recharge its batteries, word was received that the faulty explosives should be dumped overboard immediately. But U.S. Navy Commander Charles "Chick" Parsons, known at AIB as Q-10 and the leader of the landing party, refused to obey the order. The explosives would be needed desperately on Luzon, and he intended to see that they got there.

Tension pervaded the sub during the remainder of its transit. The anxious, perspiring crew and passengers rode in almost total silence. Each unexpected noise set hearts thumping. Finally, the submarine reached a dark beach on Luzon, where it was met by Filipino guerrillas. Twenty-four hours later some of the explosives were used to blow up a Japanese ammunition dump.[5]

The "underground" war in the Philippines was also an "underwater" war. For more than two years, hundreds of thousands of weapons of all types, millions of rounds of ammunition, tons of explosives, vast quantities of radio equipment, and piles of medical supplies were delivered surreptitiously by MacArthur's small flotilla of submarines. Not surprisingly in such an enormous and intricate supply operation, there were occasional blunders. Stock numbers on one box indicated it contained Thompson submachine guns, ideal for the close-in jungle fighting and hit-and-run raids carried out by guerrilla forces, but instead the box held outmoded U.S. Cavalry sabers. Disappointed but undaunted, the Filipino partisans distributed the weapons among themselves, and soon Japanese commanders were receiving reports of convoys and outposts being attacked by shouting Filipino "terrorists" wielding long curved swords.

By mid-1944 every major island, as well as numerous smaller ones, had armed and organized guerrilla forces in action. To buttress the morale of his guerrillas, and possibly to taunt the Japanese, General MacArthur began broadcasting announcements that began "To my commanders in the Philippines."

There were now 182,000 organized and armed guerrillas in the archipelago, as well as a clandestine network of 126 radio stations and 27 weather-reporting stations. Thousands of these partisans would not live to see the liberation of their country. Prices were put on their heads, and many not shot or bayoneted on sight were hurled into the bleak dungeon at Fort Santiago in Manila, then dragged to the scaffold and decapitated.

As fall approached, the AIB's war of nerves with the Japanese in the Philippines was at full pitch. AIB had struck special stamps for a Guerilla Postal Service, and when they were shipped into the islands by the hundreds of thousands, the partisans began using them in outlying areas. Many reached the Manila post office, where workers, affecting not to notice them, routinely processed letters with the bogus stamps.

"I shall return!" was crudely painted on walls in hundreds of *barrios* (villages), as well as on the sides of city buildings, and postal workers risked their lives stamping it on mail—even on letters marked for delivery to Japanese posts. The dawn breaking over Manila would often find a large billboard with "I shall return!" painted on it in huge letters. Sheets of paper bearing the fighting words would mysteriously turn up in Japanese files. They could even be found on stickers pasted on the backs of military buses and trains, at the entrances to theaters and post offices, at railroad stations, even in brothels.

American spies and guerrilla leaders were especially vulnerable to exposure and death, as their Caucasian features set them off from the population. One of those constantly on the run was the swashbuckling Navy commander, Chick Parsons. His old shipmates would never have recognized him. The most-wanted American "terrorist" wore what he called his "business suit": old, dirty, and torn trousers and shirt, along with a tattered, saw-toothed straw hat. He went barefoot and had a two-week's growth of beard. Parsons never carried a gun, preferring to use his agility—mental and physical—to evade the *Kempei Tai*. In mid-1944 he was operating in the midst of the Japanese on Leyte, the large undeveloped island south of Luzon, where he had been setting up a chain of clandestine radio stations. Parsons was unaware that his reports flashed to Australia were of special significance: Leyte had been chosen as the site for MacArthur's return to the Philippines after an absence of more than two years.

Commander Parsons had become well known to the *Kempei Tai* after weeks of espionage activities on Luzon and Leyte, and there was a price on his head—fifty thousand American dollars in gold, an incomparable fortune. Yet the natives regularly provided Parsons with food and shelter, not only disdaining the huge financial reward for betraying him but risking death if the American's presence in their homes was ever discovered.

While Chick Parsons was operating on Leyte and Luzon, for nearly two months, an American Army doctor, Captain James L. Evans, and a Filipino who had once been on the staff of a San Francisco luxury hotel, Major Vincent Zapanta, had taken refuge with one of the world's most primitive tribes, the Manobos, on the island of Mindoro. After shaking off early fears that they would find themselves on the Manoba dinner menu, the two men had come to feel at home in their aboriginal surroundings.

Early on the morning of September 12, 1944, Dr. Evans was awakened by an excited young tribesman wearing a bone through his nostrils. Powerful airplane engines could be heard, and Evans dashed outside and squinted into the sky. There were some seventy planes—*American* warplanes. "MacArthur's back!" the physician shouted joyfully.

A wild celebration, featuring copious amounts of local *tuba* juice, erupted in the straw-hut village and lasted far into the night. Not knowing what they were celebrating, the Manobos nevertheless joined in with zeal. As the *tuba* juice flowed, the celebrating natives clapped each other's shoulders and shouted, "Muck-artur back! Muck-artur back!"[6]

3

Eagles Soar Over Manila

In late August 1944, another command dispute, centered in the Pentagon and reaching ten thousand miles westward into the Pacific, rocked the United States armed forces at the highest levels. With his forces about to spring northward to the Philippines—where they would converge with Nimitz's land, sea, and air forces island-hopping westward —MacArthur became increasingly concerned about the split command in the Pacific. Cannily, he signaled Washington that he would be willing to step down if the Joint Chiefs would appoint a single supreme commander.

In the Pentagon, MacArthur's long-time foe, Admiral Ernest King, scoffed at the proposal. "More MacArthur theatrics," he snorted. King, whom Roosevelt privately called the "Old Bear," knew that the president would never approve of replacing a national hero like MacArthur.

Army Chief of Staff George Marshall proposed MacArthur as sole supreme commander. The Navy professed to see no need for unification of command; if it came to that, King had a candidate: Admiral Nimitz. Marshall refused to agree to an admiral's appointment, and King became enraged each time MacArthur's name was proposed. So the flawed command structure in the Pacific remained.

Five thousand miles east of the Philippines on August 24, the 45,000-ton battleship *New Jersey*—whose 32-knot capability would permit it to keep up with even the fastest aircraft carriers—sortied out of Pearl Harbor, Hawaii, and set a westward course, escorted by three destroyers. On board was four-star Admiral William F. "Bull" Halsey, Jr. Halsey, the epitome of the old sea dog, was the most celebrated American admiral on the home front, and well he might have been. In the early, bleak days of the war, Halsey's ships had trounced the Imperial Navy in several engagements that slowed the progress of the Rising Sun toward Australia. Despite these successes, Halsey, almost alone among senior admirals, shared MacArthur's strategic view. "The Philippines are indispensable," he had told the chief of naval operations, Admiral King. Halsey, like MacArthur, was in favor of invading the Philippines and establishing a base there as a springboard toward Japan.

Bull Halsey's lone stand, as well as his peppery personality and fighting heart, had endeared him to MacArthur. But when the pair of strong-willed commanders had met in MacArthur's office several weeks earlier to coordinate an operation, a heated shouting match had erupted. Outside the office, where the two men were closeted alone, staff members eavesdropped shamelessly; they had never known *anyone* to speak to the general like that. Yet when the two four-star commanders emerged, they were beaming and warmly pumping each other's hand. Staff members, who ducked back to their work, later agreed that the verbal shootout had been a draw.

Doug and Bill. They would carry America's banner, ground into the dust more than two years previously, back to the Philippines. But Halsey and his powerful Third Fleet would be operating independently of MacArthur, continuing to take their orders from Admiral Nimitz at Pearl Harbor.

Off the Philippine island of Mindanao on September 7, the young skipper of an American submarine had a large Japanese freighter, the *Shinyo Maru*, in his periscope. The vessel had no markings on it, but presumably the enemy was using it to shuttle war material back and forth between Japan and the Philippines. Minutes later the order to "Fire!" rang through the sub, and two torpedoes burrowed through the water, striking the *Shinyo Maru* broadside.

There was a mighty explosion; the *Shinyo Maru* keeled over, then plunged to the bottom. Going down with it were some six hundred and seventy-five American prisoners of war who had been captured on Bataan and Corregidor and were being shipped from the Philippines to Japan. Eighty-five other POWs managed to reach shore and were rescued by Filipino guerrillas.

On September 9, two days after that tragedy at sea, Bull Halsey launched carrier-based aircraft against the central Philippines. Halsey had ordered his warships to edge in so close to shore that from the bridge of the *New Jersey* the admiral could see the hazy outlines of the mountains on the island of Samar.

Delighting in the chance to bring the war back to the locale in which the Japanese had inflicted a humiliating defeat on America, Halsey's eager pilots roamed the central Philippines, bombing and strafing. On that first day alone, twelve hundred sorties were flown, a number that was equalled the following day. After the final warplane had been recovered aboard its carrier at the end of a third day of air assault, a beaming intelligence officer rushed up to Halsey. "Here's the box score!" the excited officer exclaimed.

Halsey scanned the figures and let out a low whistle. His pilots had shot down 173 Japanese planes, destroyed 305 more on the ground (some of which may have been dummies), sunk 59 Japanese vessels, and inflicted enormous damage upon enemy installations. Halsey's losses: 8 warplanes and 10 men.

The admiral was dazzled by these figures. In his elation, he fired off a signal to all carriers:

> Because of the brilliant performance my group of stars has just given, I am booking you to appear before the best audience in the Asiatic theater.[1]

That "audience" was Manila, which had the largest concentration of Japanese warplanes in the Philippines. Cheers rang out in the pilots' ready rooms when word was received that a thrust would be made into the belly of the Imperial dragon.

Admiral Halsey's decision to stir up the hornets' nest in Manila was not reached lightly, nor in the euphoria of the moment. American commanders in the Pacific had long known the necessity of watching for signs of Japanese weakness and exploiting it promptly. Halsey intended to probe just as an infantry patrol would probe, until resistance was met that could not be readily overcome.

At that moment in the central Philippines, the enemy had just been dealt a devastating blow by Halsey's pilots, and enemy defenses appeared to have been reduced to a shell. The time might be right not only for a strike against Manila, but perhaps to alter the existing plans for invading the Philippines in order to save many months and thousands of lives.

Halsey reflected as to whether he dared recommend to the highest levels that MacArthur scrap his plans for invading the southernmost island of Mindanao and, instead, shift his offensive to Leyte in the central Philippines. And, he wondered, did he dare set off more debate on high by proposing that the November 15 target date for the invasion of the islands be moved up two months, to September 15?

He would.

Admiral Halsey knew that his recommendations would upset a great many people, and that he was putting his nose into something that was outside his jurisdiction. But he was convinced his proposals were militarily sound. He called in his long-time chief of staff, Rear Admiral Robert B. "Mick" Carney, and his flag secretary, Commander Harold E. Stassen. "I'm going to stick my neck out," he told them. "Send an urgent dispatch to CINCPAC [Commander in Chief, Pacific—Admiral Nimitz]."[2]

As the Bull had anticipated, he could almost hear the applecarts being overturned—at MacArthur and Nimitz's headquarters, in the Pentagon, even in London, halfway around the world.

Halsey's proposal eventually came to rest in Quebec's stately old Frontenac Hotel, overlooking the broad expanse of the St. Lawrence Seaway. There, perhaps providentially, President Roosevelt, Prime Minister Churchill and the combined chiefs of staff (American and

British) were convened in a global strategy conference. Admiral King read the signal from Halsey to the assembled dignitaries and military personnel, possibly taking satisfaction in the fact that one of his admirals was telling Douglas MacArthur how to run the war in the Pacific.

But MacArthur didn't see it that way. His warm, if sometimes volatile, relationship with Halsey now paid off. For the first time in the war, the supreme commander in the southwest Pacific put his complete trust in an admiral's view—an admiral who was not even under MacArthur's command. He sent his own signal to Quebec, stating that he was already prepared to shift his plans to Leyte and to land on October 20. His message reached Quebec at night while General Marshall, Admiral King, General Hap Arnold, and Roosevelt's military advisor, Admiral William Leahy, were being entertained at a formal dinner by Canadian officials. The Joint Chiefs hastily excused themselves to discuss MacArthur's message. Within ninety minutes after the signal had been received, MacArthur and Nimitz had received their instructions: attack Leyte on October 20. It may well have been the swiftest strategic decision of any magnitude reached by the Joint Chiefs of Staff during World War II.

In the meantime, Halsey was in position to strike Manila for the first time since America had been driven from the Philippines over two years before. On the night before he would unleash his full complement of warplanes against the Japanese-held capital, Halsey called in his Filipino stewards. Pointing to targets on a map of the city, the admiral said, "I want you to know what we're going to do, because many of you have relatives in Manila. All of us pray that none of them are injured."

The chief steward, Benedicto Tulao, who had been with Halsey for two years, solemnly asked the admiral, "Those are Japanese installations there, sir?"

"Yes."

"Bomb hell out of them!"[3]

Shortly after dawn on September 21, American fighter bombers began lifting off from their carriers forty miles east of Luzon and just over a hundred and forty-five miles from Manila and its environs. In less than an hour the first flights were approaching Clark and Nichols airfields—both of which Mitsubishi bombers had virtually destroyed, along with most of the U.S. aircraft in the Philippines, in a one-hour attack on December 10, 1941. Halsey's pilots caught the Japanese with their flaps down. A Japanese colonel on Clark Field squinted into the sun, pointed a finger at the approaching planes, and exulted to an aide: "See our splendid war eagles. How swiftly they fly. How gracefully they maneuver." Moments later bombs began exploding.[4]

Wave after wave of carrier-based aircraft swept over Manila that day. So overpowering—and unexpected—was the assault that only a handful of Zero fighter planes got into the air to challenge it. The next day, Halsey's planes were out in force again over Manila, but the admiral had to cancel the last two strikes due to a lack of suitable targets.

Again a box score for the two-day rampage against the Philippines capital and environs was totaled up: 405 Japanese airplanes destroyed or damaged, 103 ships sunk or damaged, Clark and Nichols Fields demolished, Manila harbor littered with wrecks. Only fifteen U.S. planes were lost.

In Halsey's name, his chief of staff, Mick Carney, had a signal sent to all ships:

> The recent exceptional performance yielded gratifying gate receipts, and although the capacity audience hissed very loudly, little was thrown at the players. As long as the audience has a spot to hiss in, we will stay on the road.[5]

These were exceedingly busy, even hectic, days at General MacArthur's newly constructed headquarters on the banks of Lake Sentani, a beautiful body of water in the Cyclops Mountains above Hollandia, Dutch New Guinea. The impending return to the Philippines, code-named King II, would be the largest combined operation in the Pacific war up to that time. King II was bold, original, and far-reaching—more extensive even than the Allied invasions of North Africa and Sicily. Longstanding plans for hitting Mindanao had to be scrapped and new ones created for the Leyte operation—*and* the timetable had to be speeded up by thirty days. Inwardly, Douglas MacArthur knew that not only the lives of his men but his reputation was at stake. After more than two years of trumpeting "I shall return," what if he should fail?

MacArthur was grimly determined to succeed, however. His air chief, Lieutenant General George C. Kenney, whose personal courage had never been questioned, called on the supreme commander one day to remind him that the Leyte plan had one serious flaw: until landing strips could be scraped out or recaptured from the Japanese, Americans would be fighting five hundred miles beyond fighter cover. Always before this, Kenney pointed out, MacArthur's men had fought within range of land-based aircraft.

As was his custom while contemplating matters, MacArthur paced the floor of his office. Suddenly he halted and turned toward Kenney. "Goddamn it, George," he exclaimed, "I'm going back there if I have to paddle a canoe with you flying cover for me in your B-17!"

End of discussion.[6]

Along a six-thousand-mile arc of Japanese Pacific defenses, Allied blows had been falling thick and fast. For the Imperial high command in Tokyo there was no choice but to ponder where the next amphibious assault would strike. Eventually, Japanese leaders concluded it would probably be at the Philippines.

On October 6, Tokyo received an alarming signal from their ambassador to Moscow. A high-level official in the Soviet Foreign Office had let it slip to the Japanese emissary that the United States air forces in China had been ordered to launch attacks "in the near future" designed to "isolate the Philippines." This was the clinching piece of intelligence the Tokyo leaders needed—and it came from an ostensible American ally, Russia. (The Peoples Commissariat for Foreign Affairs had undoubtedly been aware that his leak could result in disaster for the Americans in the Philippines, or at the least in heavy American casualties. The Russian aim was to prolong the war in the Pacific until the Kremlin had decided the time was right to leap in and stake out postwar territorial claims.)

On October 7, Admiral Soemu Toyoda, chief of the Imperial Navy, visited Manila for a conference with Army and Navy commanders. Armed with the information from the Russian official, Toyoda made his predictions on American intentions. Reconnaissance planes and submarines had reported a heavy concentration of American warships and other vessels in Hollandia and Wakde, twelve hundred and fifty miles south of the Philippines in Dutch New Guinea, and this impressive armada would strike at Leyte during the final ten days of October, the admiral warned.

Three days later, on the morning of October 10, Lieutenant General Tomoyuki Yamashita strode into the modern office building overlooking the Pasig River in east Manila that served as headquarters of the Japanese Fourteenth Army, the unit charged with the defense of the Philippines, and assumed command. Capable, tough, and powerfully built, Yamashita was a folk hero in Japan, and certainly the empire's most celebrated general. Flamboyant and dynamic, he was, in the eyes of his country, the Japanese counterpart to General George C. Patton. Known as the "Tiger of Malaya" for his dramatic capture of Malaya and the "impregnable" fortress of Singapore (which Prime Minister Winston Churchill had described as "the worst British military disaster in history"), Yamashita had been banished to bleak Manchuria by Premier Hideki Tojo, who was jealous of his sudden fame. But now, with MacArthur in striking distance of the Philippines, the disgraced Tojo's successor, General Kuniaki Koiso, needed a popular leader in Manila, someone in whom the nation had great faith, and he had found his man in the colorful, confident—and victorious—Tomoyuki Yamashita.

The new commander began energetically preparing a hot reception for the eventual return of Douglas MacArthur, a hated foe whom Yamashita considered to be arrogant; he intended to teach the American a lesson. Much in the Patton manner, Yamashita electrified the Japanese homefront with his first pronouncement on taking command in the Philippines: "The only words I spoke to the British commander during the negotiations for the surrender of Singapore were, 'All I want to hear from you is yes or no.' I expect to put the same question to MacArthur."[7]

Yamashita's confidence that MacArthur's looming return to the Philippines would be drowned in a sea of American blood was shared by the Japanese high command. Months earlier, Tokyo military leaders had created a plan code-named *Sho-Go I* (Operation Victory). The plan called for all the resources Japan possessed to be pressed into one gigantic effort aimed at preventing the Americans from establishing a foothold in the Philippines.

The Philippines were crucial to Japan. Should the Imperial forces lose control of the archipelago, shipping lanes to the East Indies, where the Japanese war machine got its oil, would be severed. Lieutenant General Shuichi Miyasaki, chief operations officer in the Imperial high command, regarded holding the Philippines as "the one essential."

Admiral Toyoda agreed. He was prepared to sacrifice his entire fleet in an effort to bar MacArthur from retaking the Philippines. "What good would our fleet be," he told staff officers, "if it doesn't have any fuel?"

Field Marshal Hisaichi Terauchi, supreme commander in the southwest Pacific, was confident that MacArthur would strike at Leyte, but Terauchi was covering all bets: he strengthened his forces at points throughout the Philippines. There were now some three hundred thousand Japanese troops in the chain of islands, all of whom venerated Emperor Hirohito and considered it an honor to die in battle for him.

Although the Tiger of Malaya was prepared to slug it out with the American invaders on whatever island MacArthur chose to hit, he was mainly concerned with holding Luzon. That island was more important to Yamashita (and to the Imperial high command) than anything else in the archipelago. Even if the Japanese were to be driven out of Mindanao and Samar and Leyte, Yamashita would cling to Luzon to the last man.

On the same day that General Yamashita took over the defense of the Philippines, the huge American fleet that would bring MacArthur and his men back to the Philippines weighed anchor in the wide, blue bays of Hollandia and Manus and began sailing northward. The convoys would aim for a nautical position called Point Fin off the entrance to the Gulf of Leyte.

There were 738 ships in Vice Admiral Thomas C. Kinkaid's Seventh Fleet, which was under MacArthur's direct control. Seventh Fleet had fewer ships than had participated in the Allied invasion of Normandy the previous June 6, but carried a heavier striking power. When Admiral Bill Halsey's Third Fleet (which was under Admiral Nimitz's orders) of eighteen aircraft carriers, six battleships, seventeen cruisers, and sixty-four destroyers were added, this was the most powerful naval force yet assembled. Still, it would be a tedious trip for the troops jammed into the holds of Kinkaid's ships; A-Day on the Leyte beaches was still ten days away.

On October 11, at the Emperor's Palace in downtown Tokyo, Hirohito, impeccably attired in formal clothing, was ready to receive a delegation of high-ranking military and government officials. To reach the palace, their limousines would have to cross the Imperial Plaza, the traditional parade ground where for centuries the emperor's elite guard had marched. It was in this Imperial Plaza, Tokyo Rose had reminded the world, that "the war criminal MacArthur" would be hanged.

Formal dress was reserved for state occasions. Hirohito customarily shuffled about the long halls and ornate rooms of the sprawling palace clad in old casual clothes, scuffed shoes, and in need of a shave. In recent weeks, he had become increasingly alarmed as he read daily reports furnished him by the military clique in control of the Japanese government. American submarines, now operating from new advanced bases, were being sighted astride the crucial sea lanes between the Dutch East Indies oil fields and Japan, sinking tankers at the rate of two a day; American warplanes were matching that figure. Halsey's carrier-based planes were swarming all over the Philippines and other Japanese-held locales.

Shipping losses during 1944 had been staggering: more than two million tons. Japan's shipyards could replace only half of that loss. Short of oil, minerals, food, and even lumber, and her armed forces at bay on all fronts, the Empire was in a pinch.

Now, in the palace in Tokyo, generals, admirals, and government officials, subdued and with hats in hand, were confessing their failures to the introverted, slightly stooped Hirohito, who, for nineteen years, had been struggling to make a success of the throne he had inherited at age twenty-five from his father. All was not lost, the brass assured Hirohito. The bleak picture would be reversed when all available army, air, and naval forces were hurled against the Americans in the decisive battle for the Philippines that was soon to begin.

Said Radio Tokyo that night: "High officials received by the emperor have promised supreme efforts to ease His Majesty's august mind."[8]

Eleven thousand miles from Tokyo, in Washington, another mind was in need of being eased. General George Marshall, the Army chief of staff, was alarmed to learn from a secret source that New York Governor Thomas E. Dewey, the Republican opposing Franklin Roosevelt in the forthcoming November election, was planning to publicly reveal one of the most closely guarded secrets of the war: the fact that the Americans had cracked the "unbreakable" Japanese Purple code. Dewey planned to loose this bombshell to support campaign charges that Roosevelt's administration had been "slack" in not interpreting Japanese intentions in time to thwart the Pearl Harbor disaster.

The complex Purple code had been broken by a brilliant cryptographer, Colonel William F. Friedman of the Army's top-secret Signal Intelligence Service (SIS), just prior to America's entry into the war. Later, U.S. naval intelligence had broken the Japanese naval code. Crucial information obtained from monitoring and deciphering Japanese messages had been of enormous assistance to MacArthur in his lengthy campaign up the rugged spine of New Guinea, and to Nimitz in his island-by-island drive westward across the Pacific. If the Republican presidential aspirant now revealed this crucial secret, the Japanese would change codes, and MacArthur, on the verge of invading the Philippines, would be denied knowledge of enemy ship and troop movements.

General Marshall was saddled with a vexing problem: what to do about the Tom Dewey crisis? In a democracy, how does an active-duty general tell a candidate for President of the United States what he should or should not use as a campaign issue? Marshall took the bull by the horns. He sent Governor Dewey a hand-delivered letter, explaining to him how the breaking of the Japanese codes had already saved untold lives and would shorten the war; how the road to Tokyo would be even bloodier if the Japanese became aware that their codes had been broken; and how new ciphers would be installed, ciphers that might take years to penetrate.

On receipt of Marshall's written plea, Dewey's initial reaction was one of skepticism. He regarded Franklin Roosevelt as the consummate politician, the master manipulator. The Republican said as much in a short reply to Marshall's note: How could the chief of staff have taken such an unusual action without the direct connivance of Marshall's boss, Franklin Roosevelt?

Marshall persisted. He fired off a second courier-delivered letter to Governor Dewey, this one even more specific as to the enormous damage that would be done to the American war effort if the Purple code penetration was revealed.

Dewey kept the general's secret and ultimately went down to crushing defeat at the polls in November. In the Pacific, on the eve of his return to the Philippines, Douglas MacArthur continued to read top-secret Japanese messages.

4

"The Empire's Fate Is at Stake"

The squat PBY "Black Cat" flying boat dropped down from the sunlit sky and taxied to a halt just off the beaches near the town of Tacloban on the western shore of the Leyte Gulf. It was a risky business. Leyte was held by the Japanese, and the lumbering aircraft was a sitting duck for enemy artillery. A door swung open and out hopped the peripatetic Commander Charles Parsons, the American masterspy. With him was a U.S. Army colonel, Frank Rouelle. It was October 10, ten days before MacArthur was to hit Leyte.

This was Parsons's eleventh mission in the Philippines, and one of the most crucial. His task was to scout the landing beaches, inform guerrilla leaders nearby of the impending invasion, and to gather intelligence for MacArthur's headquarters.

Chick Parsons had been a resident of Manila when war broke out, and by posing as an honorary consul to Panama he had managed to remain there when the Japanese invaded. In 1942 he had slipped out of the country, eventually reached New York, and was given a commander's rank by the Navy. Sent to Australia, Parsons had promptly become one of General Whitney's most successful agents.

Now, clad in soiled cotton shirt and trousers and a straw hat, Parsons headed for the small port of Tacloban, the only community on the large island of Leyte that could lay claim to any modernity. It was at Tacloban, with a population of some 25,000, that General MacArthur planned to establish his headquarters.

But Tacloban first would have to be heavily bombed and shelled—without prior warning. The Allied command was sure it was an important center of Japanese resistance or a major headquarters and supply base. Slipping into the town, the barefoot Parsons wandered up one street and down the other, soaking up everything he saw. After three hours of snooping, he stole back to his hiding place in the jungle.

"Q-10," as he was listed at the Allied Intelligence Bureau, sent an urgent message to headquarters at Hollandia: No enemy soldiers or facilities in Tacloban. The town was thereby spared destruction and the lives of many civilians were saved. Over the next week Parson's radio signals informed MacArthur's headquarters of the absence of underwater obstacles to the landing beaches, of enemy strongpoints on the heights at Carmon and other hills inland, of mines in waters around Leyte Gulf, as well as the disposition of Japanese units. Commander Parsons also contacted Colonel Ruperto K. Kangleon, one of the ablest guerrilla leaders, and found that the Filipino had already deployed his forces to knock off the Japanese as they pulled back in the face of MacArthur's amphibious assault.[1]

Even as the leading elements of Admiral Tom Kinkaid's Seventh Fleet were steaming northward from Hollandia and Manus, Admiral Bill Halsey's Third Fleet was running interference for MacArthur's Great Return. Halsey's carrier-based aircraft had already smashed much of the Japanese air strength in the Philippines, and now the Bull intended to knock out enemy air bases from which new warplanes could operate. Most of those bases were on the large island of Formosa, three hundred miles north of Luzon, while others were in the Nansei Shoto chain between Formosa and Japan.

Halsey was aware that he was sticking his head into a swarm of Japanese airpower; he would be closer to mainland Japan than any American had been since Lieutenant Colonel James H. "Jimmy" Doolittle and his little band of twin-engined land-based bombers had lifted off from the flight deck of the *Hornet* and dropped bombs on Tokyo in the spring of 1942.

To mask his planned all-out attack against Formosa, Halsey struck first at Okinawa, four hundred miles to the northeast, on October 10. In a three-day engagement between American carrier-based and Japanese land-based warplanes over Okinawa, Formosa, and the Nansei Shoto islands, the Japanese suffered crippling losses, with two-thirds of the Imperial Air Force in the South Pacific being destroyed. But the cost was heavy, as nearly one hundred American planes were shot down.

On Formosa, Vice Admiral Shigeru Fukudome, commander of Sixth Base Air Force, had been plunged into despair. But he took heart as encouraging reports trickled in from pilots who had been attacking Halsey's fleet offshore. It began to look more and more to Fukudome that the American armada had been dealt a devastating blow. The admiral's euphoria rose even higher when reconnaissance planes reported that "the remnants of the American fleet are fleeing in a southernly direction."

His work done at Okinawa and Formosa, Admiral Halsey was indeed steaming toward the south, and with his fleet virtually intact except for the cruisers *Canberra* and *Houston*, which had been badly damaged by torpedoes. Third Fleet was heading back to support General MacArthur's landings on Leyte.[2]

Word of a victory over Bull Halsey's fleet was flashed to Admiral Toyodo, chief of the Imperial Navy, who happened to be on Formosa at the time Halsey struck. Toyoda, too, was elated. He sent a message to his air commander at Manila, Vice Admiral Gizo Mikawa: "American fleet [Halsey's] retiring in defeat. Annihilate the remnants tomorrow."

The air commander on Luzon did not have to seek out Admiral Halsey's remnants the next day, October 15; the "remnants" came to him, bright and early. At 8:00 A.M., large numbers of warplanes took off from carriers in Rear Admiral R. E. Davison's Task Force 38.4, a component of Third Fleet, and launched an assault against airfields around Manila. Davison's pilots shot down or drove off the sixty or so Zeros that challenged them in a series of dogfights over southern Luzon.

At noon that day, Rear Admiral Masafumi Arima, leader of the 26th

Air Flotilla based at Nichols Field, gathered his grim-faced pilots around him and made an emotional speech. The "decisive battle" for the Philippines had commenced, he declared, and he personally would lead an all-out attack against the American carrier force (Davison's) laying off Luzon. Despite the vigorous protests of his staff, Admiral Arima vowed to sacrifice his own life by crashing his Zero fighter into an American aircraft carrier.

Masafumi Arima was no fanatic. On the contrary, he was quiet, scholarly, and dignified, and maintained a Spartan existence in keeping with the code of the Samurai warrior. Shortly before 1:00 P.M., Admiral Arima removed from his flying suit and uniform all markings of rank, a symbol to his men that he intended to die in battle. The fifty-year-old Arima walked calmly to his Zero, shook hands with a solemn-faced, tearful aide, scrambled into the cockpit, and lifted off, setting a course for Admiral Davison's task force. With him was a sizeable flight of thirteen Mitsubishi "Betty" bombers, protected by eighty-six fighters.

Admiral Arima's sacrificial mission was a failure: Davison's air patrols shot down his Zero and nineteen others, and the remainder returned to Nichols Field. None had gotten close enough to the American flattops to launch an attack.[3]

In Tokyo and other crowded locales in Japan, Jinno Tanaka (the Japanese equivalent of John Q. Public) was starved for encouraging news after two years of defeats. On the night of October 16, millions of Japanese civilians were electrified by a Radio Tokyo newscaster who was unable to conceal his exhilaration: "The glorious Imperial Navy and Air Force has annihilated a large American fleet that had attacked Okinawa and Formosa. Our brave pilots sunk eleven aircraft carriers, two battleships, three cruisers, and a destroyer."[4]

A congratulatory message purportedly from Adolf Hitler, the German führer, was read over the air. Local dignitaries ranging from cabinet ministers to a keeper in the Tokyo zoo lauded "the greatest naval victory in history." "I hope to get that man Halsey alive," the zoo keeper declared. "I have already reserved a special cage for him in the monkey house." Emperor Hirohito proclaimed a national holiday.

Shown an English translation of the broadcast, Admiral Halsey chuckled and said to staff officers on the *New Jersey,* "The zoo keeper's evidently been ruffled by my remarks [a few weeks previously] that 'the Japs are losing their grip, even with their tails!' "[5]

On the afternoon of October 16, General Douglas MacArthur and his staff boarded the cruiser *Nashville,* which had been selected as his flagship for the Leyte operation. Slower elements of the huge convoy under the command of Admiral Kinkaid had departed from Hollandia and Manus several days earlier. MacArthur was in good spirits but showed hardly a trace of the emotion and anxiety that must have attended this long hoped-for return.

As the *Nashville* and a small escort zig-zagged northward, MacArthur, wearing his famed gold-embroidered Philippine field marshal's cap and drawing on his corncob pipe, strolled the deck. Undoubtedly, these were the most poignant days of his nearly sixty-five years of life. Broad-shouldered, flat-hipped, and slightly stooped, MacArthur carried himself with soldierly grace. His step was quick and sure, and he radiated good health and nervous energy. The supreme commander, who hated neckties, winked at Army uniform regulations (as did most generals) by having pleats sewn into his regulation khaki trousers to conceal a slight paunch.

For many years MacArthur had known fame and honors. He had been "cadet captain" (student body commander) at West Point, and had graduated number one in his class, with marks so high that they would not be surpassed for half a century. At only thirty-seven years of age he had received wide recognition for his heroics as the commander of the famed Rainbow Division during World War I. He had been the youngest U.S. Army chief of staff ever.

Spearheading Douglas MacArthur's return to the Philippines would be the veteran Sixth Army, commanded by German-born Lieutenant General Walter Krueger, who was sailing northward on the *U.S.S. Wasatch.* The sixty-three-year-old Krueger was a skilled tactician who neither sought nor gained the public eye. He had assumed command of Sixth Army in early 1943 and turned it into a superb fighting outfit that saw heavy action in New Guinea, New Britain, the Admiralties, Biak, Noemfoor, and Morotai. While Eisenhower's army commanders in

Europe—Omar Bradley, George Patton, and others—had been featured on the covers of *Time* magazine, Walter Krueger remained veiled in anonymity as he and his men rolled up an unbroken string of victories.

As Admiral Kinkaid's fleet moved majestically toward Leyte, small minesweepers known as "yardbirds," which were commanded by reserve ensigns or lieutenants junior grade, led the way. But it would be five hundred men of the U.S. 6th Ranger Battalion, led by Major Robert W. Garrett, who would strike the first blow. Garrett was a tough soldier leading tough men. Formerly, the 6th Rangers had been a pack field artillery unit, and after conversion of the outfit to a commando-style unit, the men had undergone rigorous jungle training in New Guinea.

The 6th Rangers had a crucial mission scheduled for October 17—A-Day minus 3. They were to seize four tiny islands—Dinagat, Calicoan, Suluan, and Homonhon—perched at the entrance to Leyte Gulf in order to clear the way for the main invasion fleet. Air reconnaissance and guerrilla reports had indicated that the Japanese had installations on the islands; probably search radar whose electric feelers could flash word to Manila that a big American convoy was approaching.

Suluan was the first to be hit. The sweeping of the approach channel began at 6:30 A.M., and twenty minutes later General Yamashita's headquarters in Manila received an urgent signal: "The enemy is landing! Long live the emperor!"[6]

From sixty-five hundred yards offshore, at 8:00 A.M. the cruiser *Denver* opened fire and for thirty minutes pounded Suluan, thereby earning the honor of shooting the first rounds in the liberation of the Philippines. Shortly afterward, Major Garrett's Company D stormed ashore and quickly knocked out a Japanese radio station. Heading rapidly overland, the Ranger force was raked by a concealed machine-gun nest. Private First Class Darwin C. Zufall was killed and Private First Class Donald J. Cannon was wounded. Zufall had the unwelcome honor of being the first armed American soldier to give his life in the return to the Philippines.

Garrett's Rangers then charged a lighthouse, where thirty-two enemy soldiers were killed in a brief but fierce firefight. Suluan was secured.

As dusk approached, two more Ranger companies, plus a company of the 21st Infantry Regiment, landed on Dinagat against minor opposition. On the prowl for souvenirs, a Ranger pried open a trunk locker belonging to a Japanese lieutenant killed in the fighting and found a neatly folded American flag. The following morning the Stars and Stripes were formally hoisted on a crude pole, the first American flag to fly over Philippine soil since the Corregidor disaster in 1942.

At the same time, other Ranger units went ashore on Homonhon and found no enemy. "Goddamn," complained a Ranger. "Here we are with all these bullets and no Japs to shoot them at."

The following afternoon of the eighteenth, General MacArthur's flagship *Nashville* met the main King II convoy sweeping across the horizon in a seemingly limitless array of American naval might. Suddenly the *Nashville* swerved violently, just missing a floating mine.

Onboard MacArthur had a new worry. Wearing the grim look of all military weathermen reporting bad news on the eve of a major amphibious operation, his meteorologist revealed that a typhoon was heading for Leyte Gulf and might arrive there at the same time as the convoy. Whatever his concerns, MacArthur never changed expression and replied evenly, "Thank you. Keep your eye on it."

Officers on the *Nashville* traced the course of the storm with increasing anxiety. There were sighs of relief as the meteorologist, showing a trace of a smile, at last announced, "It's going to blow on past Leyte before A-Day."

The next afternoon—A-Day minus 1—Douglas MacArthur and his guerrilla and espionage chief, General Courtney Whitney, were standing at the rail surveying the spectacle of ships stretched out in every direction. "General," Whitney observed, "it must give you a sense of great power having such a mighty armada at your command."

"No, Court, it doesn't," MacArthur replied softly, drawing on his pipe. "I cannot escape the thought of fine American boys who are going to die on those beaches tomorrow morning.'"[7]

Alerted by the lookout on Suluan, and by air reconnaissance, that an American armada of over seven hundred ships, stretching out for a hundred miles, was heading for the entrance to Leyte Gulf, Lieutenant General Sosaku Suzuki was confidant that MacArthur's highly advertised return to the Philippines would meet with disaster. Suzuki, commander of the Thirty-fifth Army in the central islands, was almost euphoric as he told his staff: "My only worry is that the American leader [MacArthur] might attempt to surrender only the troops in this operation. We must demand the capitulation of MacArthur's entire forces, those in New Guinea and other places as well as on Leyte."[8]

In Tokyo, Prime Minister Kuniaki Koiso, brimming with confidence engendered by what he believed to be the monumental disaster inflicted in recent days on Admiral Halsey's fleet at Formosa and Okinawa, took to the airwaves to assure his countrymen. "The coming battle of Leyte will be the greatest Japanese victory since the Battle of Tennozan in 1592."[9]

Not all Japanese military commanders were so confident of victory, however. As dusk settled over Luzon's Mabalacat Field on October 19, a black automobile carrying Admiral Takijiro Onishi drew up in front of the headquarters of the 201st Air Group. Leader of the First Air Fleet, Onishi was regarded as Japan's foremost authority on air warfare.

A hasty meeting of the 201st's staff officers was called. Admiral Onishi explained to them that the situation was "so grave that the fate of the entire Japanese empire depends on the successful defense of the Philippines." He pointed out that a powerful Japanese fleet under Admiral Takeo Kurita was racing to intercept the American warships in Leyte Gulf, but until Kurita arrived the First Air Fleet was to "render enemy aircraft carriers ineffective for at least one week."

Then he paused to survey the roomful of listeners, who were hanging on his every word. The admiral continued by observing that the Japanese position was such that the Nipponese could no longer win by employing conventional methods of warfare. Again he paused. There was nearly complete quiet in the crowded room. Then Admiral Onishi dropped his bombshell: "In my opinion, the enemy can be stopped only by crashing on their carrier flight decks with Zero fighters carrying bombs!"[10]

The admiral's words stunned his audience. He was suggesting mass suicide by his fighter pilots.

At the conclusion of Onishi's talk, the 201st Air Group's executive officer obtained permission to consult privately with his squadron leaders. When he advised them of the proposal that they and their men become human missiles, none protested. They said little; all were willing to die for their country and emperor.

Lieutenant Yukio Seki, an honor graduate of the Naval Academy at Eta Jima, was asked to lead the first suicide attack. Seki had been married only a few hours before leaving Japan for the Philippines. He bowed his head for several moments, then said evenly, "Please appoint me to lead the attack."

All over the Philippine islands that day other Japanese pilots were being recruited for the "special attack corps." When MacArthur struck, there would be scores of *kamikaze* suicide pilots waiting for him.

Based on decoded Japanese signals, American naval intelligence had been aware for several weeks that the enemy considered the looming Philippines invasion "the decisive battle" in the Pacific. It was clear that the Imperial high command intended to throw all available land, sea, and air forces into the showdown. But from where and when the Japanese—particularly their powerful fleet—would launch the all-out effort to destroy MacArthur's invaders remained unknown.

Seeking an answer to these questions were listeners along a U.S. Army and Navy chain of intelligence radio posts that ringed the Japanese empire from Alaska to Australia. These posts were key components of one of America's closely-guarded war secrets, Operation Magic (the cover name given to safeguard the source of the intelligence gained by American cryptologists who had been eavesdropping on coded Japanese signals). Over the last couple of months, hundreds of enciphered messages had been picked out of the air by the radio monitors in an effort to obtain Japan's plans. These, in turn, had been fed by teleprinter to a team of codebreakers at Commander Laurence F. Safford's OP20G unit in Washington's naval headquarters (NEGAT), and to Lieutenant Commander Joseph J. Rochefort's group posted at Pearl Harbor, known as the Pacific Fleet Combat Intelligence Unit (HYPO).

Commander Rochefort, a former enlisted man, had combined a thorough grasp of the Japanese language with a natural aptitude for his work to play a central role in breaking the Japanese naval code, an effort that had required an enormous memory for details and a knowledge of Japanese naval operations acquired through years of studying. The leader and guiding light of the eight-man staff at Pearl Harbor's HYPO, his little group had worked around the clock for many months, "sealed off from the rest of the world like a submarine," as one of its officers put it, toiling relentlessly in the windowless basement of the new Administration Building. Sharp-eyed sentries, under strict orders to shoot to kill, guarded the lone wooden door marked simply COMBAT INTELLIGENCE UNIT.

The intense efforts to uncover Japanese military secrets at Pearl Harbor's HYPO and at Washington's NEGAT were being matched at General MacArthur's headquarters in the Southwest Pacific, whose code-breaking unit had been named BELCONNEN. These small but indispensable outfits had been of incalculable value to MacArthur's drive northward, as well as to Nimitz's westward offensive. But now, with the invasion of Leyte and the "decisive battle" underway, the secret gatherers of American intelligence hit a dry spell. Possibly suspicious that their naval code had been cracked, the Imperial General Headquarters in Tokyo had changed its cyphers, created a deception plan, and imposed radio silence during certain times.

Unknown to American electronic eavesdroppers, high ranking officers of the Imperial Army and Navy were meeting at the swank Navy Club in Tokyo on the night of October 19 to coordinate plans for smashing the American invasion of the Philippines. Almost at once a disagreement surfaced and, as the evening wore on, descended into name-calling. The navy was determined to launch one final, all-out effort to smash Halsey's Third and Kinkaid's Seventh fleets, then to bombard and destroy the American beachhead on Leyte.

No! cried the generals. The chance for success was minimal, and the Imperial fleet could be wiped out, leaving the Japanese homeland defenseless.

"If the fleet does not take the offensive now, the war will be lost," a Japanese admiral countered.

The meeting broke up with its participants stomping out of the room. The Imperial Navy, it appeared, would cast one final roll of the dice.

Just before midnight on October 19, at about the same time the heated strategy debate was breaking up in Tokyo, the American armada reached its position just outside Leyte Gulf. The night was moonless and quiet. Only the gentle breezes sweeping over the Philippine Sea could be heard. On every ship nervous soldiers, sailors, and marines paced the decks or lined the railings, peering through the darkness toward Leyte and conjecturing what fate awaited them with the dawn.

These were tough times for admirals and seamen, generals and privates. Below, in stuffy holds, infantrymen checked and rechecked their rifles, Tommy guns, and Browning automatic rifles (BARs), then checked them again. Last-minute letters to home were dashed off. Pocket bibles were read intently. Here and there lips moved in silent prayer. Men with special missions studied plans—for the dozenth time.

General Krueger's Sixth Army would make two main assaults on Leyte's eastern coast. Major General Franklin C. Sibert's X Corps (24th Infantry and 1st Cavalry divisions) would come ashore in the north, just below Tacloban. Simultaneously, eleven miles to the south, Major General John R. Hodge's XXIV Corps (7th and 96th Infantry divisions) would hit the beaches near Dulag. The two bridgeheads were to link up quickly, after which the Americans were to drive generally westward across the rugged terrain of Leyte.

At 1:00 A.M. on A-Day, an aide tip-toed into General MacArthur's cabin on the *Nashville*. The supreme commander was fast asleep with an open Bible in his lap.

5

"Believe It or Not, We're Back!"

The sun rose out of a yellow haze off toward Samar island, illuminating the calm waters of Leyte Gulf. Mist dissolved from the heavily forested mountains, and the palm-lined beaches became clearly visible to thousands of anxious eyes on hundreds of vessels. It was October 20—A-Day.

At 8:00 A.M. offshore from the northern beaches near Tacloban, the venerable battleships *Maryland*, *West Virginia*, and *Mississippi*, along with three destroyers, opened a thunderous fire from their main batteries. Shells hit the beaches and crashed into the thick, green underbrush covering the hills beyond. The crescendo of noise reverberated for miles. Great rolling clouds of black smoke and dust stretched up and down the beach, as the guns of other warships joined in the barrage, and swarms of carrier-based Hellcats flew through the pall, bombing and strafing.

On the *Nashville*, General MacArthur had been awakened by the opening rounds of the bombardment. He was unaware that only minutes earlier the captain had had to swing her helm violently in order to dodge two floating mines. General Whitney entered MacArthur's cabin and saw him slipping an old revolver into his trousers pocket. "That, Court, belonged to my father," he explained, not without regard for the theatricality of the gesture. "It's just a precaution—just to make certain that I am never captured alive."[1]

MacArthur went to the captain's bridge. There, wearing his trademark gold-braided cap and sunglasses, he puffed on his corncob and took in the extravaganza unfolding on all sides. As the smoke cleared, he peered off behind the beaches and spotted Tacloban. A curious feeling welled up in him. Forty-one years previously, as a young lieutenant fresh out of West Point, he had arrived at Tacloban on his first assignment. His task: to make a survey of Tacloban's potentialities in case of war.

Now, with no response from the enemy on shore, MacArthur had a growing sense that his "hit-'em-where-they-ain't" strategy had paid off again. A war correspondent asked him, "How do you think it's going, General?"

Without taking his eyes off the beach, MacArthur replied evenly, "It's going fine." Then he turned to the reporter, his jaws clenched, and said, "It's the Sixteenth Division we're up against, the outfit that did the dirty work on Bataan."

He turned to look at the smoke-covered beaches, then added solemnly, "We'll get 'em. We'll get 'em."[2]

Nearby, on the transport *James O'Hara*, tense troopers of the 7th Cavalry Regiment, 1st Cavalry Division, heavily-laden with combat gear and their weapons, were listening to a final exhortation by their leader, Colonel Walter E. Finnegan. Waving his clenched fist, Finnegan urged his men to uphold the tradition of the regiment, a tradition that dated back to Civil War days, when the 7th Cavalry, commanded by Lieutenant Colonel George A. Custer, was massacred by Indians at the Little Big Horn River in 1876.[3]

At 9:30 A.M. the shore bombardment had built up to a feverish climax, and then the guns fell silent. By now Colonel Finnegan's men had scrambled over the railings of the *O'Hara*, struggled down rope ladders, and dropped into tiny landing craft. Waves of assault boats formed up quickly, and with a raucous revving of engines they headed for the Tacloban beaches, seven miles away.

47

Precisely at H-Hour (10:00 A.M.), the Higgins boats crunched onto the beach, lowered their ramps, and Finnegan's troopers charged inland. Disposing of small rear-guard groups, the 7th Cavalry pushed on to its first objective, a small airstrip outside Tacloban. This strip would be crucial to the success of the invasion, for on it would be based General Kenney's fighter-bombers.

Just to the left of the cavalrymen, Colonel Aubrey S. "Red" Newman's 34th Regiment of the 24th Infantry Division had been racing for the shore. Huddled in a Higgins boat in the first wave were Private First Class Silas Thomas, an American from North Carolina, and Corporal Ponciano Dacones, a Filipino. The two men had won a drawing to determine who would plant the American and Philippine Commonwealth flags on the Leyte beaches. As soon as their boat's ramp was lowered, Thomas and Dacones dashed toward a line of trees and imbedded the two standards, side by side, in Philippine soil.

At the same time that Sibert's X Corps assault troops were landing at Red and White beaches, the 7th and 96th Infantry Divisions of Hodge's XXIV Corps were splashing ashore on Violet and Yellow beaches eleven miles to the south near Dulag. The green but spirited 96th Infantry Division dashed over the beach without a shot being fired at its leading elements, although several men were killed and wounded by mortar shells. In less than an hour, Hill 120, a key terrain feature, was seized and the 96th Division was nearly a mile inland.

Nearby, the 7th Infantry Division gained a mixed reception. The 184th Infantry Regiment was almost unopposed, and it rapidly seized Dulag airfield, a key objective. A sister regiment, the 32nd Infantry, ran into stubborn machine-gun crews, and only with the aid of a few tanks was the deadly obstacle wiped out.

Aboard his flagship in Leyte Gulf, General Krueger could not believe his good fortune. Opposition along all of the landing beaches had been minimal. Krueger had no way of knowing that the enemy commander on Leyte, General Suzuki, had learned from previous American invasions in the Pacific that no beach defense could survive the thunderous air and naval bombardments. On Leyte, Suzuki's would be a defense in depth, with strongpoints in the hills overlooking the beaches that could be pulled back under pressure.

Off the northern beaches that morning, General MacArthur had eaten an early lunch in his cabin, then reappeared in a fresh khaki uniform on the captain's bridge. As he surveyed the invasion armada stretching as far as the eye could see, his thoughts flashed back to mid-March 1942. Then, as a result of a presidential order, MacArthur had been forced to escape from Corregidor in Navy Lieutenant John Bulkeley's decrepit PT 41. MacArthur, a proud man, had been defeated and humiliated. Yet his heart had been with the Battling Bastards of Bataan he had had to leave behind. As far as he was concerned, those had been America's blackest days since Valley Forge.

Now, thirty-three months later, he was returning on the 10,000-ton, six-hundred-and-fourteen-foot cruiser *Nashville*, at the head of a veteran army that would number 200,000 men, to keep a sacred pledge. As aides clustered around him on the bridge, he used his corncob to point over the glassy green water of the Gulf of Leyte at the greatest fleet ever assembled in that part of the world.

It was time for the third wave to go ashore, and MacArthur would go in with it. With a dexterity belying his sixty-plus years, he climbed down a ladder and into a barge. Staff officers and a bevy of correspondents scrambled on board after him. MacArthur took up position in the stern; only his confidant Courtney Whitney noticed the bulge of the revolver in his trousers pocket.

The coxswain (the sailor steering the barge) headed for the transport *John Land* to pick up Philippines President Sergio Osmeña (who had succeeded the late Manuel Quezon) and Resident Commissioner Carlos Romulo. After Romulo had struggled down a rope ladder and was still gasping for breath, a high-spirited MacArthur clamped an arm around his shoulder and exclaimed, "Carlos, my boy! How does it feel to be *home?*" Romulo beamed as tears streamed down his cheeks. He was too filled with emotion to reply.[4]

President Osmeña, reticent and inscrutable, appeared far less emotional on the threshold of The Return. He did, in fact, feel much like a fifth wheel. He would be returning to his beloved Philippines in the shadow of Douglas MacArthur, a man regarded by most Filipinos as a near deity who would return to deliver them from their oppressors. And how would the man who had replaced their shining symbol of freedom, Manuel Quezon, be received by the people?

General MacArthur was a model of composure and good humor as his barge raced toward Red Beach. Behind the shore could be heard the occasional crack of rifles and the *ker-plunk* of exploding shells. The organized pandemonium of an amphibious landing raged on all sides, with boats dashing to and from the beach. Overhead and behind the beaches roared Navy Hellcats, orbiting like mother hens over the Americans down below who were pushing inland through the forbidding jungles and treacherous swamps.

As MacArthur sat erect in the stern of his barge, there was a sudden crunching noise as it grounded in shoal water fifty yards from shore. "Lower the ramp," the general ordered. He turned to his long-time chief of staff, Lieutenant General Richard K. Sutherland, who had escaped with him from Corregidor, and remarked, "As Ripley would say, Dick, believe it or not, we're here!"[5]

MacArthur walked down the ramp and began wading ashore. Water came up to his knees, and the sun glinted off the golden "scrambled eggs" on his trademark cap. His entourage was hard put to keep pace with his long strides through the surf. In the brush behind the beaches, in foxholes and propped in trees, Japanese snipers were plentiful. Reaching the dry coral sand, MacArthur moved to one side of the others and onto a low sandy mound. Standing motionless and erect, a conspicuous target, he gazed about the pock-marked terrain and slowly lighted his pipe. The pungent odor of cordite from the thousands of exploding shells wafted over the shoreline.

Along the beach and a short distance inland, GIs were crouched behind palm trees and firing intermittently into the brush and up into the trees. A Japanese automatic weapon suddenly opened fire. MacArthur did not even duck. As he casually strolled around looking for the command post of the 24th Infantry Division, his air chief, diminutive General George Kenney, heard him murmur, "This is what I've dreamed about!"[6]

Heavy firing broke out inland, and MacArthur walked in that direction. He reached a squad of 24th Infantry Division men who were wide-eyed on seeing a four-star general at the front lines. "How do you find the Nip?" MacArthur inquired. Spotting four or five newly dead Japanese, the general walked over and turned the corpses with his foot to see their insignia. With a look of satisfaction he remarked to his companion, Carlos Romulo, "Sixteenth Division. They're the ones who did the dirty work on Bataan!"

Bataan and Corregidor. Corregidor and Bataan. Douglas MacArthur's mind would never ease until he had eradicated that stain on America's honor.

MacArthur strolled to a spot where signalmen were setting up a portable broadcast unit that would carry his message by radio to hundreds of thousands of Philippine homes, as well as to the rest of the world. Taking the microphone, the general was outwardly composed. He had waited and struggled for this moment through two and a half years. Only his nearby confidants—Whitney, Sutherland, and a few others—noticed that his hand trembled slightly as it held the microphone.

To the Filipinos, his first words were the fulfillment of a promise: "This is the Voice of Freedom." That was how the last American radio programs from Corregidor had begun.

Now deep emotion began to surface, but his voice remained strong and resonant: "People of the Philippines, *I have returned!* By the grace of Almighty God, our forces stand again on Philippine soil—soil consecrated in the blood of our two peoples. . . .

"At my side is your president, Sergio Osmeña, worthy successor to that great patriot, Manuel Quezon, with members of his cabinet. The seat of your government is therefore now firmly re-established on Philippine soil. . . ." Off in the distance could be heard the angry rattle of rifle fire. MacArthur continued:

"Rally to me. Let the indomitable spirit of Bataan and Corregidor lead on. . . . Let no heart be faint. Let every arm be steeled. The guidance of Divine God points the way. Follow in His name to the Holy Grail of righteous victory!"

Taking President Osmeña by the arm, MacArthur walked a short distance inland, where the two men sat on a fallen log and for an hour held an animated discussion while sharp-eyed infantrymen cautiously tracked down Japanese snipers along and behind the shore. Down the beach a Japanese plane sneaked in to drop two bombs. Neither MacArthur nor Osmeña looked up or missed a syllable.

The supreme commander and the Philippine president then climbed into a jeep and drove inland past thick underbrush and tangled jungle to inspect forward troop elements, going all the way to Tacloban airfield, which was being assaulted by Colonel Finnegan's 7th Cavalry troopers.

Returning to his barge, MacArthur and entourage headed back for the *Nashville*. As the little craft burrowed through the calm green waters, someone aboard shouted "Look!" and pointed a finger toward the sky. A Japanese torpedo plane had swooped low over the barge and was headed for the light cruiser *Honolulu*. Called the "Blue Goose" by her crew, the *Honolulu* had bombarded the shore all morning and was now standing by to fire on call.

The Blue Goose had long led a charmed life, having been involved in countless engagements and escaping unscathed time and again as sister ships around her went to the bottom or were severely damaged. Incredibly, she had never lost a man—to enemy action or to accidents.

Now, there were shouts from lookouts on board: "Torpedo plane! Torpedo plane! Port quarter!" The cruiser's skipper, Captain H. Ray Thurber, who was getting his hair cut in his cabin, dashed out onto the bridge and saw the low-flying warplane heading directly toward him. Moments later, he saw the dropping of a torpedo, the splash as it hit the water, and a wake coming toward the *Honolulu*. Thurber shouted orders to take evasive action, but it was too late. There was an enormous explosion and the cruiser shook violently. The torpedo had ripped into the ship on the port side just forward of the bridge, gouging out a jagged hole twenty-by-twenty-five feet.

Lady Luck had finally turned her back on the charmed life of the Blue Goose: sixty officers and sailors were killed, many others wounded. But the vessel refused to go down. The *Honolulu* limped away under her own power to the relative protection of the shoal water near the beach.

Late that morning at Mabalacat Field on Luzon, Admiral Onishi, the air warfare expert, learned that a powerful American force had struck at Leyte. Onishi summoned the twenty-four pilots who had volunteered to be human missiles and addressed them, his voice quivering with emotion: "Japan faces a terrible crisis. The salvation of our country is beyond the power of ministers, the general staff, and lowly unit commanders like myself. It is now up to spirited young men such as you."

Tears welled in Onishi's eyes as he looked at bridegroom Yukio Seki, who had agreed to lead the other grim pilots in suicide attacks against the American fleet. He concluded, "I ask you to do your utmost and wish you success."

That night Colonel Ruperto Kangleon, the Filipino guerrilla chief in eastern Luzon, held a makeshift radio to his ear in a small thatch hut deep in the jungle. His heart skipped a beat as the voice came over the air: "To my leaders behind enemy lines." It was Douglas MacArthur himself! "The campaign of occupation has commenced. It is desired that your forces be committed to action with the specific mission of harassing the movement of enemy troops. . . . The time has come to rally as a unit!"

While American "dogfaces" (as foot soldiers proudly called themselves) were digging foxholes in which to spend their first night on liberated Philippine soil, out on Leyte Gulf admirals and seamen alike were growing nervous, knowing that the Japanese air force liked to strike at night, and that even the most hastily trained young pilot could hardly miss hitting one of the hundreds of immobile vessels.

At sunset an order was flashed: "Begin smoke operations." Smoke generators on many ships began grinding away to lay a blanket over the standing fleet, an operation that continued until midnight. If the smoke shielded the ships from interloping Japanese warplanes, it also made nervous anti-aircraft gunners even more edgy. Their anxiety grew more intense as a result of periodic calls over loudspeakers: "Flash red!" (unidentified aircraft approaching). None was ever actually sighted. Still, a few American gunners opened fire—at American ships in Leyte Gulf. At 7:31 P.M. an unknown ship raked the wounded *Honolulu* with 20-millimeter projectiles. Five men were killed and eleven wounded on the Blue Goose. Less than ten minutes later an LSD, the *Lindenwald*, was struck with an American five-inch shell that killed one sailor and wounded six.

Back in the United States, the homefront absorbed the news that MacArthur and his men had landed in the Philippines. By now, every child in school knew the saga of Bataan and Corregidor, and how a defiant Douglas MacArthur had pledged to return at the head of an army.

Meanwhile, the telephone was jangling continuously at the home of Mrs. Elizabeth Holley of Skaneateles, New York. Mrs. Holley was the mother of Mrs. Jonathan Wainwright, the wife of the American general who had been a prisoner of war since surrendering Bataan and Corregidor in the spring of 1942. Adele Wainwright, called Kitty by her husband, had been living with her mother. Now, reporters were telephoning in droves, seeking her reaction to MacArthur's return to the Philippines. But the general's wife was too excited to make any comment; her mother responded to reporters' questions instead. General Wainwright's liberation, she said, appeared to Kitty to be "just around the corner," for he was thought to be imprisoned on Formosa, three hundred miles north of the Philippines on the road to Tokyo.

At that precise moment, General Skinny Wainwright was a long way from Formosa. In anticipation of an American invasion of the Philippines, Wainwright and other prized captives had been shipped from Formosa to cold and forbidding western Manchuria two weeks prior to A-Day at Leyte. The prison camp, a hundred miles from the major city of Mukden, was depressing. Wainwright had nearly given up hope. His weight had dropped from its normal 165 to less than 120; his gaunt frame and pinched face gave him a skeletal appearance. What little food he and his fellow prisoners were served consisted of mush for breakfast, thin, watery soup (some said there were worms in it on occasion) for lunch, and half-rotten vegetables for supper.

Skinny Wainwright's spirits and physical strength had nearly hit bottom. There was endless conjecture among the American captives as to when they would be liberated, which intensified their depression. Wainwright was convinced that his release, and that of his companions, would not come until United States armed forces invaded and conquered Japan. That could take from two to five years! Could he survive? He doubted that he could.

On reaching the Philippines, Douglas MacArthur had been silent on the subject of Wainwright, the old pal whom the supreme commander had assured during those dark days on Corregidor that he would return at the head of a strong army. MacArthur was back, but there was no mention, even off the record, of General Wainwright.

Locked away in the Pentagon files and marked TOP SECRET was the answer to this riddle that puzzled many reporters: MacArthur had been antagonistic toward Wainwright since Bataan and Corregidor had fallen in June 1942. Hardly had the capitulation taken place than MacArthur, in Australia, blamed Wainwright for many of the casualties. Wainwright, MacArthur had told a handful of confidants, had not obeyed his orders to attack northward out of Bataan and then scatter and conduct guerrilla warfare.

While still in this sour frame of mind, MacArthur had received, in July 1942, a signal from General Marshall in the Pentagon seeking his approval for awarding a Congressional Medal of Honor to Wainwright for his stubborn fight at Bataan. (In March 1942, just after his escape from Corregidor, MacArthur himself had been awarded the Medal of Honor, partly to offset the drumfire Japanese propaganda that "the cowardly MacArthur deserted his men on Bataan and fled.") Much to Marshall's consternation, MacArthur had hotly opposed the idea. Awarding General Wainwright the nation's highest military decoration, MacArthur had declared, would be a "grave injustice" to other deserving generals who had fought on Bataan. The supreme commander's condemnation of Wainwright's actions was so vitriolic that Marshall had ordered the message to be kept under lock and key indefinitely.

Now, at the close of A-Day at Leyte, MacArthur went to bed early. It had been a long, emotional, and exciting day, and the long tramps through heavy surf and over sandy, brush-covered terrain had taken their toll. He slept through the night, even though a short time before retiring Radio Tokyo had announced that he was aboard the *Nashville*. The Imperial Japanese Air Force had vowed, the broadcast declared, that the *Nashville*—and MacArthur—would never leave Leyte Gulf.

6
Death of the Mighty *Musashi*

On the bridge of the *Nashville* on the morning of A-Day plus 1, Douglas MacArthur and his air chief, General George Kenney, were looking skyward at perhaps fifty Japanese warplanes that had taken off from Luzon to pounce on Leyte Gulf. The aircraft dodged and weaved as gunners on the water sent automatic weapons fire up toward them. The din was deafening, and the blue sky quickly became pock-marked with the puffs of black smoke from exploding shells. Kenney was growing increasingly nervous, especially when Navy officers began conjecturing that the target seemed to be MacArthur's flagship.

"A sailor's life is not for me, particularly in wartime," Kenney told MacArthur above the roar of airplane motors and the barking of scores of guns. "I will cheerfully trade my comfortable quarters and excellent mess on the *Nashville* for a tent under a palm tree on shore and a box of canned rations!" General MacArthur laughed, then grinned again moments later when Kenney inquired, "By the way, general, when are you moving your headquarters to shore?"[1]

Just after 10:00 A.M., MacArthur and Kenney went ashore to visit Major General Verne D. Mudge's 1st Cavalry Division. They climbed into a jeep and headed along a trail where the troopers had dug in the night before. On the way the jeep halted: off to one side of the trail crouching GIs were firing intermittently at a sniper in a tree, just sixty yards or so from the path. MacArthur was impatient to go on, but aides convinced him he should wait a few minutes. The sniper was shot, and the jeep lurched forward. A short distance ahead, MacArthur's vehicle again ground to a sudden halt. This time Mudge's cavalrymen were dueling with a tank that was blocking the road. Twenty minutes later the all-clear sign was flashed, and the supreme commander's jeep moved forward past the burning Japanese tank and the charred body of a crewman hanging grotesquely out of the turret.

When the inspection of the 1st Cavalry Division's frontlines was completed, General Kenney indicated he wanted to look over a nearby Japanese airfield. His ardor cooled, however, when he learned that a fierce firefight was in progress there, with GIs and Japanese soldiers at opposite ends of the field blazing away at each other. But MacArthur decided to go. Once at the airfield, he strolled casually about as swarms of Japanese bullets hissed overhead.

"How soon can you make this field operational," MacArthur asked Kenney above the ear-splitting racket.

"I'm not sure, general," the air chief replied. "But I'd like to find out under more favorable conditions."

MacArthur laughed and stopped to light his corncob.[2]

With little more than a toe-hold on Leyte, MacArthur turned his attention toward officially redeeming his pledge to return to the Philippines. At noon the following day, October 22, a ceremony was held in the Commonwealth Building at Tacloban for this purpose. Shy, reticent Sergio Osmeño was duly sworn in as president of the Philippine Commonwealth, and Tacloban was designated as the temporary capital pending the recapture of Manila. MacArthur and Osmeña spoke over a broadcast network that carried throughout the islands, and troopers of the 1st Cavalry Division hoisted the American and Philippine flags simultaneously on adjoining poles.

Then General MacArthur and his brass climbed into jeeps and sped off in a swirl of dust. Left behind was a bewildered President Osmeña, who not only lacked a ride but didn't even know where he would sleep that night.

MacArthur and his entourage headed for a two-story stucco mansion in the heart of Tacloban known as Price House. It belonged to an American businessman, Walter Price, who at the time was imprisoned at the Santo Tomás internment camp in Manila. Price's beautiful Filipino wife had also been imprisoned, but had escaped and for months had been hiding out in the jungle.

Price House was a commodious structure, so large that the Japanese had used it as an officers club, where, according to Taclobans, "a little bit of everything" had taken place. Due to its size and location, Price House was a prime target for enemy action.

That night an announcer over Radio Tokyo declared, "General MacArthur and his staff and General Kenney have established their headquarters in Price House, right in the center of Tacloban. Our brave aviators will soon take care of that situation." Kenney and some staff officers proposed moving to a less conspicuous command post. MacArthur scoffed at the suggestion.

In the meantime, Admiral Soemu Toyoda, chief of the Imperial combined fleet, was at his headquarters in the Naval College outside Tokyo putting the finishing touches on a bold tactical plan for the looming showdown in the Philippines. If successful, the Japanese navy could inflict a crushing defeat on both the American navy and General MacArthur's bridgehead on Leyte Gulf. On the other hand, if Toyoda's strategy backfired, it might result in a debacle and the beginning of the end for the empire. All the chips would be on the table.

In developing his hasty plan, Admiral Toyoda had been aided by a flagrant security lapse—an uncoded message sent out by an American commander and picked up by Japanese monitors—that had given him information on the disposition of the Americans' 221 warships around the Philippines.

Toyoda's main fleet, under Vice Admiral Takeo Kurita, would assemble at Brunei Bay, North Borneo, southwest of the Philippines. Kurita's fleet represented sixty percent of Japan's remaining naval strength and consisted of seven battleships, thirteen heavy cruisers, three light cruisers, and a few destroyers. It would be divided into two groups for the all-out effort against the Americans at Leyte Gulf. The smaller flotilla, to be known as Southern Force and led by Vice Admiral

Teiji Nishimura, would weave through the islands of the middle Philippines and into Surigao Strait, which empties into Leyte Gulf from the south. The remainder of Kurita's warships, known as Center Force and under Kurita himself, would knife through San Bernardino Strait, north of Leyte Gulf. The two powerful naval forces would then converge on MacArthur's beachhead in a pincer movement, with the upper jaw (Center Force) coming down from the north and the lower jaw (Southern Force) swinging upward from the other direction.

There was one unknown in Toyoda's tactical equation: Could Admiral Bull Halsey and much of his Third Fleet be lured away from the Philippines long enough to permit the Central and Southern forces to sneak into Leyte Gulf and inflict a mauling on the Americans? Admiral Toyoda was gambling that he could entice Halsey away; indeed, he was betting the entire operation on his ability to do so.

The Japanese navy chief hoped to coax Halsey northward by dangling tempting bait before the American admiral—Japan's remaining six aircraft carriers, four of them aged ones, formed into the Northern Force, under Vice Admiral Jisaburo Ozawa. Northern Force would be sacrificial; Toyoda expected it to be wiped out. But if Halsey went after it, Kurita's Central Force could sail unmolested through San Bernardino Strait.

X-Day (Execution Day to Japanese planners) for Imperial warships to storm into Leyte Gulf was set for October 25.

On the eve of departure from Brunei Bay for the naval slugfest that would decide who owned Leyte, the fifty-five-year-old Admiral Kurita learned that his senior officers had grown depressed, even rebellious, over the looming operations. They would be sailing into the teeth of American air and sea power, would have no air cover of their own, and would be launching an attack in Leyte Gulf in daylight instead of at night when their warships would be less visible targets.

Takeo Kurita secretly shared their concerns. But outwardly he was a tower of confidence. He assembled his top officers and told them: "The Imperial General Headquarters has given us a glorious opportunity. . . . You must all remember that there are such things as miracles. What man can say that there is no chance for our fleet to turn the tide of the war in a decisive battle?"[3]

At 8:00 A.M. on October 22, Admiral Kurita's Center Force sailed majestically out of Brunei Bay. Kurita, who had been an admiral since 1938, stood on the bridge of his flagship *Atago* in crisp white uniform and surveyed his powerful fleet. He could not miss his pair of monster 64,000-ton battleships, *Yamato* and *Musashi*, the largest of their mammoth 18-inch guns soon to be unloading on MacArthur's beachhead. The older battleships *Kongo*, *Haruna*, and *Nagato* also had enormous firepower, with 14- and 16-inch main batteries.

Shortly after midnight somewhere between Brunei Bay and Leyte, American submarine skippers Commander David H. McClintock of the *Darter* and Commander Bladen D. Claggett of the *Dace* were standing on the decks of their respective craft, some fifty yards apart, conferring by megaphone. The two boats had been prowling for targets as a team for a few weeks. Suddenly a shout came from the *Darter*'s conning tower: "Radar contact, one three zero degrees, thirty thousand yards!" The contact was ships, the radar operator added. McClintock passed the information by megaphone to Claggett on the *Dace*.

"Okay, let's go get the bastards!" came the reply from the blackness. Within minutes, the *Dace* and *Darter* were racing toward the enemy task force, that of Admiral Kurita.[4]

At first light on October 23, the *Dace* and *Darter* raised periscopes and caught their first glimpse of the enemy fleet. Commander McClintock in the *Darter* attacked first, sending ten "fish" (torpedoes) at the line of Japanese warships.

Admiral Kurita and his staff were in the flag plot (operations center) of the *Atago* when a series of explosions rocked the vessel—five of the *Darter*'s fish had found their target. Kurita and the others in the plot were knocked down. The admiral struggled to his feet and saw that the *Atago* had been mortally wounded—the cruiser was belching flame for almost its entire length, and thick black clouds of burning oil engulfed her.

The *Atago* began to list badly, and hundreds of crewmen were soon jumping overboard. Officers on the bridge hastily destroyed classified materials and a coding machine. Admiral Kurita—after assigning two officers to rescue the emperor's portrait—and his staff slid over the side of the sinking *Atago* and were fished out of the water by crewmen of the destroyer *Kishiami*. Sister ships rescued an additional 710 officers and men, but 18 officers and 339 sailors went to watery graves.

The *Darter*'s torpedoes had also crashed into the cruiser *Takao*, but, although damaged severely, she managed to limp back to port.

In the meantime, Commander Claggett's *Dace* had torpedoed the cruiser *Maya*, which promptly began to list and break up. She went under within minutes, but two destroyers raced up to rescue nearly 775 of the crew of 1,000.

Thus began the opening round in what would be the greatest sea battle in history. The round was overwhelmingly American. The main Japanese fleet, which had been "lost" for months by U.S. naval intelligence, had been unmasked and three of its warships had been eliminated. Admiral Kurita, recognizing that the odds for success had been reduced even more, ordered full steam ahead for the Philippines from his new flagship *Yamato*.

Alerted by submarine skippers McClintock and Claggett, Admiral Halsey on the *New Jersey* sent out air patrols, which soon spotted Kurita's Central Force and Nishimura's Southern Force, the latter three hundred miles south of Leyte. But where were the "missing" Japanese carriers?

All that day, October 23, Bull Halsey paced the bridge of the *New Jersey* and fretted. Unless the enemy carriers were located, they could strike Third Fleet or MacArthur's bridgehead unimpeded, with devastating impact. Halsey had no way of knowing that the Japanese carriers presented no real threat, that they had only a hundred aircraft among them, and that they were merely sacrificial ploys trying to be "discovered." That same day, Admiral Ozawa's flattops had sailed down from Japan and now were only two hundred miles north of Luzon, but somehow American search planes had not detected them.

Shortly after dawn the following morning, Commander David McCampbell and six of his pilots from the carrier *Essex* lifted off in Gruman Hellcats to intercept an approaching flight of fifty-nine Japanese bombers, fighters, and torpedo planes. McCampbell, at age thirty-four, was considered ancient by his youthful pilots, yet they regarded him as the finest fighter pilot on the *Essex*. He had been an intercollegiate diving champion while at the Naval Academy, and Clarence

"Buster" Crabbe, the famed 1932 Olympic gold medal winner (and later movie star) had been best man at his wedding.

The Hellcat squadron quickly located the Japanese flight, and although outnumbered fifty-nine to six, flew into the enemy formation with machine guns blazing. For ninety minutes a series of dogfights swirled in sky. McCampbell's Hellcats had a field day, and when the Americans finally had to break off the fight, which raged almost all the way back to Manila, only eighteen Japanese planes were still in formation.

McCampbell had shot down nine planes and had seen two others raked by his guns trailing smoke and plunging toward the sea. His wingman, Lieutenant Rushing, got six kills, and the other five pilots downed a pair of aircraft each. Nearly out of fuel, McCampbell had to land his Hellcat on another carrier. Just as his wheels touched down, the engine sputtered and went dead on its last thimbleful of gasoline. Nine rounds remained in his machine guns. Unaware that he had set an American record for the most planes shot down by one pilot on a single mission, Dave McCampbell walked nonchalantly to the debriefing room. Just another day at the office.[5]

A short while later, a flight of Hellcats was preparing to land on another of Halsey's carriers, the *Princeton*, when a lone glider bomber dropped through a hole in the clouds and loosed a five-hundred-pound bomb. It struck the *Princeton*'s flight deck, plunged through three decks, and exploded in the bakery, killing the ship's bakers. The blast reached the hangar deck, which was soon a gasoline-fired inferno. Torpedoes already loaded on aircraft exploded, rocking the doomed carrier. Many crewmen jumped into the water and reached nearby destroyers. Some drowned. Other men in the water were carried away by the currents, and machine gunners on rescuing ships had to keep away menacing sharks.

Captain John H. Hoskins was on the *Princeton* in order to take over command from the skipper, Captain William H. Buracker, in a few days. An explosion mangled Hoskins's foot so severely that the ship's doctor, himself wounded, cut it off with a sheath knife. Captain Hoskins was put on a stretcher and carried through the flames to the main deck, but before allowing himself to be lowered over the side to a waiting whale boat, he spotted Bill Buracker. Hoskins smiled weakly, saluted Buracker, and inquired, "Have I your permission to leave the ship, sir?"[6]

At 3:23 P.M. a tremendous explosion blew off most of the *Princeton*'s stern. Steel debris rained down on the ill-fated carrier and on the cruiser *Birmingham*, which had moved alongside the *Princeton* to help fight the raging fire. Nearly everyone remaining on the carrier was killed by the blast. The *Birmingham*'s topside had been jammed with officers and men. Captain Thomas B. Inglis, skipper of the cruiser, and his executive officer, Commander Winston Folk, were both struck by debris and knocked down.

Inglis and Folk, both dazed, bloody, and dust-covered, struggled to their feet. Folk was sent to assess the damage. He was shocked by what he saw. Nearly all of the main deck was covered with dead, dying, and wounded. Bits and pieces of human bodies were strewn about. Blood ran freely down the waterways. Men with arms and legs blown off, with gaping wounds in their sides, with intestines spilling out on deck, with the tops of heads pitted with pieces of metal, insisted to medics, "I'm okay, take care of him over there." Folk felt he was having a horrible nightmare and wished he could wake up.

One man, hideously mutilated and ashen faced, called out to a surgeon, "Don't waste your morphine on me, Doc. Those other guys need it more. Just hit me over the head with something."

Commander Folk staggered up to the bridge to report to the captain. He found Inglis with a broken arm and in severe shock. Folk tried to give the skipper first aid. "Don't bother with me," Inglis grunted. "There's others hurt a lot worse."

The *Princeton* was now a gutted, floating wreck, beyond salvation. After surviving crew members had been removed, another American ship was ordered to finish her off with torpedoes. As the *Princeton* sunk beneath the waves, her skipper, Bill Buracker, looked on forlornly from the deck of the corpse-strewn *Birmingham*. Tears streamed down his cheeks.

One lucky bomb hit on the *Princeton* had caused the bloody catastrophe. On the *Birmingham*, 229 officers and bluejackets (enlisted men) were killed, 431 were wounded. Nearly half of *Princeton*'s crew was lost.

While the *Princeton* had been struggling for her life, planes from Vice Admiral Marc A. "Pete" Mitscher's carrier-heavy Task Force 38 (a component of Third Fleet) were pouncing on Kurita's Central Force. Flying through virtual curtains of flak (each Japanese battleship mounted a hundred and twenty anti-aircraft guns), the American planes singled out the *Musashi* for special attention.

Eventually, two bombs and a torpedo detonated inside the monster whose crew thought her to be unsinkable. But the *Musashi*, some 20,000 tons heavier than U.S. battleships, shook off the explosions as an elephant would a swarm of gnats. An hour later another wave of Mitscher's warplanes swept down upon Kurita's force. In rapid succession the *Musashi* was hit by a bomb . . . then a torpedo . . . then four more torpedoes . . . then four more bombs. The dreadnought began reeling, but refused to go down. It slowed, however, and fell twenty miles behind, inviting a knockout punch. Now a third wave from the *Lexington* and the *Essex* roared in. Admiral Kurita's flagship *Yamoto*, almost as heavy as her sister ship *Musashi*, was hit by two bombs, but kept going. A bomb knocked the turret off the battleship *Nagato*; she too sailed onward.

Admiral Kurita's worst fears had been realized: his force had been caught by American warplanes with no air cover. He transmitted an urgent signal: "Request land-based air force to make prompt attack on enemy carriers." The plea for help went unanswered.

In desperation, Kurita ordered experimental *Shanshikidon* shells to be readied for firing from the *Yamato*'s guns. These shells were designed to explode into fragments and knock down aircraft up to ten miles away. Kurita had not used the *Shanshikidon* earlier for fear of destroying the gun barrels. As a flight of seventy-two American planes approached, the order was given to fire the *Shanshikidon*. The blast from the awesome 18-inch guns rocked the *Yamato*. But the targets flew onward unscathed and headed for the grievously wounded *Musashi*. The Hellcats and Avengers sent seven torpedoes into her, making a total of thirteen torpedoes and seven bombs she had absorbed.

At 3:20 P.M. the *Musashi* was in her death throes. Her skipper, Captain Toshihei Inoguchi, received a signal from Admiral Kurita: "Go at top speed to [run] aground on nearest island and become land battery." The order could not be carried out. Three of her four engine rooms were flooded and she was listing badly. Inoguchi gave the order to abandon ship.

At 7:35 P.M. the battleship gave a final shudder and plunged to the bottom. She went under so swiftly that 39 of the 112 officers and 984 of the 2,287 sailors were pulled down with her. As the *Musashi* disappeared beneath the waves, Captain Inoguchi stood on the bridge, choosing to go down with his ship.

7

"Where in Hell Are Their Carriers?"

While violence unfolded at sea around the Philippines, a crucial strategic decision had been reached at Imperial General Headquarters in Tokyo. Field Marshal Hisaichi Terauchi, supreme commander in the South Pacific, had long held that initially MacArthur would strike the Philippines at the southernmost island of Mindanao—and consequently had poured in reinforcements there. But when the Americans skirted Mindanao and hit Leyte, Terauchi was faced with an entirely new picture.

Terauchi's commander in the Philippines, General Yamashita, had planned to fight "the decisive battle in the Pacific" on the rugged terrain of Luzon, some three hundred miles northwest of Leyte, where Yamashita had some hundred and fifty thousand veteran troops and nearly all of his warplanes on first-class airfields. But on October 22, the six-foot-two, two-hundred-and-ten-pound Tiger of Malaya was overruled: the Japanese would fight desperately for every inch of Leyte, instead.

Although convinced that Count Terauchi had reached the wrong decision, within hours General Yamashita began loading troops from Luzon into ships and rushing them to Leyte in support of the ten thousand men of Major General Shiro Makino's hard-pressed 16th Division, the only unit on Leyte when the Americans had landed.

When word was received from Tokyo of the plan to heavily reinforce Leyte, the mood of General Sosaku Suzuki, commander of the Thirty-fifth Army in the central Philippines, was transformed from one of depression to that of euphoria. Suzuki told his staff, "We'll retake Tacloban in ten days!" He again expressed the conviction that not only would the Japanese smash the American invaders, but that he would capture General MacArthur and force a mass surrender of all his forces in the southwest Pacific.[1]

Meanwhile, on October 24, in the flag plot of the *New Jersey*, Admiral Bull Halsey was still receiving reports of Kurita's Central Force milling about in confusion and possibly pulling back. Halsey and his staff were convinced that the Japanese carriers would still appear. Periodically throughout the day, a staff officer, Lieutenant H. Douglas Moulton, pounded a huge chart and called out, "Where in the hell *are* their carriers?"[2]

If Halsey was growing increasingly frustrated over the failure of his search planes to locate the Japanese carrier force, the boss of that sacrificial flotilla, Admiral Ozawa, was equally thwarted—but for a different reason. Having resigned himself to the fate of a watery grave, Ozawa was distressed that his desperate efforts to attract Halsey's attention had been in vain.

On the night of October 23, Ozawa had sent a long radio message from his flagship *Zuikaku*, convinced that the American fleet would pick it up. But inexplicably, Halsey's monitors had failed to detect the signal. Thinking he'd have better luck if he changed course, Ozawa ordered a change of direction toward the southwest at 6:00 A.M. on October 24. By now only some two hundred miles north of Luzon, he had still not been sighted by American submarines or reconnaissance planes.

At just past 4:00 P.M. that day, Jisaburo Ozawa's lookouts made a discovery that elated the would-be martyr: a lone American patrol plane far off in the distance. Monitors on board the *Zuikaku* eavesdropped on the American radio transmission and learned that it was reporting the sighting of the "lost" Japanese carriers 195 miles west of Luzon's Cape Engaño. On the *New Jersey*, a relieved Admiral Halsey told his staff, "Now we've got all the pieces of the puzzle."

When Halsey fitted the pieces together they told him that all three Japanese fleets (Ozawa's Northern, Kurita's Central, and Nishimura's Southern) were converging on the Philippines at a leisurely fifteen knots, which indicated to Halsey that they had a prearranged time and meeting place. Halsey theorized that the Central and Southern Forces were to rendezvous with Ozawa's carriers.

But he had no intention of standing by idly while theories were being tested. He prepared to do battle. Scouting plane reports had indicated that the approaching Southern Force was weak and therefore could be handled by Tom Kinkaid's Seventh Fleet, whose mission it was to protect the American landing in Leyte Gulf. Halsey's pilots had informed him, mistakenly, that Kurita's Central Force that day had received enormous topside damage, especially to its guns and fire-control instruments, so that it too could be readily handled by Kinkaid's largely defensive force. And, Halsey knew, if the carriers could be destroyed it would break the back of the entire Japanese navy.

The Bull's mind was made up. At 7:05 P.M. he signaled his boss, Chester Nimitz, in Hawaii: "Central Force [Kurita] heavily damaged according to strike report. Am proceeding north with three groups to attack carrier force at dawn."[3]

It was a fateful decision. Bull Halsey had swallowed the "bait."

Before hoisting anchor, the Third Fleet commander signaled all hands: "We go north and put those Jap carriers down for keeps!"[4]

In the blizzard of signals that flew back and forth between Halsey, Nimitz, and Kinkaid, both Nimitz and Kinkaid had gained the false impression that Halsey planned to leave behind his powerful Task Force 34 to block the crucial San Bernardino Strait and prevent Admiral Kurita's formidable Central Force from sailing through it and reaching the American beachhead on Leyte Gulf. If that were to occur, some eighty thousand of MacArthur's soldiers would be trapped ashore, exposed to the big guns of Kurita's battleships.

Relishing the chance to annihilate the Japanese navy's carrier force,

Halsey saw no need to leave part of his fleet behind. He headed north-ward at full throttle.

At thirty-five minutes after midnight on October 25—X-Day at Leyte Gulf—Kurita's Central Force was plowing through the Philippine Sea heading for the San Bernardino Strait. Every ship was at general quarters (full alert and at battle stations) expecting a fight. But not a single American vessel would be there to give battle.

On the battleship *Yamato*, Admiral Matome Ugaki, leader of Central Force battleships, was in his cabin, penning grim observations in his diary. He had been crushed by the loss of the "unsinkable" *Musashi*, and wrote:

> *This is like losing a part of myself. Nothing I can say will justify this loss.* Musashi, *however, was the substitute victim for* Yamato. *Today it was* Musashi's *day of misfortune, but tomorrow it will be* Yamato's *turn.*
>
> *My sorrow over* Musashi's *loss knows no end, but when one conducts an unreasonable operation these things must be expected.*
>
> *Since I have already made up my mind that* Yamato *should be my place of death, I firmly resolve to share the fate of my ship.*[5]

Earlier, on the afternoon of October 23, Admiral Kinkaid had informed General MacArthur, still on the *Nashville*, that a battle was looming at the southern entrance to Leyte Gulf (in the Surigao Strait) and that the *Nashville* would be needed in the fight. Kinkaid related a gloomy estimate of American chances in the looming clash, intending to stress the need for the *Nashville*'s guns.

"Of course, Tom," MacArthur replied. "Send her in."

"But I can't do that, send the supreme commander into a naval fight," Kinkaid protested.

"Don't be ridiculous, Tom," the general replied. "I've never been in a major naval engagement, and I'm anxious to see one."

Defeated in the verbal skirmish with his boss, the Seventh Fleet commander returned to his own flagship. But the next morning Kinkaid was back on the *Nashville*. His mood was grim. The Japanese force coming up from the south (Nishimura's) toward Surigao Strait was even stronger than first reported and the *Nashville*'s guns could be the decisive factor, the admiral told the general.

"All right, Tom," a disappointed MacArthur said. "You win. I'll go ashore."[6]

Two hundred miles to the south of Kurita's Central Force, Admiral Nishimura's Southern Force was steaming to the northeast and by darkness of October 24 was a hundred and fifty miles from Surigao Strait, which empties directly into Leyte Gulf. Tipped off by reconnaissance planes to the approach of Southern Force, and believing that Halsey had San Bernardino Strait blocked, Admiral Kinkaid had rushed almost the whole of Seventh Fleet's gunnery and torpedo boats, under Rear Admiral Jesse B. Oldendorf, to intercept and destroy Nishimura's oncoming flotilla.

Taking advantage of geography, Admiral Oldendorf laid an ambush. Some forty PT boats were deployed to either side of the entrance to Surigao Strait at a point where the Japanese would have to reform into a column to negotiate the narrow passage. Behind the PT boats, Oldendorf strung his six battleships, eight cruisers, and twenty-eight destroyers across the eleven-mile-wide strait.

Onward through the blackness came Admiral Nishimura's Southern Force into the noose fashioned by Jesse Oldendorf. Lurking in the night, American gunners stood by for the order to fire. On the cruiser *Louisville*, Oldendorf was savoring every old salt's dream: an enemy force moving blindly into an ambush. Finally, the admiral gave the order: "Open fire!"

An enormous crescendo of noise erupted, punctuated by jagged, lightning-like flashes that illuminated the seascape and the shoreline for miles. Every gun on the battleships *Maryland*, *California*, *Tennessee*, *West Virginia*, and *Mississippi*, along with those of the cruisers and destroyers, poured shells into the hapless, staggering Japanese warships. American gunners concentrated on the *Yamashiro*, and repeated salvos crashed into her, knocking out three gun turrets and setting her afire. Explosions deep below decks rocked the battleship. From the battered *Yamashiro*'s bridge, with exploding American shells nearly drowning out his voice, Shogi Nishimura shouted an order over the ship-to-ship communications system: "Proceed and attack all enemy ships!"[7]

Moments later a shell struck the bridge, killing Admiral Nishimura. His second in command took over and, following his chief's final order, directed the *Yamashiro*, now an inferno, to continue to move forward. Twenty minutes later, with a gigantic shudder, the battleship plunged to the bottom of Surigao Strait.

In its charge through Surigao Strait, Nishimura's Southern Force was virtually wiped out. With the light of day there would be little remaining of the once formidable fleet: one badly damaged vessel, pieces of floating wreckage, and streaks of oil on the calm waters.

At dawn, Admiral Kinkaid sent a warm congratulatory signal to Jesse Oldendorf for ambushing and annihilating Nishimura's force, believing that to be the only threat against him at Leyte Gulf. But soon reconnaissance airplanes were sending him alarming reports: San Bernardino Strait was wide open. At 6:30 A.M. a frantic Tom Kinkaid fired off an urgent signal to Halsey: "Is [your] Task Force 34 guarding San Bernardino Strait?"

Halsey was puzzled. He replied: "Negative X. It is with our carriers now engaging enemy carriers."[8] Halsey was not unduly alarmed. He was convinced that Kinkaid's Seventh Fleet was strong enough to hurl back or destroy Kurita's effort to break through San Bernardino Strait.

Another signal from Kinkaid was received by Halsey at 8:32 A.M.: "Urgently need fast BBS [battleships] Leyte Gulf at once."

This signal irritated Halsey. He reflected that it was not his mission to protect Kinkaid's largely defensive Seventh Fleet, but rather to destroy the Japanese carrier force that threatened the entire Philippines strategy. However, Halsey sent a message to Rear Admiral John S. "Slew" McCain, whose formidable task force of five carriers, four heavy cruisers, and several smaller warships was refueling far to the east: "Strike enemy at [coordinates of San Bernardino Strait) at best possible speed."

Earlier, however, at 4:00 A.M., Admiral Takeo Kurita's Central Force, the most powerful congregation of Japanese warships since the Battle of Midway in 1942, steamed unmolested through San Bernardino Strait. By dawn it had entered Leyte Gulf and set a course at full throttle for General MacArthur's beachhead.

At 7:00 A.M. lookouts on the battleship *Yamato* spotted masts just over the horizon. They turned out to be a handful of light American vessels, and Kurita was convinced that they were all that stood between his powerful battleships and heavy cruisers and American transports off the Leyte landing beaches. An elated Kurita, hardly able to believe his good fortune, radioed Admiral Toyoda at Combined Fleet headquarters: "By heaven-sent opportunity we are dashing to attack enemy carriers."

The masts that had been sighted by the *Yamato*'s lookouts were those of Rear Admiral Clifton A. "Ziggy" Sprague's six small escort carriers and six destroyers, a group known as Taffy 3. As Admiral Kurita had deduced, Sprague's little force was indeed all that blocked the Japanese drive to MacArthur's beachhead.

Now it was time for an American suicide mission. Ziggy Sprague knew that the only way to halt Kurita's force short of the landing beaches was to hurl his little group directly at the oncoming fleet, which is what he intended to do. Grim-faced, Sprague told staff officers he doubted if Taffy 3 would "last fifteen minutes" against such overwhelming strength. "But we can delay this enemy force's descent on Leyte Gulf until help comes." Then he added, "Of course the end will come sooner for us."[9]

Getting word of the suicide mission to save General MacArthur's beachhead, one of Sprague's skippers, Commander Amos T. Hathaway on the destroyer *Heermann*, remarked drily to his navigator, Lieutenant Robert T. Newsome, "Buck, what we need is a buglar to sound the charge!"

Emerging ghostlike through the heavy morning mists, the Japanese dreadnoughts fired salvo after salvo with their 14- and 16-inch guns. Brightly colored geysers began to spurt skyward around Sprague's vessels from shells loaded with red, yellow, green, and pink dyes to aid spotting. "Fer chrissake," exclaimed a young gunner on the escort carrier *White Plains*, "the bastards are shooting at us in technicolor!"

The destroyer *Johnston*, under Commander Ernest E. Evans, a husky, determined part-Cherokee, sped directly toward the enemy fleet, firing her 5-inch guns. Two of her torpedoes found their marks, and a Japanese cruiser began to burn fiercely. Then, in rapid succession, the *Johnston* was struck by three 14-inch shells and three 6-inch projectiles. Instead of withdrawing, Evans ordered his gunners to continue to blast

Crucial conference with President Roosevelt—"Mr. Big"—in Honolulu, to decide whether the Philippines would be bypassed. Admiral Chester Nimitz points to map as (left to right) General Douglas MacArthur, Roosevelt, and Admiral William Leahy listen. (U.S. Army)

A small portion of MacArthur's invasion fleet in the Admiralty Islands, before it sailed for Leyte in the Philippines. (U.S. Navy)

General Douglas
MacArthur (left) and
General Walter Krueger.
(U.S. Army)

Top naval brass. From left:
Admiral Chester L.
Nimitz, Chief of Naval
Operations Ernest J. King,
and Admiral William F.
Halsey. King and Nimitz
were engaged in ongoing
disputes with General
Douglas MacArthur
through most of the war.
(U.S. Navy)

Vice Admiral Takeo Kurita of Central Force that nearly reached the Leyte beachhead. (U.S. Navy)

Admiral Soemu Toyoda, chief of the Japanese combined fleet and architect of brilliant Leyte Gulf operation. (U.S. Navy)

Vice Admiral Jisaburo Ozawa, who led carrier decoy force at Battle of Leyte Gulf. (U.S. Navy)

General Douglas MacArthur and staff with Filipino officers, wading ashore at Leyte Gulf. (U.S. Army)

Towering columns of smoke at Leyte Gulf are the result of a pounding by American carrier-based warplanes and naval guns. (U.S. Navy)

Leyte had some of the worst terrain Americans were forced to fight over in the Pacific. Here GIs of the 1st Cavalry Division attack through a waist-deep swamp. (U.S. Army)

Rear Admiral Clifton A. F. "Ziggy" Sprague. His light force thwarted Japanese naval invasion of Leyte Gulf. (U.S. Navy)

Rear Admiral Ralph E. Davison, whose carrier planes pounded Manila. (U.S. Navy)

Troopers of the 1st Cavalry Division shoot it out with an enemy force in a Leyte village. (U.S. Army)

U.S. carrier Sewanee *hit by kamikaze off Leyte.* (U.S. Navy)

Rear Admiral Theodore E. Chandler, killed in action. (U.S. Navy)

Father of the kamikazes, Admiral Takijiro Onishi. (U.S. Navy)

Vice Admiral Thomas C. Kinkaid, leader of "MacArthur's Navy," the Seventh Fleet. (U.S. Navy)

Kamikaze pilots. Their average age was twenty. (U.S. Army)

American vessel hit by a kamikaze off Mindoro. (U.S. Navy)

Badly burned victim of a kamikaze crash receives first aid. (U.S. Navy)

Commander David McCampbell receives the Medal of Honor from Vice Admiral Aubrey W. Fitch. The decoration was for shooting down nine Japanese planes, the most by any American pilot on a single mission. (U.S. Navy)

Vice Admiral Daniel E. Barbey. (U.S. Navy)

Rear Admiral Russell S. Berkey. (U.S. Navy)

Major General Oscar W. Griswold. (U.S. Army)

Rear Admiral John S. "Slew" McCain. (U.S. Navy)

Major General Franklin C. Sibert. (U.S. Army)

Major General John R. Hodge. (U.S. Army)

Major General Inis P. Swift. (U.S. Army)

Lieutenant General Tomoyuki Yamashita, defender of the Philippines. (U.S. Army)

Emperor Hirohito. (U.S. Army)

Field Marshal Hisaichi Terauchi, MacArthur's opposite number. (U.S. Army)

Rear Admiral Jesse Oldendorf's heavies bolt into Lingayen Gulf prior to the Luzon landings. The battleship Pennsylvania *is in the lead, followed by another battleship and three cruisers.* (U.S. Navy)

Filipinos arrive to greet American troops landing on Lingayen Gulf.
(U.S. Coast Guard)

A Japanese Shinyo *suicide boat was packed with TNT set to detonate on impact.*
(U.S. Navy)

Aboard landing craft on way to Nasugbu Bay invasion. Lookouts were watching for kamikazes. (Eyewitness sketch by Sergeant James Vignola, 11th Airborne Division)

GIs and jeep with radio, near Garcia's Mansion, while Manila burns in background, across the bay. (Eyewitness sketch by Sergeant James Vignola)

TOP: *Lieutenant General Walter Krueger pins the combat Legion of Merit on Major Henry Burgess, 11th Airborne Division, who led the parachute battalion that rescued prisoners at the Los Baños internment camp.* (Author's collection)

LEFT: *Lieutenant Colonel George N. Pearson, 11th Airborne Division, whose battalion helped recapture the Leyte airfields seized by Japanese paratroopers.* (Author's collection)

BOTTOM: *Filipino reception committee welcomes 11th Airborne Division in its amphibious assault at Nasugbu, south of Manila.* (U.S. Navy)

away. By now the *Johnston* had taken fourteen hits and only two of its guns remained operational. Killed and wounded men were sprawled about the ship where they had fallen.

Still another shell knocked Commander Evans down, blew off most of his clothes, and killed three officers on the bridge beside him. Dazed, he struggled to his feet to continue the fight. Thirty minutes later a shell hacked off two of Evans's fingers, peppered his back with steel fragments, and sliced up his face and neck. Covered with blood from head to foot, he angrily rejected pleas from fellow officers that he go below for medical aid.

Evans continued to direct the fight, even though several more shells battered the *Johnston*. By now all her guns were knocked out and the ship was aflame. At 9:45 A.M. Commander Evans gave the order: Abandon ship. In ten minutes all survivors were off the destroyer, and she rolled over as the last man departed.

Some two hundred and fifty *Johnston* survivors were floundering in the water on small rafts and pieces of wreckage. Before they could be rescued, forty-five died of exposure, drowned, succumbed to wounds, or were killed by sharks. One of those who perished was Commander Ernest Evans.

Admiral Sprague's flagship *Fanshaw Bay* was hit six times, refused to go down, and fought on. The escort carrier *Gambier Bay*, turned into a smoking hulk by Japanese naval artillery, plunged to the bottom. Under Commander L. S. Kintberger, the destroyer *Hoel* had one engine knocked out, her rudder jammed, and her guns destroyed. She charged the Japanese armada to loose her torpedoes and was struck several more times. At 8:55 A.M. the *Hoel* rolled over and sank. Nineteen of the *Hoel*'s crew were killed, and 252 more were missing; only 82 survived. The destroyer *Samuel B. Roberts* was left a burning, twisted metal platform.

All the while, Avenger pilots from Sprague's escort carriers had been pounding Kurita's fleet, sinking one warship and forcing another to withdraw. Out of torpedoes, bombs, and bullets, the Navy airmen had launched dummy runs against Japanese vessels to divert enemy attention from Sprague's remaining ships.

Heavily outgunned and outnumbered, Admiral Sprague's puny David fought tooth and nail for two hours to keep the Japanese Goliath from reaching MacArthur's vulnerable beachhead. But the cost in casualties and ships was heavy: hundreds of Americans dead, wounded, or missing, and all thirteen of Sprague's vessels either hit or sunk.

While American warships were fighting desperately in Leyte Gulf, Admiral Halsey had launched his first strike wave against the carrier force he had been chasing through the night. Admiral Ozawa, baiting the trap expertly, was withdrawing, presumably in the face of a superior force, but in reality luring Third Fleet even farther away from Leyte Gulf.

Just after 8:00 A.M. a flight of one hundred and thirty warplanes launched torpedo and bombing attacks against the Northern Force, concentrating on the carrier *Zuikaku*, the only survivor of the Pearl Harbor attack and Admiral Ozawa's flagship. Pounded steadily for an hour, the *Zuikaku* was soon a roaring inferno and listing badly. At the same time, another wave of one hundred and seventy aircraft struck the carrier *Chitbose*, leaving her a motionless wreck. Two other carriers and their destroyer escorts were badly damaged. Just after 9:00 A.M. Admiral Ozawa left the burning *Zuikaku* and climbed aboard a destroyer.

Onboard the *New Jersey*, Bull Halsey was rubbing his hands in glee as he prepared to launch the *coup de grace* against Ozawa's battered force. This was the opportunity he had been dreaming of since his Annapolis cadet days: the annihilation of an entire enemy fleet.

Shortly after 9:00 A.M. he was handed a decoded signal from his boss, Chester Nimitz: "Where is Task Force 34? The world wonders."

Halsey was stupified. He could not believe Nimitz would send him such an insulting message. His hands trembling, he snatched off his cap and slammed it to the deck, letting loose a long string of curses.

Admiral Nick Carney rushed over and grabbed his boss by the arm, shaking Halsey as a mother would an unruly child. "Stop it, Bill!" Carney shouted. "What the hell's the matter with you? Pull yourself together!"[10]

Halsey was so furious he could not reply. Only now did he realize that Admiral Nimitz, and presumably Admiral Kinkaid, were under the mistaken impression that Halsey had left behind his Task Force 34 to guard the gate at San Bernardino Strait.

The liability of the divided American command in the Pacific had come home to roost and MacArthur's beachhead was in mortal danger.

(Only later would Halsey learn the reason for Nimitz's apparently sarcastic signal. To make it more difficult to break the American code, most signals were padded at either end with meaningless gibberish. In this case Nimitz's encoding officers had added the phrase "The world wonders," and, for some reason, Halsey's decoders had failed to discard the padded wording, as they customarily would have.)

At 11:00 A.M., still smarting from the apparent rebuke by Nimitz, Bull Halsey ordered his battleships and cruisers to reverse course and head south at full throttle to "rescue" Kinkaid's Seventh Fleet. But Halsey left three of his fast-carrier groups under Admiral Pete Mitscher to pursue and destroy Ozawa's surviving vessels.

The aggressive Mitscher (only Halsey and a few close officers knew he had suffered a heart attack a few days previously) promptly sent wave after wave to pounce on Admiral Ozawa's stragglers fleeing northward. At 1:55 P.M. the carrier *Zuikaku* was sent to the bottom, followed in quick order by the *Zuiho* and the *Chiyoda*. Only two flattops, two cruisers, and six destroyers in the Northern Force escaped the fury of Mitscher's swarming warplanes. Aboard one of the surviving destroyers was Jisaburo Ozawa, second highest-ranking officer in the Imperial Navy.

Earlier that morning of October 25, at an airfield outside Manila, Lieutenant Yuro Seki was steeling his spirit for the ordeal he now had to face. Seki knew that before the sun set, he would be dead. Only a few days earlier the young bridegroom had accepted the honor—as the Japanese military viewed it—of leading the first human-bomb attack against the mighty American invasion fleet.

Yukio Seki was hardly aware that he was the forerunner of a revolutionary type of warfare—suicide missions by piloted aircraft—that would eventually threaten the American victory in the Pacific. He and the hundreds more who would volunteer for suicide missions had been named *kamikazes*. The name, meaning "divine wind," was derived from a watershed event in Japanese history. In 1570 a Mongol emperor organized a huge amphibious force for the invasion of Japan, a small nation at the time that was virtually defenseless. But the gods sent a heavenly wind in the form of a typhoon that scattered the Mongolian fleet and blew back toward the China coast all vessels that had not been sunk.

Now, nearly four centuries later, Lieutenant Seki was reading the first *kamikaze* order issued by Admiral Takijiro Onishi, founder of the desperation Special Attack Corps:

It is absolutely out of the question for you to return alive. Your mission involves certain death. Your bodies will be dead, but not your spirits. The death of a single one of you will be the birth of a million others. You must not leave behind you any cause for regret, which would follow you into eternity . . .

Another *kamikaze* pilot, Lieutenant Akio Otsuka, arose early, did his customary strenuous exercise routine, and dashed off a letter to home:

I wanted to send you parings of my nails and a few locks of my hair. But I had my hair cut yesterday and my nails are already too short. I am sorry, but unfortunately it is too late. Neither my nails nor my hair have grown overnight. . . . Do not weep because I am about to die.

On the Luzon airfield, maintenance men were scouring the cockpit of each *kamikaze* plane. It was their belief that the cockpit would be the pilot's coffin and as such it should be spotless.

Just before 10:00 A.M., Lieutenant Seki and four other pilots climbed into their Zeros. Strapped to the wings of each suicide aircraft were bombs. As the five Zeros taxied into position for final take-off, ground crews, their eyes brimming with tears, trotted along with hands on the wingtips, a final gesture of admiration, grief, and farewell.

Fifty minutes later, Yukio Seki's squadron flew in at one thousand feet over Admiral Sprague's battered, weary, and depleted Taffy 3. Each Zero pilot picked out a target, peeled off, and dived. A terrific racket echoed across Leyte Gulf as hundreds of anti-aircraft guns opened fire on the five intruders.

Four of the five suicide pilots missed their targets—barely—and plunged to their deaths in the water. The fifth Zero smashed into the flight deck of the escort carrier *St. Lo,* and a mighty explosion rocked the ship. Thirty minutes later, twisted and burning, the *St. Lo* sank.

Two hours later the tide turned drastically in the battle for Leyte Gulf. Admiral Slew McCain and his strong task force, sent racing for San Bernardino Strait by Halsey, reached the scene and launched planes at Admiral Kurita's now beleaguered fleet. Fearful that the Americans would bolt the San Bernardino Strait gate behind him, Kurita pulled his remaining vessels back through the narrow passage under cover of night.[11]

By midnight of October 25, the three-day series of naval actions and counteractions around the Philippines was over. Japan's navy had been crushed. Admiral Toyoda's combined fleet had lost four carriers, three battleships, six cruisers, twelve destroyers, hundreds of airplanes, and some ten thousand sailors and airmen.

America too had paid a stiff price to break the back of the Imperial Navy. Three thousand of her men were killed, more than two hundred planes destroyed, and a light carrier, two escort carriers, and three destroyers sunk.

The following night, October 26, Douglas MacArthur and staff officers were having dinner at the general's Tacloban residence, Price House. MacArthur heard others at the far end of the table making highly critical remarks about Admiral Halsey for "abandoning us on the beachhead while he chased off to the north."

"That's enough!" a red-faced MacArthur shouted, banging his fist on the table in a rare display of temper. "Leave the Bull alone. He's still a fighting admiral in my book."[12]

8

Bloodbath at Breakneck Ridge

Ten days after the invasion, the struggle for Leyte had turned into a brutal, bloody, slugging match. American foot soldiers, supported on occasion by a few tanks, had been pushing steadily inland, but Japanese resistance stiffened as General Yamashita began shuttling in reinforcements. Japanese strategy in the Philippines by now had become clear to Douglas MacArthur and his field commanders: the defense of the primary island of Luzon was going to be fought on Leyte.

Due to the rugged nature of this mountainous terrain, there was no solid front line. Often the "front" in a given sector would be a three-foot-wide path over which a unit would struggle in single file. Many Japanese outfits cut off from supplies but fully armed and spoiling for a fight, were bypassed and ambushed unsuspecting Americans in "rear" areas.

To Krueger's soldiers, who were forced into the dual role of fighters and pack mules, the three weeks in the green hell of Leyte seemed an eternity. The thick jungles were hot and humid, and razor-sharp rocks cut through boots and slashed feet. Rot lay just underneath the lush greenery. Decaying vegetation emitted a sour, nauseating odor that often caused tension-burdened soldiers to vomit. Dampness, thick and heavy, hovered everywhere, penetrated clothing, and increased the general misery.

Through this horrible terrain Krueger's soldiers struggled down gorges, clawed up treacherous mountains, and edged along narrow, slippery cliffside paths. Drenching rains and seventy-mile-per-hour winds lashed Leyte, turning its tangled jungles into quagmires. At night the blackness grew even more ominous for the GIs, filling them with a hundred fears. All the while the Americans were confronted by a wily, enigmatic, and tenacious foe. Always there was the haunting specter of sudden death or mutilation.

All over northern Leyte bitter clashes raged. On the morning of October 28, elements of the 17th Infantry Regiment, 7th Division, attacked the town of Dagami, ten miles inland from the invasion beaches, where several hundred Japanese were strongly entrenched. Wading waist deep through a swamp, the Americans were raked with machine-gun and rifle fire, and pounded by mortars. Typically, the action boiled down to tiny knots of GIs trying to root out Japanese in concealed spider holes and bunkers naturally camouflaged with vegetation. It was a bloody business, and the casualties piled up.

Private Leonard C. Brostram, enraged by seeing his comrades gunned down around him, charged a pillbox and its two machine guns alone. A slug tore through his stomach, knocking him down. Holding in his intestines with one hand, he continued to move forward. Two more bullets plowed into his abdomen. He crawled on and pitched grenades through the pillbox portals, silencing the weapons. While Brostram was drawing Japanese fire, his comrades slipped around the side and wiped out the strongpoint from the flank. The next morning, the 7th Division GIs cleaned out Dagami.[1]

Early on the morning of October 30, Colonel Red Newman's 34th Regiment of the 24th Infantry Division jumped off from the flimsy village of Jaro to seize the key town of Carigara, near the northern coast of Leyte twenty miles northwest of the invasion beaches. The leading elements, supported by a few tanks, could not even get out of Jaro. The Japanese had dug in on the outskirts and now raked the advancing GIs with heavy small-arms and mortar fire. Several Americans were cut down and the column was forced to pulled back.

Colonel Newman immediately sent a platoon to renew the attack, but after advancing less than a hundred yards it was pinned down by heavy fire. Newman rushed forward to see for himself what was holding up the attack. With bullets hissing past, the colonel walked past the prone GIs and toward the Japanese positions. Someone shouted, "Let's follow the colonel!" The men immediately leaped to their feet and advanced on Newman's heels.

A mortar shell exploded next to the colonel, blowing a GI to smithereens. Newman was knocked to the ground and his uniform saturated with blood from a gaping stomach wound. The enemy fire grew heavier. Grimacing from pain and flat on his back in the mud, Colonel Newman ordered a lieutenant to "send word for some artillery and mortar fire," then added, "Leave me here." His men refused to abandon him, and the ashen-faced colonel was dragged to the rear on a poncho. Red Newman would survive his grievous wound.

The following morning, the 34th Infantry reorganized and renewed the attack. The fighting was bitter, but the GIs slugged ahead yard by bloody yard and drove the Japanese back toward Carigara. At daybreak on November 2, American artillery pounded Japanese positions in front of the town, to no avail: the shells were exploding on areas vacated by the Japanese during the night. GIs jumped off on the heels of the barrage and occupied Carigara.

On November 3, the 34th Infantry Regiment continued its advance westward along the coastal road from Carigara. Morale was slightly higher, for the drenching rains had ceased and a warm sun was shining. Leading elements of the regiment soon bumped into an approaching Japanese reconnaissance battalion, which, although as startled by the contact as were the Americans, rapidly formed a defensive line behind a stream. A hasty order was issued to the GIs: cross the river and wipe out the enemy force.

Sergeant Charles E. Mower was leading his squad when he was hit by a bullet in midstream. Bleeding profusely, he refused to go down or retreat, continuing to urge his comrades ahead instead. Pointing out enemy weapons so effectively, Mower now became the center of attention of the enemy force. The sergeant was hit time and again, and finally went under, leaving a slick of crimson on the surface. Inspired by Sergeant Mower's example, the assault battalion stormed across the stream and routed the Japanese force.[2]

In the meantime, General Frank Sibert, commander of X Corps, was ordered by Sixth Army to attack southward from Carigara Bay toward the key Japanese-held port of Ormoc on Leyte's west coast, some twenty-five miles away. As long as the Japanese held Ormoc, General Yamashita's convoys could land troops and supplies on the island. Just inland from Carigara Bay and directly in the path of X Corps's advance was a long, craggy ridge, a natural defensive barrier guarding northwest Leyte. Dug in on this steep elevation were more than four thousand men of Lieutenant General Tadasu Kataoka's crack 1st Division.

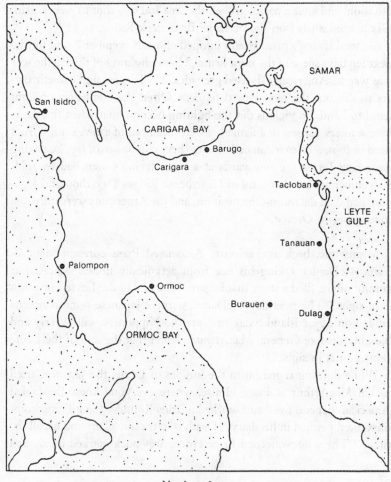

Northern Leyte

On the crest and forward slopes the Japanese had camouflaged scores of machine guns, and to the rear were large numbers of mortars and artillery pieces. With typical ingenuity, they had hastily constructed an interlocking system of trenches, spider holes, and firing pits, each situated to cover a possible approach. Rock outcroppings had been constructed into crude pillboxes, and in the defiles that sliced into the rugged terrain they had cut down trees and arranged them into miniature fortresses.

The task of driving the Japanese off of this gun-studded ridge was handed to Major General Frederick A. Irving's workhorse 24th Infantry Division, and after a patrol probed the area and was shot to pieces, grim GIs pinned a label on the obstacle: Breakneck Ridge.

General Irving's main assault jumped off on November 7, and for the next ten days some of the most brutal, bloody fighting of the Pacific war was waged. American GIs used grenades, TNT, rifles, and flamethrowers to dig out the tenacious defenders. Often the combatants fought hand-to-hand. So vicious did the fighting become that when five Japanese soldiers, targets of a flamethrower, raced out of a cave on fire from head to foot, an American called out, "Fry, you bastards, fry!" Clawing their way forward a few yards at a time, Irving's men had by mid-November achieved control of Heartbreak Ridge. Two thousand Japanese had died defending the position, and the Americans were only one mile closer to Ormoc.

Meanwhile, back at Tacloban, Associated Press correspondent C. Yates McDaniel, taking his cue from a typically upbeat MacArthur communiqué, filed a story that began: "The end of the Leyte campaign is in sight." The next day McDaniel wrote: "Japanese reinforcements landed on Leyte island today indicate the Nipponese will bitterly and bloodily dispute General MacArthur's belief that the end of the Leyte campaign is in sight."

While fighting raged on in the jungles of Leyte, the Japanese tried to kill MacArthur at Price House, where everyone knew the fabled American general lived and worked. Carlos Romulo, the Filipino commissioner, penned in his diary: "Death is in the air, all around us, all the time."[3] The white-stuccoed Price House was pock-marked inside and out from repeated strafings. Shells had left yawning holes in the walls. Visitors were ingenious in hastily concocting reasons for their required presence elsewhere. The Japanese had pinpointed MacArthur's headquarters as a special target but had been unable to hit the bull's-eye. Their strenuous efforts had come close, however; twelve Filipinos had been killed in a building adjacent to Price House, and two civilian correspondents met their deaths in a structure to the other side.

At one point General MacArthur was working alone at his desk when a flight of Zeros zoomed in at tree level and riddled Price House with .50-caliber bullets. A worried staff officer dashed into MacArthur's office and called out excitedly, "Did they get you?"

Still seated at his desk, MacArthur removed his pipe and replied evenly, "Not this time," then pointed to a bullet hole in the wall about a foot above his head.[4]

On November 27, MacArthur convened a strategy session at his Tacloban headquarters. The subject was his coming leap to Mindoro, the last stepping-stone on the long and tortuous jungle road back to Corregidor and Bataan and Manila—destinations that had obsessed MacArthur for two and a half years. Mindoro, two hundred and sixty miles northwest of Leyte, would be needed for land-based planes to support another leap-frog attack on Luzon, just to the north.

All the senior officers in the Philippines were present: General Walter Krueger, the ground commander; General George Kenney, the air chief; Admiral Tom Kinkaid, MacArthur's naval leader; Lieutenant General Robert L. Eichelberger, soon to take command of the newly formed Eighth Army, as well as various other top staff officers. Almost at once the session became heated, with red-faced brass shouting and pounding the table. General Kenney, somewhat sheepishly, admitted that if the weather was overcast his Leyte-based planes would not be able to protect the Mindoro amphibious operation. MacArthur was far from pleased. For many days ambitious George Kenney had been arguing that Bull Halsey's carrier-based aircraft were no longer needed in Leyte Gulf—not the kind of talk Douglas MacArthur liked to hear. As he had told Kenney weeks before, he was going to invade Luzon if he had to row a boat there alone with Kenney flying cover in a B-17. Now the irritated supreme commander called on Admiral Kincaid to express his views.

Only a few days earlier, the "co-commander" in the Pacific, Admiral Chester Nimitz, had balked at MacArthur's request to provide warships and other vessels for the Mindoro invasion. Before he would risk his ships, Nimitz had declared, MacArthur would have to assure him that there was adequate land-based air power to guard against *kamikaze* attacks. Furious at Nimitz, MacArthur had called in his navy commander. Kinkaid was caught in the crossfire between the Pacific's "Army Theater of Operations" (MacArthur) and the "Navy Theater of Operations" (Nimitz). Kinkaid, whom MacArthur liked, was a symbol of a recalcitrant and timid Navy, as MacArthur saw things. The general read him the riot act. Kinkaid stood there mutely, much like a schoolboy being admonished by the headmaster, as MacArthur ranted and waved both arms. "Warships, what are they for?" the general bellowed. "They have to take risks just as my soldiers and tanks have to take risks." Warming up to his tirade, MacArthur declared that "the Navy has a moth-eaten tradition that an officer who loses his ship is disgraced."[5]

Now, at the tension-packed Tacloban conference, MacArthur was in for another unpleasant surprise. Kinkaid, despite the tongue-lashing he had been forced to absorb from the general on behalf of the United States Navy a few days earlier, vigorously opposed any idea of threading his aging battlewagons and slow, thin-skinned baby flattops through narrow Surigao Strait in order to reach the Mindoro landing beaches. It was in Surigao Strait that Admiral Jesse Oldendorf had ambushed and wiped out Nishimura's Southern Force the previous month. "We will be sitting ducks for Jap land-based air," Kinkaid declared.

This was the same argument that Nimitz had put forth. But there was a difference: Kinkaid took his orders from MacArthur. "Well, Tom," MacArthur replied evenly, "that's a chance you're going to have to take."

All through the heated meeting, enemy warplanes had been pounding targets in and around Tacloban. American anti-aircraft guns were barking so furiously on all sides that voices at the conference table were often drowned out. Periodically, there was the *crump* of exploding bombs and the rattle of the Zeros' machine guns. Puffing on his corncob, Douglas

MacArthur affected to ignore the violent air raids. The other generals and admirals therefore assumed the pretense that they didn't hear bombs dropping and ack-ack guns going off, either.

That night General Eichelberger wrote to his wife Em: "The noise was terrific, but the Big Chief went right on talking."[6]

While MacArthur's eye was on a leap to Mindoro, General Tomoyuki Yamashita's gaze was focused on a complex of three American airfields, known as San Pablo, Buri, and Bayug, and located inland from the invasion beaches in eastern Leyte. If he could knock out those airstrips, the Tiger of Malaya might yet pull victory out of apparent defeat.

9

Japanese Paratroopers in Suicide Jump

Operation *Wa* was the code name for a daring Japanese airborne and ground offensive designed to seize the initiative on Leyte. Named after Lieutenant General Takaji Wachi, Thirty-fifth Army chief of staff who had developed the plan, *Wa* had been hatched a month earlier and was to be implemented if the situation on Leyte became desperate. The situation was now desperate. General Yamashita thus ordered *Wa* to be put into effect. The principal target would be three American airstrips on Leyte, San Pablo, Buri, and Bayug, where it was hoped American land-based air power could be destroyed.

Operation *Wa* would develop over a period of ten days, beginning with landings by twin-engined transport planes filled with eighty men each of the Kaoru Airborne Raiding Detachment on Bayug and Buri airstrips east of the town of Bureuen. Their mission was to blow up U.S. aircraft and facilities, then withdraw westward into the mountains. Then the 2nd Parachute Brigade, recently rushed from Formosa to Lipa Airfield on southern Luzon, would make a night drop and seize the three American strips. It would be the Japanese army's first airborne operation since February 1942.

The next day General Suzuki, Thirty-fifth Army commander on Leyte, would attack eastward with his 11th and 26th Divisions and link up with the paratroopers. At the same time, remnants of the 16th Division, the outfit that had done "the dirty work on Bataan," would infiltrate down from the mountains of eastern Leyte and join in the coordinated assault against the three airfields.

Shortly after midnight on November 27, the men of the Kaoru Airborne Raiding Detachment, each loaded with explosives, waddled aboard four transports at Lipa. The morale of the raiders, under Lieutenant Shigeo Naka, was high, despite the suicide nature of their mission. After a flight of about two hours, Lieutenant Naka reported by radio that the raiders were nearing the targets. In actuality, only one transport was over the airfields, and all aboard were killed when it crash-landed with jarring impact on the Buri airstrip.

Two Japanese transports crash-landed on beaches south of Dulag, far off-target, and most of the dynamite-loaded raiders decamped into the black jungle. At the same time, a bored sentry of the 728th Amphibious Tractor Battalion was manning a lonely post along the Leyte Gulf shoreline. The soldier's thoughts were 8,046 miles away (the distance to the United States) when he suddenly heard a swishing sound similar to that given off by an airplane as it glided in for a landing. Then he caught a glimpse of the shadowy outline of an aircraft landing on the water just offshore.

Presuming that it was a friendly plane in distress, one forced down by engine trouble or lack of fuel, the sentry plunged into the surf, swam to the bobbing aircraft, and climbed on a wing to offer assistance. The occupants were decidedly ungrateful, even to the point of tossing hand grenades at the puzzled Good Samaritan, who leaped back into the water and swam for shore. The grenade explosions awakened the sentry's comrades, and there was a mad scramble for weapons. When the Japanese on the floating transport plane reached land, they were greeted by a fusillade of small-arms fire. A brisk fight followed in which several Japanese were killed and the remainder of the intruders slipped off into the countryside. The mission had been a failure.

In Manila, no further word was heard from Lieutenant Naka and his raiders. But apparently the raid had been at least a partial success,

Yamashita's headquarters believed, for American aircraft over Leyte diminished in numbers the next day. So that night Radio Tokyo blared the good news to the homefront: The Kaoru Airborne Raiding Detachment had occupied key positions on the American airfields by means of suicide tactics and had accomplished its mission.

Not far from the airfield complex on December 1, General MacArthur was working alone in his Price House office when ack-ack guns opened fire at Japanese aircraft heading for Leyte Gulf. An errant shell punched through the general's bedroom wall and came to rest on a couch, a dud. Later, MacArthur found the projectile, and the next morning at breakfast he placed the shell in front of the responsible officer and said evenly, "Please ask your gunners to raise their sights just a little bit higher."[1]

The following night, December 2, General Walter Krueger was studying battle maps at his CP (command post) at Tanauan and assessing the Leyte situation after six weeks of slugging it out with General Sosaku Suzuki's Thirty-fifth Army. On the maps it looked good for the Americans. His Sixth Army now controlled most of Leyte, except for the San Isidro peninsula in the northwest corner of the island and a semicircular sector with a twelve-mile radius from the port of Ormoc. In addition, Suzuki's Thirty-fifth Army was in bad shape, Krueger's G-2 had concluded. It had lost 24,000 men, but still had some 35,000 tough, veteran soldiers to defend the northwest Leyte pocket. Krueger's losses had been 2,260 killed and missing, plus thousands more incapacitated due to wounds, injuries, dysentery, trench foot, skin rashes, malaria, and other ills encountered in tropical locales.

At the San Pablo airfield on the afternoon of December 4, Major Henry A. Burgess, acting G-3 (operations officer) of the 11th Airborne Division, received what was called a "crystal ball report." Burgess, a twenty-six-year-old rancher from Sheridan, Wyoming, had never heard of a crystal ball report. He rushed the message to Major General Joseph L. Swing, the fifty-year-old, white-thatched leader of the airborne outfit whose headquarters was at the airfield.[2]

Swing, a no-nonsense type, frowned as he read the message. It warned that the Japanese were planning to launch an airborne attack against the three American airfields. Even though the crystal ball reports had been "remarkably accurate" in the past, Swing scoffed at this one (as did other American commanders on Leyte). The general did not know that the reports were the work of American code-busting agencies, whose very existence was known but to a few at the highest levels.

Should the Japanese strike from the sky, however, the vital airfields would be in danger, for they were by air corps, engineer, signal, and headquarters troops, instead of regular infantry. The newly arrived 11th Airborne infantry regiments, two gliders and one parachute, were either fighting in the inhospitable Mahonag Mountains far to the west or guarding XXIV Corps rear installations along the landing beaches.

On the night of December 4, the G-2 of General John Hode's XXIV Corps issued an analysis of the situation in the airfields area: "Organized resistance has about ceased." Thirty-two hours later, just before dawn on December 6, soldiers of the Japanese 16th Division, who had slipped down from the mountains, crept into a bivouac area at the Buri airstrip and pounced on the sleeping men of a construction battalion. Many dozing Americans were bayoneted on the ground. The raiders then dashed into the battalion headquarters, where nine construction officers were sleeping. Each of the nine was shot in the head before he could unzip his hammock.

Despite the shock of the surprise assault, many construction soldiers grabbed weapons and, barefoot and in their underwear, fought the Japanese hand-to-hand. An angry cook shot five men trying to loot his kitchen. But soon the construction soldiers, not trained for combat, scattered into the surrounding jungles. Other Buri service troops, mainly signal and ordnance men, were chased from their bivouacs.

At mid-afternoon that day, at Lipa and Angeles airstrips on southern Luzon, the fourteen hundred men of the Japanese 2nd Parachute Brigade had finished a feverish day of preparations for the do-or-die assault on the American airfields. There was a shortage of transport planes, so only one of the brigade's two regiments would participate in the initial drop, with the other to follow the next day. The 3rd Parachute Regiment, led by Lieutenant Colonel Tsunehiro Shirai, would lead off the operation, but it would jump in three waves. Each wave would be separated by the several hours required for the transports to return to

Luzon, refuel, load up with more paratroopers, and return to Leyte.

Shirai's diminutive but tough parachutists were in high spirits. Each had been provided with a bottle of liquor to heighten their morale. The bottles carried a label with a strict order: "*Not* to be consumed until plane is in the air."

Knowing that assembling in the blackness was difficult once the paratroopers had jumped, planners had devised a system of identification that included horns, whistles, bells, gongs, wooden clappers, flutes, bugles, flares, and even distinctive songs for each small unit. Strips of a luminous substance were worn on uniform sleeves. Many officers spoke passable English. Each man carried a new parachute, and much of the equipment had not been used before. Everyone was heavily burdened with automatic weapons, land mines, and TNT. In their pockets were neatly folded slips of paper with taunting phrases in English, such as, "Go to hell, beast!"

It was hoped by the mission's planners that an element of surprise could be gained on approaching the airfields at dusk by the fact that the twin-engined Japanese transports bore a resemblance to the American DC-3 cargo plane and might be mistaken by air defense gunners for a friendly flight.

By 3:30 P.M., three-hundred-fifty paratroopers in the first wave were loaded onto twenty-six transports, and ten minutes later the aircraft sped down the runway and lifted off for Leyte. In the first plane was Lieutenant Colonel Shirai, who was carrying a battle flag personally inscribed two days earlier by Lieutenant General Kyoji Tominaga, commander of air operations in the Philippines. The inscription read: "Exert your most for your country." Shirai himself was in an elated mood, proud to be leading the attack that would drive the Americans off Leyte and out of the Philippines. Most of his paratroopers were to drop on Buri, the northernmost of the airfields, with others jumping on San Pablo and Bayug.

A few hours later, at twilight, General Joe Swing had finished a fried chicken supper at his CP on San Pablo airfield and was sitting idly outside, seeking a breath of fresh air in the oppressive heat. The husky, ramrod-straight general, who had played on the West Point football team along with another halfback named Dwight D. Eisenhower, gazed at two flights of transport planes approaching the airfield at about seven hundred feet. Swing thought they were DC-3s. So did Major Henry Burgess, who had just strolled outside. As the aircraft approached, Burgess was startled to see that the planes were lighted and that a man was standing in the doorway of each one. Those on the ground could not believe their eyes: these were Japanese paratroopers and they were ready to jump. The crystal ball warning of two days earlier had been accurate once again.

In a chow line nearby Captain Kenneth A. Murphy, a tall, solidly built former football player at the University of Minnesota, was also watching the approaching flight. As San Pablo was far behind the "front lines," neither the twenty-five-year-old Murphy nor the others lining up for supper were carrying their weapons. Suddenly Murphy heard General Swing call out: "Look at those Jap planes! They've even copied our flight formations!"[3]

When the two flights were directly over the airfield the American saw the grayish sky filling with parachutes. Cries of "They're Japs!" rang out. Supper was forgotten; mess kits were sent flying in every direction. There was a wild scramble as men dashed for their tents to retrieve rifles, carbines, Tommy guns, and BARs. The descending Japanese paratroopers came down right on top of the 11th Airborne CP and the airstrip nearby.

Most of the paratroopers landed on San Pablo, instead of on Buri as had been planned. Perhaps fifty Japanese, including Colonel Shirai, dropped on Buri. None of the parachutists landed on Bayug. Several were killed when their parachutes failed to open properly.

On both San Pablo and Buri, some of the invaders went about systematically torching and blowing up light aircraft, gasoline dumps, and buildings. But most seemed to be confused, drunk—or both. In the shadows cast by the flickering blazes, Japanese paratroopers ran madly about San Pablo screaming *Banzai!*, shooting off flares at random, and sounding their horns, clappers, whistles, horns, and gongs.

Others, however, rapidly organized into small groups. At one end of San Pablo, about forty of Swing's paratroopers, mainly headquarters and supply soldiers, had been packing bundles and rigging parachutes for an aerial resupply drop to comrades in the mountains. Lieutenant

David M. Carnahan and the others saw the Japanese parachutists descending and quickly broke open several bundles, got out machine guns and ammunition, and set up the weapons. A short time later, after night had fallen, Carnahan, crouched behind a machine gun, discerned the outline of a column of men, rifles slung over their shoulders, marching along the airstrip toward the tense Americans and singing what sounded like an old American favorite, "Sweet Adeline." No doubt these were 11th Airborne men sent to reinforce his little band, Carnahan reflected, but why all the crazy singing in this perilous situation?[4]

When the approaching soldiers reached a point twenty yards from Carnahan and his men, the marchers halted and the leader moved forward a few steps, aimed a flashlight beam at Carnahan, and asked, "Is this the machine gun at the west end of the airstrip?" The American felt a chill race up his spine. The officer spoke with an accent. "Yes, sir!" Carnahan called out, then squeezed the machine gun trigger, raking the intruders. The paratroop officer toppled over with a bullet through the head, still clutching the shining flashlight. Other Japanese were cut down by the burst, and the remainder fled into the darkness.

In the meantime, back at Lipa Airfield on Luzon, Colonel Shirai's second wave took off at 10:00 P.M., but after flying a short distance had to return to the field due to turbulent weather. The third wave never lifted off, resulting in Shirai fighting deep in American-controlled territory with less than half of his paratrooper regiment.

At San Pablo pandemonium reigned, as confused American 11th Airborne headquarters men and equally mystified Japanese paratroopers, alone, in pairs, and in tiny groups, were entangled in a lethal cat-and-mouse game. Wild shootouts erupted continually; streams of tracer bullets zipped through the black night; orange grenade blasts pierced the air. No one could be certain if a shadowy figure was friend or foe. At one point, Parachute Captain Ken Murphy was stalking the enemy and being stalked in turn. Then, just ahead, a bright chain of tracer bullets erupted and zipped past his head. Murphy leaped into a deep, two-man foxhole that was already occupied by a shadowy figure. Murphy was glad to have a comrade; not even the toughest fighting man liked to be alone in the blackness in a dangerous situation. Neither the captain nor the other man spoke a word, each being aware that the enemy was all around and that any sound could result in a shower of grenades.

After what seemed an eternity to Murphy, gray tinges in the sky to the east heralded a welcome dawn. Glancing at the dim figure beside him, Murphy noticed that the silhouette of his helmet had a curious configuration. Suddenly, he felt a surge of concern: this was a Japanese soldier. At the same time, the enemy paratrooper had apparently arrived at the identical conclusion with regard to Captain Murphy, for he raised his rifle with its fixed-bayonet and gave the American a vicious hack on the side of the neck. Murphy tried to raise his carbine, but a split-second later another blow of the razor-sharp bayonet sliced into the captain's left shoulder. The bayonet was raised for yet another, possibly fatal, slash when Murphy fired his carbine. The bullet caught the Japanese in the head, and he crumpled in a bloody heap to the bottom of the hole.

Captain Murphy took a silk flag and pistol from the dead paratrooper. Then, bleeding and dazed, Murphy managed to pull himself from the foxhole and joined others in organizing a defense until relief arrived later that morning.[5]

General Joe Swing, assuming the role of company commander, rounded up a motley crew of cooks, clerks, MPs, and headquarters soldiers that morning and led them in killing or chasing off the invaders remaining on the San Pablo airstrip. But many of them who had jumped on San Pablo moved over to the nearby Buri airstrip, where they joined Lieutenant Colonel Shirai's smaller force and elements of the 16th Division and seized control of the facility.

In the meantime, a 187th Glider Infantry battalion, led by Lieutenant Colonel George N. Pearson of Sheridan, Wyoming, rushed to the scene and joined in the fight at Buri. At noon on December 7, a battalion of the newly arrived 38th (Cyclone) Infantry Division reached the airport complex and was greeted by General Swing. "We've been having a hell of a time here," he declared with customary candor. "But I want the Japs kicked out and Buri Airfield secured by nightfall."

Wading through deep swamps, the Cyclone division battalion reached the edge of the Buri airstrip, where they clashed with dug-in Japanese paratroopers. Private Ova A. Kelly's platoon was pinned down by heavy machine-gun fire. Kelly scrambled to his feet and charged the enemy weapons. He killed eight Japanese before he himself was struck by a bullet. His wound was not serious, but medics dragged him into a shallow ditch until Kelly could be removed to an aid station. While waiting there, Private Kelly was hit by a stray bullet and killed.[6]

Outnumbered and outgunned, the Japanese paratroopers and 16th Division soldiers hung on doggedly against elements of four battalions until December 10, when one final coordinated assault by the Americans killed or drove off the remaining defenders and recaptured Buri Airfield.

Still the Japanese refused to give up. One group charged down the road to Bureuen and, using captured American automatic weapons, began firing into Major General Ennis P. Whitehead's Fifth Air Force headquarters building. An irate air corps staff officer phoned an infantry unit nearby and demanded that "this promiscuous firing cease at once." Informed that it was Japanese doing the shooting, the rattled air corps officer exclaimed that "the bullets are coming right through the general's office." Deeply annoyed by now, the infantry voice shouted back, "Then tell the goddamned general to get down on the goddamned floor!"

Operation *Wa*, which had been launched with high hopes, had by now fallen apart. The Japanese 11th and 26th Divisions, which were to have attacked eastward to link up with the paratroops, got bogged down by tangled, slippery mountain trails and thick jungle, and then bumped into elements of Swing's 11th Airborne Division in the Mahonag Mountains. General Yamashita's final roll of the dice for victory on Leyte had ended in dismal failure. But the bloodletting would continue unabated.

10

Killer Typhoon

Before dawn on December 7, while Joe Swing's 11th Airborne men were tracking down die-hard Nipponese paratroopers, a Seventh Fleet task force of warships and transports was lying off Leyte's west coast, three miles south of the key Japanese port of Ormoc. Under Rear Admiral Arthur D. Struble, the flotilla had made the 225-mile end run from Leyte Gulf through Surigao Strait and up into the Camotes Sea without detection.

Waiting nervously on transports were the assault waves of Major General Andrew E. Bruce's 77th Infantry Division, known as the Statue of Liberty division, because nearly all of its original members were from New York City, Brooklyn, or Jersey City. But Bruce's men called themselves the "Old Buzzards." Many were family men, and at induction their average age had been thirty-two, some eight years older than the average American foot soldier.

This would be another of MacArthur's "hit-'em-where-they-ain't" operations. The supreme commander hoped to split General Suzuki's formidable force in two by having Bruce's division land and drive due north, linking up with American elements pushing southward from the bloody Breakneck Ridge region. H-Hour had been set for 7:07 A.M. (the stocky, long-chinned Andy Bruce liked sevens for his battle-tested 77th).

At 6:38 A.M. Admiral Struble's destroyers opened up a heavy shore bombardment; after twenty minutes, LCIs (landing craft, infantry) equipped with scores of rocket launchers deluged a twelve-hundred yard stretch of beach. Promptly at 7:07 the first assault boats crunched up onto the sand and lowered their ramps; Bruce's leading troops dashed onto the beach without a casualty. Three hours later the Japanese air force struck violently and in substantial numbers, engaging twin-boomed Army Lightnings (P-38s) and Marine Corps fighters. For nine hours savage dogfights filled the sky above Ormoc Bay.

Three years earlier to the day, at Pearl Harbor, the ancient destroyer transport *Ward*—"the old bucket of bolts," as her crew affectionately called her—had fired the first American shot of the war and sunk a midget submarine. Now, in Ormoc Bay, three *kamikazes* dove on the old vessel. The first suicide plane struck the *Ward* just above the water-line and an enormous explosion rocked the ship. Within minutes she was a solid sheet of flame.

Admiral Struble ordered the crew to abandon ship and for the vessel to be sunk by American gunfire. As crewmen floundered about on rafts and rescue boats, tears welled in the eyes of men who had been a part of the gallant gray lady since Pearl Harbor. The Stars and Stripes were still waving over her as the *Ward* slipped beneath the waves.

In the meantime, on shore, the 77th Infantry Division pushed rapidly inland, opposed by scattered bands of Japanese who fought until killed and by periodic air attacks. Three days later the Old Buzzards captured the port of Ormoc, making it impossible for General Yamashita to reinforce and supply his beleaguered troops on Leyte. But General Suzuki, commander in the central Philippines, had no intention of surrendering; capitulation was out of the question. Suzuki led his men into the mountains and defied the Americans to come and get him.[1]

While the fireworks were erupting in Ormoc Bay, the 11th Airborne's 511th Parachute Infantry Regiment, led by thirty-six-year-old Colonel Orin D. Haugen, jumped off from positions in the Mahonag Mountains east of Ormoc in an attack that would hopefully reach Leyte's west coast. Hardly had Haugen's paratroopers begun moving forward than they were confronted with the customary bugaboos—

torrential rains, steep mountains, tangled jungles, and a clever and tenacious foe. The fighting was bitter. Three times the 2nd Battalion tried to seize a key hill but was driven back. Company E was assigned to cover the battalion's third pullback from the hotly contested elevation.

One of the E Company troopers was Private First Class Elmer E. Fryar, a quiet, unassuming son of the Deep South and, at age thirty-two, "old" for a rifleman. Fryar was the company barber, and often had remarked that after the war he hoped to return to his small town and open his own shop. In an outfit where profanity and hard-drinking were the norms, Elmer Fryar shunned both. Had a vote been taken by E Company troopers to choose the least likely hero, the well-liked and respected Fryar would have won easily.

Now, in the green hell of Leyte, while protecting 2nd Battalion's withdrawal, E Company was suddenly assaulted by a Japanese force screaming *Banzai!* Elmer Fryar spotted an enemy platoon trying to slip around the company flank. He dashed forward to an exposed hillock and was promptly struck and knocked down by Japanese fire. Dazed and bleeding, he pulled himself into a kneeling position and blazed away at the enemy platoon, killing twenty-seven Japanese and disrupting their charge.

Private Fryar, moving back to rejoin his company, came upon a seriously wounded comrade lying in the jungle. Despite his own painful wounds, Fryar managed to pick up his friend and began carrying him. Minutes later he met his platoon leader, who was kneeling over to give first-aid to another wounded parachutist. The four 11th Airborne men started toward the rear together. Suddenly, a Japanese soldier leaped out into the narrow path, raised his rifle, and took aim at the platoon leader. Elmer Fryar leaped in front of the parachute officer to shield him and a bullet intended for the lieutenant tore into Fryar's body.

Private Fryar, with blood spurting from his chest, collapsed onto the ground. Somehow he managed to pull the safety pin from a grenade and hurl it at the Japanese soldier, killing him. But soft-spoken Elmer Fryar would never open his small-town barber shop. Minutes later he let out a faint gasp and died.[2]

Another 511th Regiment trooper fighting in the mountains east of the port of Ormoc, Lieutenant Jack G. Barker, received word that he was to report immediately to 11th Airborne headquarters. At the time,

Barker, of Norman, Oklahoma, and a few of his men were stalking snipers. Although in combat but a short time, Barker was frustrated: he had yet to bag a Japanese soldier.

Trudging back to his regiment's CP, Jack Barker, a free spirit, conjectured as to how he had goofed up now. But there was another reason for his call back: he was being sent home to the States and a permanent assignment. A brother, also a paratrooper, had been killed in Normandy, and another brother, a bomber pilot, was missing after a raid over Germany. So the War Department had ordered Jack Barker, the remaining brother, back home.

Hastily saying good-bye at the forward command post, Lieutenant Barker joined a patrol of fifteen men that included two Marine fighter-bomber observers attached to the parachute regiment. Along the trail the lead scout spotted ten Japanese and opened fire. The enemy patrol ducked for cover, and so did the Americans. Barker, with a one-way ticket home in his grimy shirt pocket, leaped to his feet and dashed after a Japanese soldier crawling through the jungle, waving his carbine as he ran.

"Goddamned!" exclaimed Private First Class Jack S. Burns of Beverly Hills, California, who was stretched out on the ground nearby, covering Barker with a rifle. "What's Barker trying to do, club the bastard to death?"

When Lieutenant Barker was within twenty feet of his quarry, the crawling enemy soldier rolled over and leveled his rifle at the officer. Jack Burns shot him through the head, saving Barker's life.

But Barker felt cheated. Then he saw another soldier creeping toward high ground. The lieutenant, an ex-half-miler on his track team, gave chase. At a distance of twenty yards, he and the Japanese raised their weapons simultaneously. The enemy soldier fired twice at Barker, but missed. Barker's covering bodyguard, Burns, sent a bullet into the man's throat.

Now Lieutenant Barker was really angry. Again he had been cheated. He saw a third enemy soldier and raced after him. This time Barker was on his own—he had run into a growth of underbrush out of sight of the sharp-shooting Burns. Three quick shots rang out from the vegetation into which the parachute officer had disappeared. Burns and the others were alarmed. Had Barker's oversupply of luck run out?

There was a heavy rustling in the underbrush ahead. Burns and the others braced for a Japanese charge. Moments later Lieutenant Barker came into sight, yelling happily, "I got my Jap! I got my Jap!"

A Marine, who had been lying on the ground beside Private First Class Burns during the entire episode, turned toward Burns and, gesturing toward Lieutenant Barker, exclaimed, "You paratrooper bastards are crazy. Your whole goddamned outfit is crazy!" Jack Burns grinned as the Marine continued. "Look at that Lieutenant. He's especially crazy. He's got a ticket home. So what does he do? He chases Japs all over the goddamned mountain!" Early in December, American brass in the Pacific came to grips with the fact that they were being confronted by a revolutionary method of warfare, one that presented a serious threat to the future conduct of the war: swarms of *kamikazes* were wreaking havoc with American vessels in Philippine waters. No longer could the suicide attacks be shrugged off as isolated acts of desperation. A worried U.S. admiral confided to a newsman on December 10: "They're beating the hell out of us!"

In the seven weeks since the Leyte invasion, *kamikazes* had struck:

- the carrier *Intrepid*, killing 69, wounding 142, and causing heavy damage;
- the carrier *Cabot*, killing 36 and wounding 16 seriously;
- the carrier *Essex*, inflicting 18 casualties;
- the battleship *Maryland*, killing 31 and seriously wounding 40;
- the destroyer *Aulick*, killing 32 and wounding 64;
- the cruiser *Australia* (hit three times), inflicting many casualties;
- the destroyers *Mahan* and *Ward* (sunk), causing heavy loss of life;
- the battleships *Colorado*, cruisers *St. Louis* and *Montpelier*, destroyers *Saufley*, *Drayton*, *Liddle*, and *Lamson*, attack transports *Alpine* and *O'Hara*, as well as a score of large landing craft, inflicting heavy casualties and damage.

So serious was the menace that General MacArthur and Admiral Nimitz had ordered a news blackout to prevent the Japanese high command from learning of the enormous damage and casualties its suicide pilots were inflicting, and to keep the American homefront from panicking.

Meanwhile, at the Emperor's Palace in the heart of Tokyo, Prime Minister Kuniaki Koiso, who had been summoned by the emperor, was trying to explain to Hirohito what had gone wrong on Leyte. Three months earlier, a confident Koiso, who had just replaced the disgraced General Tojo, had called on Hirohito and assured him that when MacArthur struck the Philippines the Imperial armed forces would gain their greatest victory since the Battle of Tennozan in 1582. Now the customarily mild-mannered Hirohito was angry. How would he explain to the people the impending fall of Leyte? A flustered Koiso mumbled that this pledge would still be fulfilled when MacArthur struck at Luzon.[3]

General MacArthur indeed had his eye on Luzon. But first he would have to invade Mindoro, the large, wild, mountainous island separated from Luzon on the north by the seven-mile-wide Verde Island Passage. Mindoro's northern point, Cape Calavite, lay only ninety miles from Manila, Corregidor, and Bataan. But the proposed landing beaches along Mindoro's southwestern coast were about a hundred and ninety miles south of Manila. Near those beaches, designated White 1 and Blue 1, were four abandoned airstrips outside the village of San Jose. These were to be seized and converted into air bases to cover the invasion of Luzon.

Pentagon brass had sternly warned MacArthur that the leap to Mindoro was "too risky." Mindoro, they pointed out, was some two hundred and sixty miles northwest of Leyte Gulf, and therefore out of range of American air power based near Tacloban. In order to reach Mindoro, the invasion fleet would have to sail past Japanese-held islands, and even when the four San Jose airstrips were captured and operational they would still be surrounded by Japanese air bases on adjacent islands.

Douglas MacArthur disregarded the warnings from Washington, as he had become increasingly prone to do, and set December 15 as N-Day for the invasion of southern Mindoro. MacArthur was banking on General Yamashita leaving Mindoro lightly defended and husbanding the Imperial armed forces considerable strength on Luzon for the final showdown to determine who would be landlord of the Philippines.

Fortunately, MacArthur's intelligence had been remarkably accurate. On all of Mindoro there was only a hodge-podge Japanese force of some one thousand men, including about two hundred survivors of offshore ship sinkings who had struggled onto the beaches, been handed guns, and told they were infantrymen. They were about to face 11,878 American combat troops, mainly the 19th Regiment of Irving's 24th Infantry Division and the independent (that is, not a part of any division) 503rd Parachute Infantry Regiment. Also going ashore on N-Day would be 9,578 Army Air Corps men and 5,901 service troops, the latter to build airstrips and other facilities.

Leader of the ground forces for the Mindoro invasion would be stocky, black-haired Brigadier General William C. Dunckel, and there was little doubt he was the right man for the job. His intimate knowledge of the Philippines was legendary at MacArthur's headquarters. In prewar tours of duty, Dunckel had inspected countless islands in the chain, jotting down notes and memorizing tactical details. In 1931 he had driven around Mindoro in a Model T Ford. His sketch maps from memory of key locales on Leyte had been better than anything previously available.

The Mindoro invasion force of old battleships, cruisers, destroyers, and a few "jeeps" (baby flattops), under Admiral Arthur Struble, edged out of Leyte Gulf on December 12 for the five-hundred-and-fifty-mile trek through the island seas. The night was undisturbed. The next morning, too, was so calm that navy crewmen and troops grew jittery. They could smell a rat. Shortly after 5:00 P.M. they spotted it—Japanese warplanes.

Out of the sinking sun, swarms of *kamikazes* pounced on the American flotilla. One suicide plane crashed into the cruiser *Nashville*, exploding a few feet from the cabin Douglas MacArthur had occupied during the Leyte invasion. (Tokyo Rose had boasted that the Imperial Air Force would never permit the *Nashville* to leave Philippine waters.) The enemy pilot was loaded to kill; the two bombs he carried exploded with enormous impact. The *Nashville* was rocked from stem to stern; the deck closest to the explosions was covered with pieces of human bodies; blood was everywhere. Among the 131 killed were Admiral Struble's chief of staff, Captain E. W. Abdill; General Dunckel's chief of staff, Colonel Bruce D. Hill; and Colonel John T. Martha, commander of the 310th Bombardment Wing. The 192 wounded included General

Dunckel and several of his key staff officers. Dunckel refused to be evacuated, however, and was patched up by a medical officer. "I'm not going to miss this show," the ground force commander told the attending doctor.

Struble, Dunckel, their surviving staff officers, and twelve war correspondents transferred to the destroyer *Dashiell*. The ashen-faced and shaken reporters were deeply disappointed; they would not be permitted by censors to file one of the biggest stories of their lives—an eyewitness account of a successful *kamikaze* attack.

Less than two hours later the destroyer *Haraden* was hit by a *kamikaze*, and fourteen crewmen were killed and twenty-four wounded.

As dawn began to break on N-Day, outlining the towering peaks on Mindoro, Admiral Struble's destroyers offshore were ready to begin blasting the flat, inviting coastline. Suddenly, an urgent warning echoed through the warships: "Hold your fire!" Large numbers of Filipinos, many waving American flags, were dashing up and down White 1 and Blue 1 beaches to greet the invaders. Carabao were also lumbering up and down the sandy shore, possibly anticipating a renewal of their favorite sport, chasing and butting American soldiers.

A frustrated Admiral Struble directed his warships to fire high airbursts to warn off the beach reception committee. "Do not fire on natives or cattle," he added. At 7:10 A.M., each destroyer fired four warning shots high in the sky and, much to the relief of all hands, natives and beasts quickly scattered inland. The war could resume.

Minutes later shells and rockets began pounding the landing beaches, and at 7:31 A.M. the first assault waves went ashore standing up and dry-shod. Not a shot had been fired at them. By nightfall of N-Day, all four abandoned airstrips had been overrun. In a nearly textbook-perfect operation, the final springboard to Corregidor, Bataan, and Manila had been secured.

That night Radio Tokyo offered a different version. Lieutenant General Masaharu Homma, the "Victor of Bataan" two and a half years previously, was rushed onto the air to give his version of events on Mindoro. "The enemy was forced to make the Mindoro landing due to the terrific pressure exerted by our victorious forces on Leyte island. We have [the Americans] in a position on Mindoro to deal them a stunning blow. MacArthur, having many times escaped our traps, will not this time slip away.'"[4]

A day later, General MacArthur did indeed find his Mindoro beachhead force in a trap—this one fashioned by a fickle Mother Nature. MacArthur had taken a calculated risk in launching the Mindoro invasion beyond the range of land-based air power. The general was counting on Admiral Halsey's carrier planes to provide protection until the Mindoro airstrips around San Jose could be whipped into shape. No one could have foreseen the catastrophe that was about to upset all of MacArthur's carefully laid plans.

On the afternoon of December 18—N-Day plus 1 at Mindoro—Halsey was in the flag plot of the *New Jersey* east of Luzon, trying to mask the deep concerns that gnawed at him. He had just finished his eighth cup of coffee and lighted his thirtieth cigarette that day—both normal daily consumptions. But there was good reason for Halsey's worry: meteorologists had advised him that a typhoon was heading for the fleet.

Even before the storm struck in all its fury, chaos erupted on Third Fleet vessels. The wind quickly built to sixty-two knots. Men were washed overboard. Planes on the carrier *Monterey* broke loose from tiedowns and caught fire. The escort carrier *Kwajalein* lost her steering. Aircraft from the *Wisconsin* and *Boston* plunged overboard. Fires broke out on the flight decks of the *Cowpens* and the *Cape Esperance*.

At 2:00 P.M. the storm reached its peak. Seventy-foot waves jolted the fleet from all sides. Winds reached ninety-three knots. The rain and scud were blinding, making it impossible to distinguish ocean from air. Halsey, peering out from the bridge, could not see the bow of the *New Jersey*, three hundred and fifty feet away. A large shell had once struck the ship without Halsey even feeling its impact; now it was being tossed around as if it were a canoe. Halsey shouted to another officer, "Imagine what it's like on destroyers one-twentieth our size!" There was no response. The typhoon's roar was so loud that others in the flag plot did not hear the remark.

Indeed the destroyers were taking a severe beating. Winds pushed over their stacks until they were nearly horizontal; water poured into ventilators and intakes, shorting circuits, killing the power, steering lights, and communications, and leaving vessels adrift. Parts of destroyers were sheared off cleanly and carried away. But it was not just the steel warships that were taking a physical drubbing. So were those onboard. On the *New Jersey*, Halsey and others were slammed from one bulkhead (wall) to another, resulting in bloody and broken noses, cuts, and fractures.

At the height of the storm's savagery, three destroyers capsized:

- The 2,100-ton *Spence*, once one of the famed "Little Beavers" squadron; 24 survivors out of more than 300 officers and crew;
- The 1,395-ton *Hull*, grizzled veteran of Guadalcanal, Wake, the Marshalls and Marianas; 54 saved out of about 250;
- The 1,390-ton *Monaghan*, blooded at Pearl Harbor, veteran of the Aleutians and Marianas; 6 survivors out of 250.

Seaman Doil Carpenter, of Pasadena, California, was with a crew manning a gun when the *Monaghan* went down. The suction pulled him under and he lost consciousness. When he bobbed back up to the surface, Carpenter was faintly aware that hands were reaching out to drag him into a raft. One of those on the raft he hazily recognized was a cook.

The men spent a terrifying night on the little raft. Each time a wave would jolt it, men were swept overboard, never to be heard from again. Dawn brought a calming of the waters and renewed tragedy. The cook who had fished Carpenter from the ocean and an eighteen-year-old youngster from Texas became violently ill from drinking sea water. The stricken men thrashed about, their mouths evidencing a cream-colored foam and their tongues curling uncontrollably. The convulsions ceased only when both crewmen died. A gunners mate from the *Monaghan* had been severely injured when the ship sank, and he died shortly after daybreak. Four others on Carpenter's raft would go out of their heads and die of thirst.

Sharks moved relentlessly around survivors huddled on rafts, while other men kept afloat only by life jackets were not menaced by sharks. Three survivors from the *Spence*, all bobbing about in life jackets, tied themselves together around a life ring, drifting helplessly for hours before being rescued. All suffered from strange hallucinations: the sight of land nearby; a scantily clad Japanese girl suddenly appearing with fresh drinking water; rescue by a Russian submarine.

Nicholas Nagurney, a fireman on the *Hull*, and a few men on another raft were struck by delusions. "See how deep the water is, Nick," Glenn Wilkerson called out. Without hesitating, Nagurney thrust his arm into the water. It was bitten by a shark. Nagurney let out a loud howl and quickly pulled back his arm. Then he spotted the shark, one about eight feet long. Nagurney and the others examined his bleeding arm. The shark had bitten a thin slab off the top of the right forearm; on the under side were teeth marks half an inch deep.

A navy lieutenant on the raft became delirious and took several long gulps of sea water. Nagurney pounced on him and rammed his finger down the officer's throat to make him vomit. The deranged lieutenant bit Nagurney's finger. Nagurney later said to his bedraggled raft mates, "I guess I'm the only guy that's ever been bit by a shark and a lieutenant the same day."

As soon as the typhoon subsided, a search was launched for survivors. It soon grew dark, however, and locating a bobbing head or a tiny raft became impossible. No one was found that night. For three days, every ship and plane in Third Fleet hunted for victims of the storm in the most intensive man-overboard search in American naval history. Here and there individuals and tiny groups were fished from the waters, but the elements had inflicted a disaster upon Third Fleet such as the Imperial Navy had only dreamed about. Altogether some 790 Americans lost their lives in the storm, 200 planes were wrecked or destroyed, and 28 ships damaged.

Because of the typhoon, Third Fleet had been unable to launch a single warplane to pound the Japanese air bases on Luzon and prevent air attacks on the Mindoro beachhead or its supply convoys. Now Halsey had to notify MacArthur that Third Fleet would have to retire hundreds of miles eastward to the large base at Ulithi atoll to repair typhoon damage.

But Douglas MacArthur had escaped the "trap" at Mindoro that had been sprung by the weather's fury. So rapidly had American and Australian engineers put the four airstrips at Mindoro into operational order that by N-Day plus 2 General Kenney's land-based warplanes had flown in. The mountainous springboard to Luzon was secure.

On December 26 MacArthur issued yet another upbeat communiqué: "The Leyte campaign can now be regarded as closed except for minor mopping-up operations."

When the pronouncement trickled down to the level of those who would have to wield the "mops"—the frontline fighting men—the Leyte sky was turned a deeper shade of blue with their curses. The phrase "mopping up" infuriated the exhausted, grimy foot soldier hacking his way through the steaming jungles, always in danger of death or mutilation without warning. As he knew all too well, the Japanese under General Suzuki, although backed into the wild mountains in northwestern Leyte with no hope of escape, were still an intact fighting force (actually numbering some 27,000 men).

General Walter Krueger's Sixth Army was pulled back to prepare for the decisive invasion of Luzon, and the job of mopping up rugged Leyte was turned over to General Robert Eichelberger and his newly formed Eighth Army. Referring to MacArthur obliquely as the Big Chief or "Sarah" (Sarah Bernhardt, the legendary actress), Eichelberger wrote his wife Em that he could "never understand" MacArthur's public-relations policy of announcing victories when significant numbers of armed and organized Japanese were still resisting savagely.

Douglas MacArthur's misleading communiqué on Leyte was a great deal more truthful than those coming out of the Imperial General Headquarters in Tokyo, however. In one communiqué issued at the same time as MacArthur's, the Japanese claimed that they still held the Burauen and San Pablo airstrips (where the suicide paratroop force had been wiped out two weeks earlier).

If the beleaguered General Sosaku Suzaki had any doubt that he and his men in northwest Leyte were being abandoned to their fate, that doubt became a certainty on Christmas Day. At his jungle hideout in the mountains, Suzuki received a signal from General Yamashita in Manila. Leyte had been written off, Yamashita declared. The decisive battle would be fought on Luzon. "I shed tears of remorse for [the thousands] of my countrymen who must fight to the death on Leyte," the Tiger of Malaya exclaimed.

11
Rain of Human Bombs

General Tomoyuki Yamashita, aware that the climax of the war in the Pacific was at hand as Douglas MacArthur prepared to strike at the key island of Luzon, was a portrait of confidence as he was interviewed by reporters from Tokyo. Large in physique at six-foot-two and two hundred pounds, the Tiger of Malaya leaned back in his office swivel-chair in Manila and declared, "The loss of one or two islands does not matter. The Philippines have an extensive area and we can fight freely to our heart's content."

There was a brief pause as a flight of American fighters darted high above the Pasig River. Then Yamashita added, "I shall write a brilliant history of the Greater East Asia Co-Prosperity Sphere in the Philippine Islands."

That night, quoting Yamashita, Radio Tokyo embellished on the general's already boastful views: "The battle for Luzon, in which three hundred thousand American officers and men are doomed to die, is about to begin."

The new year of 1945 had just been ushered in, and with it General Yamashita had abandoned Manila and moved his headquarters to

Baguio, nestled in the mountains a hundred and twenty-five miles north of the Philippine capital. Baguio would be more defensible.

These early days of the new year were ones filled with emotion for Douglas MacArthur. Forced by presidential order to sneak away like a thief in the night aboard a leaking PT boat thirty-three months earlier, MacArthur would soon be returning to Corregidor, Bataan, and Manila at the head of the most powerful land, sea, and air force theretofore assembled in the Pacific—nearly a thousand ships and three thousand landing craft, in addition to some two hundred and eighty thousand men—an armada greater than those General Eisenhower had commanded for the invasions of North Africa, Sicily, Italy, and Southern France. But General Yamashita would be waiting on Luzon with the largest army the Americans had yet encountered in the Pacific: some two hundred and ninety thousand men, most of them battle-tested and nearly all of them eager to die for their emperor.

While the Tiger of Malaya had long since despaired of final victory in the Philippines, he was determined to pin down the invading Americans indefinitely while defenses were being prepared on the Japanese mainland. He knew that mountainous, jungle-covered Luzon was the ideal place to accomplish this task.

Yamashita was not certain where the Americans would hit. Military logic told the Japanese commander that MacArthur would come ashore at Lingayen Gulf, where his own countrymen had landed in December 1941. The gulf, a hundred and twenty miles north of Manila, not only provided perfect beaches and a wide anchorage, but stretching south from it toward the Philippine capital was the great central plain over which large bodies of vehicles and men could move rapidly.

Leading the American ground forces against Yamashita would be General Walter Krueger. Few men, including MacArthur, were as intimately acquainted with the military features of Luzon as was Krueger. In 1908, not long after his graduation from West Point, the then-Lieutenant Krueger, a serious-faced young man with hair parted dead in the center, was assigned to the Philippines and made a topographical inspector. As the head of a mapping party, young Lieutenant Krueger rode and tramped up and down the central plain of Luzon. Never in his wildest dreams had Walter Krueger believed that thirty-six years later he would be leading a powerful army over it, hell-bent for Manila.

While most officers clawed and scratched to obtain higher rank, General Krueger disliked the lofty impersonality forced on him by his present job as Sixth Army commander. "Hell," he exclaimed to reporters at Tacloban, "I'd rather have a regiment." Then he added, "I don't do much except think a lot, scold a little, pat a man on the back now and then—and try to keep a perspective."

At sixty-four, Krueger could outwalk men many years his junior. Once, on Leyte, a GI, watching the general scramble up the side of a rugged cliff, had called out to a comrade, "Look at that old bastard go. He must be part mountain goat." Now, more than three and a half decades after his first tour of duty on Luzon, Walter Krueger mused aloud to staff officers: "With the Japanese in possession, I think the map of Luzon needs a revision." That map-revision project, as the Tiger of Malaya suspected, would be launched at Lingayen Gulf.

S-Day was set for January 9, 1945. Two of Krueger's corps would make the assault, storming ashore at points seventeen miles apart. Major General Oscar W. Griswold's XIV Corps, consisting of the 37th Infantry Division (once the Ohio National Guard) and the 40th Infantry Division (National Guardsmen from California, Nevada, and Utah), would hit the western beaches near the town of Lingayen. Major General Inis P. Swift's I Corps, including the 6th Infantry Division (originally regular Army units) and the 43rd Infantry Division (National Guardsmen from New England), would come ashore on the eastern beaches near San Fabian.

The invasion fleet under Admiral Tom Kinkaid was so large it had been divided into four parts: bombardment and fire-support under Admiral Jesse Oldendorf; cover group under Rear Admiral Russell S. Berkey; San Fabian Attack Force, with troops for the eastern beaches, under Vice Admiral Daniel E. Barbey; and Lingayen Attack Force, with troops for the western beachhead, under Vice Admiral Theodore S. Wilkinson.

Admiral Oldendorf's heavyweights, the armored point of the spear, set sail from the central Philippines for the invasion landing beaches on January 3—S-Day minus 6. Included in the flotilla of 164 vessels were the "ghost ships," battlewagons that had been sunk at Pearl Harbor and raised from the mud. Oldendorf's mission was to bombard the beaches —to "soften" them up. Unknown to Oldendorf, the bombardment would be unnecessary, a fact that MacArthur's planners had already been told.

A few weeks prior to S-Day, U.S. Army Lieutenant Colonel Russell W. Volckmann—the leader of the guerrillas in northern Luzon—and his men had recovered documents from a crashed Japanese plane that gave away a closely guarded secret: General Yamashita would sacrifice shoreline defenses at Lingayen Gulf in order to concentrate his forces in the mountains. Volckmann had been advised by MacArthur's headquarters in late December that "invasion of Luzon is imminent." Colonel Volckman had promptly radioed back: "There will be no, repeat no, opposition on the [Lingayen Gulf] beaches." But no one at MacArthur's headquarters had paid attention to the urgent signal from the invasion site. As a result, Admiral Oldendorf was expecting to deal with heavy coastal guns, dual-purpose and anti-aircraft batteries.

On the eve of Oldendorf's departure, Carlos Romulo, the resident commissioner in President Osmeña's government at Tacloban, penned in his diary: "I can still remember the cold terror (in December 1941) when I heard over Manila Radio, 'Eighty Japanese transports have been sighted in Lingayen Gulf.' " Since that time thirty-seven months previously, the fortunes of war had changed drastically, and as Admiral Kinkaid's awesome fleet headed for the same locale, Romulo scribbled, "Now it is *their* turn to quake!"[1]

But the landlords of Luzon, with their quaint-looking helmets and World War I-style leggings, would not be the only ones quaking. Nearly everyone on Kinkaid's ships was quaking, also, for the entire U.S. fleet, with good reason, was obsessed with *kamikaze*-phobia. The affliction, peculiar to those fighting in the Pacific, would have been even more acute had the Americans been aware of a chilling factor: the Imperial High Command, in its desperation, had earmarked a hundred and twenty aircraft based at the Clark Field complex, and as many more from Nichols and other Luzon airfields, to crash into Admiral Kinkaid's Seventh Fleet as it sailed toward Lingayen Gulf.

Before dawn on January 4, even as Admiral Oldendorf's lead-off bombardment group was passing through Surigao Strait headed for the

Sulu Sea, about two dozen suicide planes were being readied at Mabala-cat outside Manila, the ground crews zealously cleansing their cockpits.

Gathered in groups in their barracks, the *kamikaze* pilots who would strike that day took inspiration from their *Song of the Warrior:*

> In serving on the seas, be a corpse saturated with water.
> In serving on land, be a corpse covered with weeds.
> In serving the sky, be a corpse that challenges the clouds.
> Let us all die close by the side of our sovereign.

As the strains of *Song of the Warrior* melted into eternity, the grim-faced suicide pilots headed for their aircraft. Many had mailed home locks of hair the previous evening. Others had sent fingernail clippings. All were now wearing white scarves around their necks. Leather helmets fit snugly about their heads, concealing the piece of white cloth each *kamikaze* pilot had wrapped around his forehead. (This headband, known as the *hachimaki,* had been worn centuries earlier by samurai warriors of feudal Japan in order to absorb perspiration and keep their hair from falling into their eyes as they fought. Centuries later, in late 1944 and early 1945, the *hachimaki* became the ceremonial symbol of the Special Attack Corps.)

Reaching their bomb-laden aircraft, the pilots climbed into the cockpits. Their average age was twenty. These were not the skilled pilots of what Imperial Navy admirals liked to refer to as "the good old Pearl Harbor days." Nearly all of the "old-timers" had been killed long ago. Rather, these flying incarnations of the Divine Wind had been rushed through flight school with minimal instruction. Most *kamikaze* pilots possessed more courage than flying skills.

On that afternoon of January 4, on scores of vessels in Oldendorf's iron-tipped spearhead, radar equipment was hard at work scanning for the dreaded *kamikazes.* Suddenly, above the escort carrier *Ommaney Bay* came a frightening screeching noise: a twin-engined bomber, undetected by either lookouts or the new radar equipment, plunged into the carrier's flight deck.

In moments the *Ommaney Bay* was a mass of fire, black smoke, and exploding ammunition. The heat was intense. Seriously wounded crewmen, most covered with hideous burns, were strapped to cots, covered with life jackets, and lowered into the water. Hopefully, someone would pick them up. The abandon-ship order was given, and the skipper, Captain H. L. Young, slipped over the side twenty-two minutes later, the last man to leave the stricken ship. Six minutes afterward, the *Ommaney Bay*'s torpedo warheads exploded and the ship was blown to pieces. She had lost ninety-three killed or missing and suffered sixty-five wounded.

All the next day, January 5, Jesse Oldendorf's flotilla ran a gauntlet of Japanese torpedo planes and *kamikazes*. One of these ships, the cruiser *Louisville*— whose proud crew called "Lady Lou"—the flagship of Rear Admiral Theodore E. Chandler, had gained a reputation as a lucky ship since being commissioned in 1931. Her intimate relationship with Lady Luck seemed about to end, however, after a *kamikaze* struck her forward gun batteries, killing one man and wounding fifty-nine. But Lady Lou sailed onward after quick repairs.

Undaunted by the enormous curtain of flak that nearly blotted out the sun, the human bombs continued to plummet out of the sky. A *kamikaze* crashed the HMAS *Australia*, killing twenty-five men and wounding thirty, but she, too, continued onward. Two Zekes, weaving violently, knifed in just above the waves toward the *Manila Bay*. Possibly, the suicide pilots had a change of heart, for at the last second they pulled up into a steep climb. But at eight hundred feet the Zekes leveled off and moments later dove on the *Manila Bay*. One crashed into the flight deck and exploded. The *Manila Bay* lost twenty-two dead or missing and suffered fifty-six wounded. But in twenty-four hours, she would catch up with Oldendorf's flotilla.

The tall skipper of the destroyer escort *Ulvert H. Moore* was standing on the bridge, scanning the azure sky with binoculars and issuing orders to his anti-aircraft gunners. Like many of those who knew they would be running a *kamikaze* gauntlet, the *Moore*'s skipper had written a letter home to his mother Eleanor, hoping it did not reflect the peril he was facing in the dash to Lingayen Gulf: his mother had enough worries on her mind, with three other sons, John, James, and Elliot, also in the armed forces. The skipper was Lieutenant Commander Franklin D. Roosevelt, Jr., son of the president of the United States.

Suddenly, there was an ear-splitting racket as guns on the *Moore* and two nearby destroyer escorts, *Goss* and *Stafford*, began blasting away at three Zekes zooming toward them. One plane plunged into the water next to Commander Roosevelt's ship, and the other crashed near the *Goss*. But the third *kamikaze* plowed into the *Stafford*, killing a pair of crewmen and wounding twelve.

That night Japanese reconnaissance planes roamed the dark sky over Admiral Oldendorf's armada. The next day, January 6, promised to be lively. At sunrise, the bombardment group, battered and banged up but full of fight, arrived off Lingayen Gulf. The battlewagons had just opened fire on the beaches when a "devil bird" (as the Americans now called *kamikazes*) sliced off the shields of two 5-inch guns on the destroyer *Richard P. Leary*. The battleship *New Mexico*, just starting to bombard the shore near San Fernando, was hit by a Zeke already in flames. Unbeknownst to him, the *kamikaze* pilot had struck a bonanza: the flagship *New Mexico* was full of American and British officers observing the operation. Lieutenant General Herbert Lumsden, Winston Churchill's personal liaison officer to MacArthur's headquarters, was killed, as were Captain R. W. Fleming, the battleship's commander, his communications officer, an aide to General Lumsden, and *Time* magazine reporter William Chickering. All had been standing on the port side of the bridge. Rear Admiral G. L. Weyler and a Royal Navy observer, Admiral Bruce Fraser, who were standing on the starboard side of the bridge, escaped unscathed. Twenty-five less heralded crewmen were killed and eighty-seven were wounded. Damage to the *New Mexico*'s superstructure was extensive—but her guns continued to blast away.

At noon four *kamikazes* went after the destroyer *Walke*. Her guns knocked down three, but the fourth slammed into her bridge. The *Walke*'s thirty-three-year-old Philippine-born skipper, Commander George F. Davis, was drenched with gasoline and moments later turned into a human torch. Crewmen rushed to Davis's aid and smothered the flames. Virtually his entire body had suffered burns, but he fought off efforts to take him below. In great pain, he continued to issue orders and direct the fight against the fires that had broken out, exhorting officers and men to save the *Walke*. Still standing, George Davis saw his guns splash yet another devil bird that had come after his wounded ship. Only when all the fires had been extinguished did Commander Davis permit his men to carry him below. He died a few hours later. (Commander Davis would receive the Medal of Honor posthumously.)

The bitter fight in Lingayen Gulf raged on. Three more ships were struck by *kamikazes*. Near sundown, a swarm of suicide planes pounced on the heavies. One struck the battleship *California*, Admiral Oldendorf's flagship, which was then raked by anti-aircraft guns from a destroyer nearby that was trying to shoot down the *kamikaze*. The *California* lost forty-five men killed and suffered a hundred and fifty-one wounded. In the same attack, the destroyer *Newcomb* was damaged by "friendly" 40-millimeter bullets and fragments from 5-inch shells. The *Newcomb* lost two killed and suffered fifteen wounded. The light cruiser *Columbia*, called the "Gem of the Ocean" by her crew, was struck by a *kamikaze* that plunged through three decks before exploding. Casualties included thirteen dead and forty-four wounded. The *Australia* was struck again, adding another fourteen killed and sixteen wounded to her high casualties of the day before. But like her neighbor the *Columbia*, she continued to fight.

The *Louisville*—"Lady Lou"—had been hit the day before and was now ripped into again by a suicide plane. Her bridge sustained heavy damage. Hideously burned by flaming gasoline, Admiral Ted Chandler helped handle a fire hose, then, when the pain became so intense he could not function, took his turn with the enlisted men in obtaining first aid. But the flames had scorched his lungs, and the following day Ted Chandler would die. Thirty-one shipmates went with him, and fifty-six others were seriously wounded.

As night drew a shroud over the bloody waters of Lingayen Gulf, Admiral Oldendorf assessed the day's events and was deeply alarmed. On this one horrendous day—S-Day minus three before the planned return to Luzon—one ship had been sunk and eleven damaged, with an American admiral, a British lieutenant general, and hundreds of others killed. The carnage had been one of the United States Navy's worst setbacks since the Battle of Tassafaronga on November 30, 1942.

If the sturdy Jesse Oldendorf, shaken by the onslaught of piloted human bombs, briefly considered withdrawing from Lingayen Gulf, he quickly abandoned any such thoughts: to pull out would give the Japanese a tremendous moral victory. At the same time, Admiral Oldendorf was a realistic man. That night he transmitted an urgent signal to his boss, Admiral Kinkaid: "If transports on S-Day receive the same treatment, the troops might be slaughtered before they can land."

Now it was Kinkaid's turn to be shaken. He immediately requested that General Kenney's land-based aircraft and Admiral Halsey's carrier-based planes pound the *kamikaze* airfields on Luzon after daylight.

Two days's sailing time behind Oldendorf's bruised bombardment group, the remainder of the invasion fleet was cutting through the blue water off the western coast of the Philippines. One of these warships was the cruiser *Boise*, flying a five-star pennant. Pacing the deck was Douglas MacArthur, who had been promoted to General of the Army two weeks previously.

On the voyage, MacArthur had spent a good part of his time sitting in the doorway of the captain's cabin. He had the air of a man whose work was already done. At one point, a photographer for *Life* magazine, Carl Mydans, happened by, and MacArthur remarked evenly, "You know, Carl, this is the same route I followed when I came out of the Philippines in a PT boat . . . exactly the same route."

Suddenly, the *Boise*'s loud-speaker crackled: "General quarters, general quarters, all hands man your battle stations, prepare for submarine attack!"

MacArthur walked over to the rail and, along with many others, saw the ominous white wake of a torpedo streaking through the water directly toward the *Boise*. The cruiser lurched to starboard, and the torpedo raced on past. With no change of expression, the general nodded his head in agreement with the skipper's evasive action, then resumed his stroll.

Nearby a destroyer was hurling depth charges. Minutes later a Japanese midget submarine surfaced, no doubt the one that had missed torpedoing General MacArthur's ship by a whisker. Black and dripping, it looked like a small whale. The destroyer *Taylor* lunged at the under-sea craft and, with an enormous crunching noise, rammed it. The submarine went to the bottom, leaving only bubbles in its wake. MacArthur, who had been watching the episode, again nodded his head in approval.

The following morning, the *Boise*'s loud-speaker summoned crew members to battle stations, and a terrific din of ack-ack fire erupted. With an eerie whining sound, a Zero dove directly toward the *Boise*. All hands watched in terrified fascination. The racing *kamikaze* came closer and closer. When just a hundred yards away, the Zero was hit by flak and exploded, shaking the *Boise* from stem to stern. Through it all, MacArthur had remained below in his cabin.

When calm was restored, Dr. Roger O. Egeberg, MacArthur's physician, went below and found the supreme commander stretched out with his eyes closed. Egeberg was convinced that MacArthur was faking. How could anyone be so calm under such perilous circumstances? Standing in the doorway, the physician timed MacArthur's respiration: sixteen breaths a minute, suggesting a tranquil pulse of seventy-two. Egeberg strode over to MacArthur's bunk and took one of his patient's wrists, awakening him. "General, how in the hell could you sleep at a time like this?" Egeberg asked.

"Well, Doc, I've seen all the fighting I need to," MacArthur replied, "so I thought I'd take a nap."[2]

At 7:55 the next morning, January 6, a *kamikaze* hit the bridge of the attack transport *Callaway*, manned largely by Coast Guardsmen and carrying 1,188 assault troops. Splinters from the Zeke and bridge sprayed everywhere, and flaming gasoline was splashed over the decks. Twenty-nine crewmen were killed and twenty-two were wounded. Not a single embarked soldier received as much as a scratch.

As the convoy steamed on, it passed close enough to Luzon for Douglas MacArthur to make out the familiar old landmarks gleaming in the sun far off on the horizon—Corregidor, Bataan, and perhaps even Manila. The sight choked him with emotion as he stood motionless at the rail, saying nothing, simply staring toward Corregidor and Bataan. One by one, MacArthur's staff drifted away. But as a coppery sunset gave way to a Stygian night, the supreme commander lingered alone at the rail.

12

On to Manila!

It was an especially clear night and the stars, so far above the violent madness unfolding below, sparkled indifferently in the tropical sky. It was a few hours into S-Day, January 9, and the invasion fleet was slipping stealthily into Lingayen Gulf. Almost everyone was alert and anxious, particularly those on watch. Word had quickly circulated throughout the fleet that the *kamikazes* usually targeted a ship's bridge.

As the dark sky gave way to the first faint tinges of dawn, the eastern and western shores of the gulf could be dimly discerned. The Iloco and Zambales mountain ranges that paralleled the shoreline were covered by low-hanging clouds. Mount Santo Tomás, at 7,407 feet, towered majestically over its neighbors and seemed to frown down on the intruders squatting in Lingayen Gulf.

On display was the steel of America: hazily outlined cruisers, destroyers, and battleships—scores of them. Command ships bristled with antennae; smaller vessels carrying messages darted to and from between the larger ships, much like waterbugs scurrying about on a farmer's pond. Pouring out over the gulf was the sound of windlasses as booms on the ships swung out amphibious craft and lowered them gingerly into the calm blue water. Ears everywhere were cocked for any sound of the dreaded devil birds. Even the most inept suicide pilot, it seemed, could hardly miss, so abundant were the massed targets in the gulf. Those whose duty stations were near their ship's bridges silently wished they were somewhere else.

At 7:00 A.M. an enormous roar swept across the water and reverberated off the towering green mountains inland. Admiral Oldendorf's heavies had begun pounding the shoreline and mostly nonexistent Japanese coastal batteries—there were only two or three guns along the coast.

Burdened with weapons and heavy combat gear, General Krueger's foot soldiers, nervous and tense, climbed over the railings of their transports, made the hazardous descent down slippery rope ladders, and dropped into gently bobbing landing craft. With a revving of engines, assault boats headed for the beaches, some forty-five hundred yards away.

At 9:50 A.M.—ten minutes behind schedule—Admiral Daniel "Uncle Dan, the Amphibious Man" Barbey's coxswains put leading elements of the 43rd and 6th Infantry Divisions onto the white beaches near San Fabian. At the same time, Admiral Ted Wilkinson's sailors landed spearheads of the 40th and 37th Infantry divisions seventeen miles to the west, near the town of Lingayen.

Except for a handful of panicky Japanese stragglers who fired rifle shots before fleeing into the jungle, there was no opposition at the beaches. But all hell broke loose offshore when the feared devil birds made their by now dreaded appearance and swarmed all over the anchored fleet. One *kamikaze* dove on Admiral Wilkinson's flagship, the *Mount Olympus*, but was splashed. Another sliced off the destroyer escort *Hodges*'s foremast and radio antenna before lunging into the gulf. An eager suicide pilot made for the light cruiser *Columbia*, already hit twice, and plowed into her gun turrets. An explosion rocked the vessel and fires erupted everywhere. An additional twenty-four crewman were killed, and sixty-eight wounded. Captain Maurice E. Curts, the skipper of the "Gem of the Ocean," ordered the shore bombardment to continue, even as fires threatened to engulf the ship. With the firing mission completed and scores of dead and mangled bodies still strewn around the *Columbia*'s decks, Captain Curts radioed his superior: "Standing by for firing orders."

A *kamikaze* picked out the battleship *Mississippi* and was met with a torrent of machine gun fire from the vessel. But the pilot kept coming and slammed into her near the bridge. In those few moments, twenty-five blue jackets lost their lives and sixty-three others were seriously injured or burned.

No sooner had this plane hit the *Mississippi* than another devil bird headed for the bridge of the unlucky *Australia*. This time the Australian warship got off lightly: the Val merely sliced off its stack before splashing into the gulf. It was the fifth time in less than a month that the ill-starred *Australia* had been hit by *kamikazes*.

In the meantime, with no obstacles except the terrain—a combination of sand and marsh—Krueger's men quickly pushed inland, consolidated their separate beachheads, seized the five-thousand-foot-long Lingayen airstrip (which was in surprisingly good condition), and set their sights on Manila, some one hundred and twenty miles to the south. By comparison with the holocaust that was raging at sea, the first act of the drama on Luzon had been tame. But the second and third acts were yet to come.

"I don't like it," exclaimed one battle-hardened veteran of the 37th Division as he rested briefly after his outfit had occupied the little town of Binmaley. "It ain't like the Japs to simply haul ass!"

Out in Lingayen Gulf, at dusk, the battleship *Colorado* was knifing through the water when she was rocked by an explosion. A 5-inch shell, fired by nervous gunners on an American ship who had mistaken the *Colorado* for an enemy vessel, exploded in her sky control, which coordinated the ship's defenses. When the bloody bodies had been removed from the shambles, shaken crewmen found that eighteen shipmates had been killed and fifty-one wounded.

There were other instances of mistaken identity in the twilight of Lingayen Gulf. A 40-millimeter shell from a strafing American fighter plane zipped through the bulkhead of the galley of the light cruiser *Montpelier*, past the heads of several cooks, and out the other side. The men were left shaking and ashen-faced, but otherwise unharmed.

Five hours after the first American soldier set foot on the Lingayen

Gulf beaches, General MacArthur stepped out of a Higgins boat into knee-deep surf and waded ashore—into bedlam. Hundreds of landing craft were strewn along the shore like beached whales. Scores of amphibious tanks, tractors, and other tracked vehicles added to the congestion. Swarms of Filipinos, many waving American flags, were parading joyously. On spotting the imposing figure with the corncob pipe in his mouth, the oversized sunglasses, and the Philippine field marshal's hat, the natives let out a rousing cheer and ran inland to spread word of the Second Coming.[1]

MacArthur climbed into a jeep that, much to the driver's embarrassment, promptly broke down. Another vehicle was secured, and that afternoon the supreme commander, protected only by a soldier carrying a Tommy gun, plunged into the thick jungles to visit the battle CPs of all four assault divisions. By nightfall, American troops had pushed nearly eight miles inland. Fifty thousand men and their equipment were ashore.

It was just after 2:00 A.M. on S-Day plus 1 when a score or more of curious-looking little vessels slipped from the shadows at a concealed anchorage at Port Saul, some ten miles northwest of the town of Lingayen. There were sixty other craft just like them hidden along the shoreline nearby. These were the latest Japanese "secret weapons"— suicide boats. Their target: the American fleet in the adjacent black waters of the gulf.

Just over eighteen feet long, made of plywood, and capable of high speeds, each suicide boat carried two 260-pound dynamite charges and mounted a light machine gun. Its crew of two or three, volunteers from the Japanese army, was the seaborne equivalent of the *kamikaze*. The operational technique was uncomplicated: slip up close enough to an American ship to either hurl the heavy dynamite charge onto or crash into the target.

At 3:20 A.M. alert technicians on the destroyer *Philip* suddenly tensed. Strange-looking blips had flashed onto their radar screen. They spread the alarm: these were not American craft. Outside the radar room, the gulf was cloaked in eerie tranquility. A short time later, nervous lookouts on the *Philip* detected the shadowy silhouette of a small boat racing directly toward her, and gunners opened fire. The first 20-millimeter fusillade was on target, and an explosion echoed over the seascape. The suicide boat, loaded with five hundred and twenty pounds of dynamite, disintegrated, shooting an orange fireball into the sky.

Pandemonium erupted in the blackness as the swift suicide boats darted about the stationary fleet in search of victims. The destroyer *Leutze* blasted two midgets out of the water, and fifty minutes later was still firing away at the elusive little boats. Streams of tracer bullets illuminated the night and periodic explosions rocked the gulf. The midgets particularly sought out the thin-skinned transports, blowing huge holes in eight of them. A large infantry landing-craft was jolted by an explosion and sank, and another LCI was so badly damaged that it had to be abandoned. Two LSTs were seriously damaged.

As high as this toll from the unexpected assault by the midget suicide boats was, it was not nearly as large as a gleeful Radio Tokyo would report later that day: twenty to thirty American vessels sunk in Lingayen Gulf.[2]

At the same time that General Walter Krueger's veteran jungle fighters were storming ashore at Lingayen Gulf, scores of American aircraft fanned out over Luzon and dropped millions of leaflets with a message that read:

> In a series of brilliantly conceived blows, General MacArthur's forces of liberation have successfully, in but a short span of time, destroyed the enemy army defending Leyte, seized firm control of Mindoro, and now stand defiantly on the soil of Luzon at the very threshold to our capital city. Thus are answered our prayers of many long months—thus is the battle for the liberation of the Philippines fully joined and the hour of our deliverance at hand. . . .

The message was signed by President Sergio Osmeña. To many Americans, it sounded like pure MacArthurese.

Douglas MacArthur's shoes were still dripping water from his wade through the Lingayen Gulf surf at H-Hour plus 5 when he began to urge General Krueger to send mechanized columns in a lightning dash southward to Manila. "I know every wrinkle of the topography, and you can do it," exclaimed MacArthur. But Walter Krueger had grown cautious. The Sixth Army commander issued orders for General Oscar Griswold's XIV Corps to advance Southward down Route 3 toward the Philippine capital and for General Inis "Bull" Swift's I Corps to protect Griswold's flank by attacking toward the east and northeast.

Strong where they had once been weak, advancing where they had once retreated, America's fighting men began pushing toward Manila, following much the same route that the 51st Philippine Infantry (the famed Philippine Scouts) armed with antiquated rifles, had taken in the hectic retreat to Bataan in December 1941. Now the American soldiers were armed with a variety of advanced weapons that had been only designers' dreams three years earlier.

For days the wily Japanese melted away ahead of Griswold's Manila-bound columns, which were snaking forward fitfully down a handful of dirt roads and jungle paths, hemmed in on both sides by thick jungles. "The 'front' here is thirty feet wide and thirty miles long," was the grim, standard joke, meaning the column was strung out for lengthy distances with no protection from attack on either flank.

General MacArthur, with his eyes focused on Manila, Bataan, and Corregidor, was growing increasingly impatient with what he regarded as Walter Krueger's snail-like progress. MacArthur had always said that a leader should avoid "back seat driving," so he carefully avoided direct criticism of his Sixth Army commander. But there were those on his staff who were more than willing to climb into the back seat and start steering. One of these was the general's long-time chief of staff, General Richard Sutherland, whose stern edicts and abrasive personality had earned him the title of "most disliked" among MacArthur's staff.[3]

Yes, Walter Krueger is far too cautious and should be replaced, Sutherland told his boss. And Sutherland had in mind a superb candidate to replace Krueger as the commander of Sixth Army—General Richard Sutherland.

Psychologically astute, Douglas MacArthur settled for a subtler tactic to goad General Krueger into moving faster: the supreme commander displaced his own CP far forward to Hacienda Lusita, resulting in the unique situation of Supreme Commander MacArthur's headquarters being thirty-five miles closer to the "front" than that of Army Commander Krueger.

Some four hundred miles to the southeast, on the island of Leyte, where his troops were still fighting the twenty-six thousand armed and organized Japanese stranded there, General Bob Eichelberger was delighted to hear that the Big Chief was unhappy with Krueger's actions on Luzon. Eichelberger and Krueger had never been friendly, and now the German-born leader of Sixth Army was getting headlines in the States while Eichelberger and his troops, battling ferociously in what had been officially labeled a mopping-up operation, were receiving no recognition at all. (With Douglas MacArthur's dramatic return to Luzon and the drive toward Manila, Bataan, and Corregidor, even the New York editors of prestigious *Time* magazine had become aware that there was a cruel, no-holds-barred war going on in the Pacific. In *Time*'s first issue following S-Day at Lingayen Gulf, the cover had a color portrait of General Walter Krueger.) No doubt with a considerable measure of glee, Eichelberger wrote his wife Em: "The Big Chief [MacArthur] is very impatient. . . . He has had to speed up your palsy-walsy [Krueger]. Your palsy-walsy doesn't even radiate courage."[4]

Meanwhile, as General Griswold's advance toward Manila gained the headlines, General Bull Swift's I Corps divisions were locked in a death struggle with Japanese defenders north and northeast of the Lingayen Gulf landing beaches. Every yard of uptilted ground captured by Swift's foot soldiers was bitterly contested. The shoreline town of Rosario, a few miles to the north of the San Fabian assault beaches, had been a no-man's-land for days and had to be battered by naval, air, and artillery bombardment before it finally fell.

As Major General Leonard F. Wing's 43rd Infantry Division and Brigadier General Hanford MacNider's 158th Regimental Combat Team tried to claw their way on to Baguio to the northeast they were pounded by big guns emplaced in the rugged hills, where the enemy clung tenaciously to pillboxes and other fixed defenses. Most of the 1,017 Americans killed during the first three weeks of fighting on Luzon died in this sector. But there was good reason for the stubborn Nipponese defense of Baguio. It was from that prewar summer resort, perched five thousand feet high in the mountains, that General Yamashita was directing the defense of Luzon.

About twenty-five miles east of the landing beaches, Major General

Charles L. Mullins's 25th Infantry Division was probing toward Highway 5, which stretched from Manila all the way to northern Luzon's coast, and which carried heavy northbound Japanese traffic. In a ferocious three-day battle, elements of the "Tropic Lightnings," as the men of the 25th styled themselves, clawed out squatters's rights in half of the town of San Manuel. The rest of the division pushed on, but the Japanese burrowed into the rubble in the other half of San Manuel and for five days resisted repeated efforts to evict them. Only after the last defender was killed did the Americans take over the pulverized little town.

On the road to Manila, the Japanese were still falling back faster than even U.S. optimists had dared to hope. Griswold's XIV Corps swept ahead, with the 37th (Ohio) Division, under Major General Robert S. Beightler, on the left, and the 40th Division, under Major General Rapp Brush, on the right; spearheads of these two outfits were approaching one of the invasion's key objectives, Clark Field, fifty miles northwest of Manila. With more than a dozen runways, Clark was the biggest air base in the south Pacific.

Manila was almost in range of Douglas MacArthur's field glasses. But the victory parade to the capital was about to grind to a halt: General Yamashita had defended the approaches to the Clark Field complex with more than thirty fortified caves. Each of these had to be cleaned out by teams of flamethrowers and infantrymen before the advance to the capital could continue.

All the while, MacArthur, who in a few days would be observing his sixty-fifth birthday, was dashing about the battlefields like a man possessed. He had now moved his headquarters forward to Tarlac, sixty-three miles above Manila. Shortly after dawn each morning he got into his jeep bearing a five-star pennant and began touring the front lines. His staff, which never ceased to be amazed by their boss, conjectured as to how long a man of MacArthur's age could maintain such a pace. General Charles Willoughby, MacArthur's G-2 and confidant, was particularly concerned over the general "being constantly in the front lines, or ahead of them." The boss had become "almost reckless," Willoughby declared in his German accent.

At one point MacArthur came upon a platoon that was pinned down and being raked by fire at an enemy roadblock. He got out of his jeep and stood erect to watch the proceedings. "For God's sake, get down, General!" a bearded young captain called out from a prone position. "We're under fire!"

Without budging, the supreme commander replied, "I'm not under fire. They're not shooting at me."

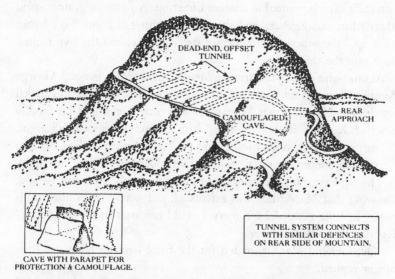

Tunnel System Near Manila. In the drive on Manila, the U.S. 37th and 40th Infantry divisions were confronted by an elaborate system of Japanese fortified caves (such as the one above) outside Clark Field and Fort Stotsenburg, some fifty-five miles northwest of the capital. (Courtesy Keith Rose)

Later, MacArthur was in a jeep with his physician, Dr. Roger Egeberg, looking for the scene of the fighting outside Clark Field, when they got lost. Continuing forward on foot, the pair came upon a GI crouched behind a tree. "Better get down!" the soldier called out. "There're Japs up ahead."

"Thank you, Corporal," MacArthur replied, continuing to stroll forward with a nervous Egeberg following reluctantly. He then suggested they locate a strand of communications wire and follow it. "That'll take us to our nearest CP."

MacArthur found a wire in a thicket, and the two men began trudging along beside it. Suddenly, a surge of panic raced through Egeberg: this was a thinner wire than the American variety—this was *Japanese* wire and they were heading for an enemy CP. Trying to keep his voice calm, an excited Egeberg pointed this out to MacArthur. The general continued walking forward, and moments later they emerged from a thicket. Three manned Japanese machine guns were spotted off to the left, their barrels pointed in another direction. A Japanese gunner spied MacArthur and Egeberg and shouted something at them. "We better back up," the supreme commander stated evenly, and the two melted back into the thicket.[5]

At one point during the drive to Manila, the air corps general, George Kenney, dropped into MacArthur's advanced headquarters and stayed for dinner. Noticing that MacArthur was only pecking at his food, a worried Kenney cautiously asked him if everything was all right. "George, I'm so damned tired I can't eat," MacArthur replied. Still, he insisted on conferring on air support with Kenney far into the night.

The next morning, Kenney had to depart shortly after sunrise and, knowing that MacArthur was exhausted, did not want to disturb his rest. "Tell the general I am sorry I could not wait to say good-bye," Kenney told a duty officer.

"Oh, General MacArthur left for the front over an hour ago," the officer replied.

Two-thirds of the way to Manila, MacArthur was shocked by a signal he received from the Pentagon: one hundred of his cargo vessels were to be taken away from him and used to carry ammunition, weapons, and supplies to the Russians at the northern Pacific port of Vladivostok. Supply was a crucial problem to any fighting force, but in the Pacific, with its astronomical distances over water, ships were of paramount importance. MacArthur needed every cargo vessel he could scrape up.

He promptly lodged a bitter protest, pointing out that his invasion force on Luzon could be jeopardized and its casualties increased by the loss of the vital one hundred vessels. His protest fell on deaf ears. A decision had been made at the highest levels of government to bring Russia into the war against Japan. Again MacArthur protested, pointing out that it would be a drastic mistake to bring the Soviets in at this late date. Nothing he could say would change Washington's decision: the one hundred ships would soon be hauling tremendous amounts of American ammunition and weapons to Vladivostok.[6]

Douglas MacArthur's sixty-fifth birthday was celebrated with little fanfare on January 26. He had secretly hoped to observe the milestone with a triumphant entry into Manila, but knew that such a projection was unrealistic.

However, the scent of victory was in MacArthur's nostrils. Like a champion boxer, the supreme commander was feinting, then landing quick, telling blows, dazzling a worthy opponent (General Yamashita) with his footwork. On his perch in the mountains outside of Baguio, the Tiger of Malaya was desperately shifting troops about in an effort to parry MacArthur's thrusts. But the American general's sights were now set on python-infested Bataan. There, in the locale of the United States's most humiliating military disaster, the Japanese might make a "historically repetitive stand," as MacArthur had been warned by General Willoughby.

At dawn on January 29, an American armada was lying to off the western coast of Luzon near the small town of San Antonio, twenty-five miles north of Bataan. On board were forty thousand troops of Major General Charles P. "Chink" Hall's XI Corps. Shortly after 7:00 A.M., Admiral Arthur Struble's warships were ready to pound the landing beaches when a "hold your fire!" order rang out. Several small landing craft loaded with Filipino guerrillas were sailing out to greet the invaders. They had been sent by Lieutenant Colonel Gyles Merrill, leader of the guerrillas in Bataan and Zambales provinces, to report that there were no Japanese in the area.

General Hall called off the bombardment and ordered his troops ashore at once. Landing were elements of Major General Henry L. C. Jones's 38th "Cyclone" Infantry Division of the Indiana–Kentucky–West Virginia National Guards (many of its officers had been businessmen), and the 34th Regimental Combat Team. The invaders were welcomed on the beaches by cheering Filipinos. Only one casualty was sustained in the assault: a GI in the 38th Division was gored by one of the notoriously ill-tempered carabao.

A regiment of the Cyclone Division rushed inland to seize the San Marcelino airstrip, but upon arrival found that Filipino guerrillas, under

Captain Ramon Magsaysay, had secured it three days earlier. Shaking hands with Magsaysay, the perspiring GIs had no way of knowing that they were greeting a future president of the Republic of the Philippines.

Not pausing to catch its breath, the 34th Regimental Combat Team sliced swiftly to the southeast and grabbed the old U.S. naval station at Olongapo. Chink Hall's other units drove eastward, and in seven days would seal off the Bataan peninsula and prevent Japanese forces in and around Manila from pulling back there for an "historically repetitive stand."

General MacArthur drove himself at a pace that would have floored most men twenty years his junior. He was obsessed with liberating Manila and Corregidor "with the fewest possible casualties," as he told General Krueger. But there were perhaps ten thousand wretched, starving, and emaciated American civilians and military men penned up in brutal camps at Santo Tomás University and Old Bilibid prison in Manila, at Cabanatuan above the capital, and near Los Baños, twenty-five miles below Manila. There was fear at MacArthur's headquarters that the Japanese might massacre the helpless men, women, and children. This specter, after the prisoners had endured so much for three years, and with deliverance at hand, shook Douglas MacArthur's soul.

13

Rescuing the Ghosts of Bataan

On the night of January 30, the emaciated American soldiers, sailors, and marines at Cabanatuan prison camp were waiting anxiously, as they had waited for more than four months—ever since they had seen the first American warplanes over Luzon. There were some five hundred prisoners in the Cabanatuan camp—located about sixty-five miles southeast of the Lingayen Gulf landing beaches and fifty miles northeast of Manila—the remnants of the "grim, gaunt, and ghostly legion of Bataan" about whom General MacArthur had spoken repeatedly and whose image seldom left him. All were sick and starving, their strength drained by more than three years of inhumane treatment and confinement in vermin-ridden barracks and bamboo huts. Every foot of ground in the Cabanatuan prison was a filled-in latrine.

In early 1942, after the fall of Bataan and Corregidor, nearly seven thousand American fighting men and a similar number of Filipino soldiers had been penned up at Cabanatuan. Later, some were shipped to POW enclosures in Formosa, Manchuria, and Japan, and in December of 1944 others were transferred to Old Bilibid prison inside Manila.

Uncounted hundreds had died at Cabanatuan over the two years since then, victims of neglect, maltreatment, and starvation diets.

Now, behind the barbed wire in the dark camp on this thirtieth day of January 1945, Colonel James Duckworth was among those guessing at what was taking place to the northwest, where the sky in recent nights had been lit with pale flashes of artillery. Duckworth, who had gained fame in the United States as a result of his heroics as a surgeon on Bataan, was the camp commandant (of inmates). Over a radio improvised from scraps of toothpaste tubes, the prisoners had caught fragmentary reports and knew that Douglas MacArthur had returned. In their ramshackle huts, they considered their chances of escape with a mixture of hope, despair, and anxiety.

The cannonading from the northwest grew audible, and drew closer that night. Over the POWs hung the fear that the Japanese might murder them. It was also conceivable that they might be wiped out by U.S. artillery or bombers if their camp was mistaken for Japanese army barracks. And even if MacArthur knew they were there, how could he rescue them so deep in enemy territory?

Leaders among the Bataan and Corregidor remnants tried to mask their concerns. Major Ralph Hubbard thought about his wife and young son back in Oklahoma City. Navy Lieutenant George W. Green reflected on how ridiculous he must look, with his naval officer's cap and tattered, filthy, long pants.

Unbeknownst to the inmates, a rescue force consisting of the 6th Ranger Battalion's Company C, led by Captain Robert W. Prince, and an attached platoon of Company F under Lieutenant John F. Murphy, had slipped forward from American lines two days earlier to work the twenty-four miles through Japanese positions to Cabanatuan. Also involved would be some two hundred-fifty Filipino guerrillas, only ninty of whom were armed. In overall command of the rescue operation was Lieutenant Colonel Henry A. Mucci, leader of the 6th Ranger Battalion.

West Pointer Mucci, son of a Bridgeport, Connecticut, horse dealer, had only sketchy details of the Cabanatuan camp layout provided by an American reconnaissance group known as the Alamo Scouts, who had reported that five hundred Japanese guarded Cabanatuan (actually, the figure was closer to three hundred). A chilling observation had been appended to their report: an enemy column thought to be a division was moving northward along the main road leading past the POW enclosure.[1]

On January 29, Colonel Mucci's force holed up about a mile from the prison camp. There Mucci, Captain Prince, and Lieutenant Murphy worked out a rescue plan. Of necessity, it was conceived hastily. Yet each Ranger and guerrilla was briefed on his specific job, as well as on the general plan of action. Total surprise would be crucial. Anything less could result in the American POWs being slaughtered and Colonel Mucci's force being wiped out.

Two Filipino guerrilla chiefs were given critical tasks. Captain Pajota was to take his native fighters one mile northeast of the POW camp along a main road and prevent a nearby Japanese force of some eight hundred men from rushing to the camp once the fireworks erupted. A second band under Captain Joson would set up a similar roadblock eight hundred yards southwest of the POW camp and hold up any enemy force trying to reach the prison camp from the town of Cabanatuan, four miles below the prison. At all costs, the guerrilla leaders were to keep the Japanese from breaking through until all the prisoners had been freed.

Meanwhile, Lieutenant John Murphy's Ranger platoon would slip up to the rear entrance of the camp and kill the guards there. Murphy's men would then signal the general attack when they opened fire. A Company C platoon led by Lieutenant William J. O'Connell was to crash through the front gate of the stockade and wipe out the guards there. Specific buildings pointed out by the Alamo Scouts were earmarked for special attention. One Ranger section would pour bazooka rounds into a corrugated tin building that supposedly housed the garrison's tanks and trucks. Another group of Rangers would charge into a large building holding the off-duty garrison, which was located just inside the barbed-wire enclosure to the rear. Yet another platoon of Company C led by Lieutenant Melville B. Schmidt had the job of opening the POW section, wiping out the Japanese, and directing the prisoners through the camp's main gate.

Guerrillas and Rangers would cut telephone lines leading out of the prison camp, and other Rangers were given the task of finding and destroying the Japanese radios. As soon as all inmates were clear of the stockade, Captain Bob Prince would fire a red flare, the signal for all Rangers to withdraw and form a rear guard for the POW column. The two guerilla forces at the roadblocks north and south of the prison camp were to stay in place until the column was at least a mile from the camp. Then Prince would fire a second red flare, a signal for the native groups to pull back and form an additional rear and flank guard for the POW column.

The Rangers would travel light and fast. They were largely pistol-packing farm boys, hand-picked for jobs like this one. They wore no helmets, but each Ranger carried two pistols, a trench knife, a rifle or Tommy gun, one canteen of water, and two days's streamlined rations. "You're not to eat your rations or drink the water," Colonel Mucci cautioned his men. "They're for the POWs you release." Then he added, "Get inside quick and knife 'em up! I don't want any of the POWs killed. Bring out every goddamned prisoner! Bring them out if every Ranger has to carry a man or two on his back!"

Shortly after 6:00 P.M., the Rangers left their assembly area one mile from the Cabanatuan camp, moving cautiously as they crossed open ground, and reached the enclosure at 7:25 P.M. Captain Prince and his company were in a shallow ditch twenty yards from the front gate, concealed only by darkness. The tense Rangers felt as if they could reach out and touch the dim silhouettes of the Japanese guards posted at the entrance. At the same time, Lieutenant John Murphy's platoon had crawled to within fifteen yards of the back entrance. The only sound was from the thousands of crickets.

In one of the rickety structures inside the compound, Private Edward S. Gordon of the 4th Marines was nibbling a piece of bread he had made from rice flour. It was 7:44 P.M. Suddenly, heavy rifle fire at the rear of the enclosure shattered the pervading nighttime silence. Gordon heard a thud and hobbled outside. A Japanese sentry, standing on a watch tower, had been shot and was down. All around him, the noise of exploding grenades mixed with the chatter of automatic weapons.

Sergeant Theodore R. Richardson of Dallas, Texas, who had been designated to breach the main gate, leaped to his feet and threw it open. That was the signal for another Ranger sergeant whose target was a sentry on the tower. One shot and the sentry stood motionless for a split-second, then fell backward, head over feet, his rifle tossed to one side. Clutching knives and pitching grenades ahead of them, Captain Prince and his men poured through the front gate. In their minds was Colonel Mucci's admonition: "Get inside and knife 'em up!"

Frantic orders were shouted in Japanese as the guards, taken by surprise, were overcome by the rush of dim figures wielding razor-sharp knives, pistols, Tommy guns, and bazookas. Screams pierced the night as Rangers fired bazooka rockets into four trucks that, by happenstance, had been loaded with Japanese soldiers only moments before the American assault erupted. Other Rangers bolted into the big building holding most of the prison camp garrison, pitched grenades, and squeezed off bursts of full-automatic fire at the startled Japanese inside.

Outside the gate, Ranger Captain James C. Fisher, the battalion surgeon, was crouched in the darkness with two of his medics, Staff Sergeant John W. Nelson and Corporal Ramsey. Doc Fisher, son of the novelist Dorothy Canfield Fisher, was one of the most popular and respected men in the battalion. His courage on the battlefield had become widely known, and his medics looked on him as "one of the boys."

"Okay, boys," Fisher now said to Nelson and Ramsey, "let's head for the gate. They might need us in there."

In the hundred yards to the front entrance, the three medics became separated. Nelson went forward alone, confident that Captain Fisher and Ramsey would make it. As he neared the gate a shell from a Japanese knee mortar exploded ahead of him, ten feet from the entrance. Nelson flopped to the ground but heard someone shout, "Man down ahead!" He scrambled to his feet and dashed a short distance forward, where a figure was crumpled on the ground. It was too dark to know who the Ranger was, for no one was wearing rank insignia. "Where'ya been hit?" Nelson asked. "Stomach," was the gasped reply.

The medic dressed the wound, and moments later a fellow medic, First Sergeant Bossard, approached. Nelson said, "Better find Captain Fisher right away; this fellow's been badly injured."

The man on the ground whispered weakly, "I am Captain Fisher."

As the noise and confusion raged around his barracks, Marine Edward Gordon, a Bataan veteran, heard someone shouting, "We're

Americans! Head for the main gate! Hurry!" The voice was that of Captain Bob Prince.

Prince's plea, and similar ones from other rescuers, got little response. The POWs, having endured three years of brutality, starvation, and the specter of imminent death, and having seen the grim fate of men who protested or tried to escape, had adopted a kind of muteness. They had pressed themselves to the brown, stinking soil or lay face down on the split bamboo floors of their huts when the sounds of battle and the shouts began. Even when the shooting was over, only a few of the Corregidor and Bataan vets moved. Finally, strong but gentle Ranger hands began hustling them to their feet.

Slowly the suspicions inhabiting wasted bodies and tortured minds began to wear off. The men who lifted them to their feet were dressed as they had never seen American soldiers outfitted before. Where were the steel pie-plate helmets the Battling Bastards of Bataan had worn in early 1942? These cloth hats were strange new Army gear, the uniforms splotched with jungle green. But the young soldiers were gentle and kind. For three years these wasted ghosts of a damaging defeat had been deprived of such gentleness and kindness. Now their own shaky voices rang out, "They're Americans! They're here! Thank God, you've come!"

Weakened prisoners hobbled on bare, swollen feet through the front entrance, past the bodies of Japanese guards. In their confusion, some POWs tried to embrace and kiss their rescuers. Rangers dashed into bamboo huts and barracks, hoisted bedridden men onto their shoulders, and trudged off through the gate with them. (Inadvertently, one POW was left behind, a soldier who was still hiding under his cot and would not be found until the next day when Filipino guerrillas swept the camp searching for Japanese survivors.)

The POWs long ordeal was not quite over yet, however. From the south, where Colonel Mucci had sent Filipino Captain Joson's guerrilla force, could be heard the angry chatter of automatic weapons fire, punctuated by shell explosions. A Japanese force, supported by at least one tank, was trying to break through to the prison camp.

At 10:15 P.M. Ranger Captain Bob Prince was satisfied that all the POWs had been rescued (there were 531 of them). He fired the first red flare, and the column of Rangers and prisoners began their withdrawal. In uneven columns the prisoners, herded along by their rescuers, staggered through rice paddies, over streams, and through fields. Guided by a nearly full moon, the POWs limped through the night, stumbling and pulling themselves up again, driven on by the prospect, finally, of freedom. One POW wiggled down from the back of a Ranger and declared, "I can walk. I'm a *soldier.*" Carried along on a makeshift stretcher was Captain Jim Fisher, ashen-faced, semi-conscious, his life ebbing away. His heavy-hearted medics took turns lugging "Captain Jim," as they called him. He would die the next day.

The ragged column's progress was slow and painful, as it stretched out for more than a mile and a half in Japanese-controlled territory. At one point, Colonel Mucci and Captain Prince suffered long, anxious minutes as soldiers and POWs were forced to move for three-quarters of a mile along a main road often used by enemy vehicles and troops. Matters were helped to a degree when carabao carts were commandeered along the way to carry the weakest of the POWs. Rangers, themselves growing weaker after many hours of fighting and marching without food, pulled some of the carts by hand.

In their trek toward American lines, the column trudged through a series of barrios, where Rangers and POWs were furnished food and water by the natives. Colonel Mucci tried numerous times to reach a higher headquarters by radio, but with no success. The sun came up hot, and the weary column kept moving. It was well that it did: unbeknownst to Mucci, Japanese units in the area had learned of the prison camp rescue and been nipping at the column's heels. Just after 8:00 A.M., the motley group staggered into the barrio of Sibul. Radio contact was finally made, and a convoy of ambulances and trucks—escorted by infantry, for they were still in enemy-held territory—reached Sibul at 11:00 A.M.

Exhausted POWs were put aboard. They tried to maintain their soldierly bearing, giving officers the regulation salute and hoping no one noticed their quivering hands. Boyish-faced GIs manning the convoy stared in awe at the bony apparitions. The men of the ghostly legion of Bataan and Corregidor tried to ignore their blistered feet, the oozing sores on their bodies, their illnesses. Most knew that they were walking skeletons, and that the sight of them was horrifying these young American fighting men. The liberated POWs passed an American flag. Enfeebled Staff Sergeant Clinton Goodbla broke into tears. Most of the others did likewise.

A price was paid for the daring raid deep into Japanese-controlled territory and the rescue of 531 American soldiers. In addition to Captain Jim Fisher, one Ranger was killed, and the Filipino guerrillas lost 26 men. Lieutenant Colonel Henry Mucci's 121 Rangers had killed 73 Cabanatuan prison guards and 151 other Japanese soldiers in the camp proper. Many other Japanese fell before the vengeful guns of the guerrillas at the road blocks to the north and south of the prison compound.[2]

Back in the United States the following day, Mrs. Ralph Hubbard, wife of the rescued major, was at an Oklahoma City children's hospital, reading to polio victims. A radio newscast electrified her. She dashed out, running all the way to the Culbertson School, and barged into a first-grade class. Spotting her son Joe, the tearful Mrs. Hubbard called out, "Your daddy's been rescued. He's safe."[3]

Two days earlier, in Oakland, California, Mrs. Caryl Picotte had been notified by the War Department that her brother had been killed fighting on Leyte. She had shed tears of anguish. Now she wept again—with relief. Her husband had been one of those rescued at Cabanatuan.[4]

14

A Mad Dash for the Capital

With several American divisions pressing down on Manila from the north and General Chink Hall's men knifing in from the west, General MacArthur was ready to plant yet another haymaker onto the forces of the burly, bullet-headed Tomoyuki Yamashita. Landing the blow would be General Joe Swing's versatile 11th Airborne Division, which would conduct a combined amphibious-parachute operation at Nasugbu Bay, fifty-five miles south of Manila.

If everything went according to plan, Swing's 187th and 188th Glider Infantry regiments would storm ashore on X-Ray Day, January 31, at the town of Nasugbu, which before the war had been a favorite resort for American military officers and their families stationed in Manila. The glidermen (who were also qualified paratroopers) would drive eastward to Route 17, which led northward into Manila. They would then advance up Route 17 toward three-thousand-foot-high Tagatay Ridge, a dominating terrain feature standing guard before the southern gateway to the Philippine capital.

As Swing's regiments approached that elevation, Colonel Orin Haugen's 511th Parachute Infantry, along with the 457th Parachute Field

Artillery and the 221st Airborne Medical Company, would bail out over Tagatay Ridge and wrest it from the Japanese. Then the entire 11th Airborne would push on northward to Manila.

Leading the amphibious assault would be the 188th Glider Infantry's 1st Battalion, led by Lieutenant Colonel Ernest H. LaFlamme. It would be a homecoming of sorts for LaFlamme, who had served in the Philippines before the war and together with his family had spent numerous weekends on the precise white beach he would soon assault.

X-Ray Day dawned warm and cloudless, and the sea was calm. Suddenly, the tranquility was shattered as guns of the invasion armada, led by Rear Admiral William M. Fechteler, began shelling the beaches. On the heels of the bombardment, Lieutenant Colonel LaFlamme's battalion splashed ashore against only sporadic machine-gun fire. By 12:30 P.M. both glider regiments and General Joe Swing were ashore.

Colonel Robert H. Soule, a husky crew-cut career officer, commanded the 188th Glider Infantry. With a battalion of the 187th Regiment attached, they rushed inland toward the Palico River bridge, the shortest and best route northward to Tagatay Ridge. Lying five miles east of the landing beaches, the Palico bridge could hold the 11th Airborne Division's heaviest loads—but it also crossed a gorge two hundred and fifty feet wide and eighty-five feet deep. If the span was blown, the division would have to take a time-consuming detour that would delay for several days the drive to Manila.

As Soule's infantry reached the bridge Japanese engineers on the far side could be seen preparing to blow the structure. Taking the chance that the bridge might be destroyed while they were on it, a platoon of troopers raced across and pounced on the enemy engineers, who had apparently been unaware of the Americans' presence. Within minutes, the Japanese band was wiped out.

By 3:00 P.M. the entire 188th Glider Infantry and the attached battalion of the 187th Infantry were across the Palico and heading for the junction of Route 17.

Once there, they kept going. Throughout the night the airborne men marched—mostly uphill—toward Tagatay Ridge.

The 11th Airborne Division's headquarters were set up for the night in an old school house, with rickety wood plank flooring covering a dark crawl space. Sergeant James V. Vignola of Carthage, North Carolina, a member of the division plans and operations section, was on CQ (charge of quarters) duty. All was eerily quiet. Seated alone in a room behind blackout curtains, with a small Coleman lantern for light, Vignola sniffed several times, then sniffed again, detecting a fishlike odor he associated with the rations carried by Japanese soldiers.

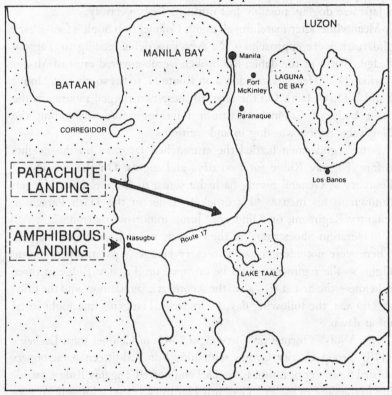

11th Airborne Landings

Grabbing his Tommy gun, Sergeant Vignola cautiously searched the room, but found no one. Then the source of the pungent smell struck him: it was coming up through the cracks between the floor planks. Japanese soldiers, either hiding or intent on blowing up the division CP, were in the crawlspace directly below Vignola's room.

The sergeant's first thought was to blast away through the floor with his Tommy gun. But he realized the sudden fusillade from inside the headquarters might set off a shootout among Americans with itchy trigger fingers. So Jim Vignola remained on duty throughout a long and anxious night, feeling as though he were sitting on a powder keg. With the arrival of dawn, Vignola and other armed comrades probed the crawlspace. The enemy had vanished. But nearby on the ground was a Japanese dogtag, possibly lost during a hasty getaway.

Meanwhile, after marching all night, Colonel Bob Soule's foot-weary glidermen were approaching the Aga Pass defile leading to Tagatay Ridge. North of the defile, the broken, scrub-covered crest of Mount Cariliao (2,100 feet) looked down on Route 17; to the south, was Mount Batulao (2,700 feet). On the faces of these two rugged mountains the main body of Colonel Masatoshi Fujishige's force defending the Nagasubu region was dug in and waiting.

Soule's glidermen battled the entrenched Japanese on the heights before Tagatay Ridge for two days and nights. On the evening of February 3, General Swing flashed a signal to Colonel Orin Haugen (known to his men as "Hardrock"), leader of the 511th Parachute Infantry Regiment, on Mindoro: "Jump tomorrow morning."

"Operation Shoestring," as the troopers called it, was aptly named. There were not enough C-47s to carry Haugen's paratroopers in one flight, so the regiment would be dropped on Tagatay Ridge in three echelons—the first at 8:15 A.M., the second at around noon, and the third at 8:00 A.M. the following day, February 4. Haugen's first flight lifted off at dawn.

In a V-of-Vs formation, forty-eight C-47s of Colonel John Lackey's 317th Troop Carrier Group with nine hundred-fifteen paratroopers aboard flew over beautiful Lake Taal and neared Tagatay Ridge. Standing in the door of the first C-47 was Hardrock Haugen himself. At 8:14 A.M. the green light came on in Haugen's aircraft and he jumped through the door, followed closely by his stick.[1] Seventeen other C-47s dropped their paratroopers at the same time. All of them came down on target, atop Tagatay Ridge.

That would be the last thing to go right in the parachute operation that day. While the trailing C-47s were still more than five miles from the drop zone, someone in the first aircraft pitched out two equipment bundles. Jumpmasters standing in the doors of the other C-47s interpreted these parachuting bundles as a signal that the flight was over the DZ (drop zone). In moments, the sky was filled with the blossoming chutes of five hundred-forty paratroopers. They jolted to earth some four and a half miles from Tagatay Ridge.

Standing on the true DZ, Colonel Haugen was furious and frustrated as he gazed into the distance and saw the hundreds of white chutes floating earthward. Then, at noon, fifty-one C-47s carrying his second serial of paratroopers approached the DZ on Tagatay Ridge. Jumpmasters looked down and saw the discarded parachutes of those who had jumped nearly five miles short of the target that morning and, presuming this to be the DZ, ordered their sticks to bail out, repeating the mistake of the previous flight.

Colonel Haugen found himself on his objective with only about a third of his troopers. But the gods were smiling on him: there was not a single Japanese soldier to be found on Tagatay Ridge.

Early the next morning, February 4, the final flight of 511th paratroopers was dropped—this time on the correct DZ. Later that day, just south of Tagatay Ridge, Colonel Soule's glidermen broke through Japanese positions on Mount Cariliao and Mount Batulao and lined up with Hardrock Haugen's parachutists. General Joe Swing now had the 11th Airborne Division together and was ready to push northward into Manila.

While the Americans drew a noose around Manila, the city was being converted into a formidable fortress. When General Yamashita had pulled out of the capital early in January, he had declared it an "open city"—the customary notice to an enemy that there would be no resistance. "I do not intend to preside over the destruction of Manila," the Tiger of Malaya had told his staff. Besides, he did not consider the capital as having much military significance. He had left behind only a small force to blow up key bridges over the Pasig River before the Americans arrived.

But hard on Yamashita's departing heels, the Imperial Navy had moved into Manila Bay in force. The fanatical Rear Admiral Sanji Iwabuchi had disregarded General Yamashita's open-city order; he promptly gave new instructions to his seventeen-thousand-man naval force, as well as to the four thousand army soldiers who had been left behind: Defend Manila to the last stone and the last bullet! To the death!

Admiral Iwabuchi plunged into the task of preparing for the destruction of all Japanese military installations and supplies in the Manila area. He liberally interpreted "military installations" to include the entire port, transportation facilities, the water supply system, and electric power plants. He ordered Manila Bay to be mined and rushed his naval combat troops to the Cavite navy base and Nichols Field. If the Americans reached the "Pearl of the Orient," Admiral Iwabuchi intended to make certain that they paid a high price in blood for the blackened shell of a once-magnificent city.

On January 30, three days after the 1st Cavalry Division had come ashore at Lingayen Gulf, its commander, forty-six-year-old Major General Verne D. Mudge, received an electrifying order from Sixth Army: race to Manila. Mudge hurriedly organized two flying columns for the sixty-mile dash to the capital under the command of peppery Brigadier General William C. Chase, leader of the 1st Cavalry Brigade. An excited Chase told reporters: "We're heading hell-bent for Manila, and we're not going to worry about what [enemy troops] we leave behind us."

Outside Clark Field, fifty miles northwest of the capital, General Bob Beightler of the 37th Infantry Division was equally eager to reach the glittering prize first. Beightler, who as a civilian had been director of the Ohio Highway Department, growled to newsmen: "We've fought our way a hundred miles, and we won't let those goddamned feather merchants [the 1st Cavalry Division] beat us in!"[2]

The modern-day cavalry charge for Manila began in a sugar-cane field, where lanky Lieutenant Colonel Haskett "Hack" Conner, leader of the 2nd Squadron, 8th Cavalry Regiment, was giving final orders to his officers. It was a few minutes before midnight on January 31. There was a murmur of excitement when Conner, speaking in a quiet voice that nevertheless carried over the sound of tank engines, revealed the mission: dash sixty miles through Japanese-infested territory, plunge into Manila, and rescue some thirty-seven hundred American men, women, and children who had been imprisoned at the Santo Tomás camp for more than three years.

Colonel Conner's flying column, seven hundred strong, would be headed by tanks and followed by cavalrymen in trucks, weapons carriers, and jeeps, along with engineering and service outfits. More tanks would bring up the rear. The vehicles bristled with .30- and .50-caliber machine guns and 20- and 40-millimeter cannon; their mobility and firepower would be used to blast a path to Manila, letting the Japanese flow back onto the route once Conner's column had passed.

At precisely midnight Conner's flying column roared southward, in what quickly became a crazy kind of operation. At some points the column attained high speeds on highways; at other times it was slowed to a crawl when forced to use carabao paths where there were no roads. The convoy crossed rivers (the Japanese had blown all the bridges) and rice paddies, and plodded through thick jungles. Often the column halted to engage in nasty clashes with ambushing Japanese, skirmishes that took a toll on both sides. As each pocket of resistance was wiped out, the cavalrymen would leap back into their vehicles like pony express riders and race onward.

Colonel Conner and his men passed through barrios in which every inhabitant was out waving, shouting "veek-tory," handing out flowers and eggs, and in turn asking for cigarettes. The cavalcade also encountered areas in which every barrio was devoid of people, pigs, and chickens. The troopers would grow tense at this sure sign of Japanese in the area.

Hack Conner's eyes were continually searching the thick trees on both sides of the road. "It's almost impossible to *avoid* an ambush in countryside like this," he remarked to a newsman in his jeep at one point. "It's like following a trail in the jungle; the first guys are bound to get knocked off."

The reporter-photographer, Carl Mydans of *Life* magazine, was no stranger to tight situations. Yet he looked ahead and to the rear, trying to assess his jeep's position in the convoy, reassured by the fact that his vehicle was in the center of the convoy. Then the soft-spoken Conner added, "Of course, if they jump on us from either side it really doesn't matter where you're riding."[3]

Suddenly, up ahead, there were explosions. The convoy lurched to a halt. Japanese positioned along a river over which a bridge had been blown had begun machine-gunning the forward vehicles. Soon Sherman tanks opened up with their 75-millimeter guns, and the firing from across the river ceased. Minutes later church bells in a village on the bank began to toll, the traditional signal that the occupiers had fled and the hamlet was again free.

Well back in the stalled column, a bearded lieutenant, resting under a tree until the roadblock was wiped out, observed tiredly: "There go the bells. Another goddamned town liberated—for a day or two."[4]

Onward rolled the convoy. As the afternoon wore on Colonel Conner grew impatient. Once, he looked at his watch and remarked, "Hell, we ought to have been in Manila by now." But as the miles remaining dwindled, the enemy fire grew increasingly fierce, and then became a constant roar. Machine guns and cannon were turned to both sides of the road and, as the flying column moved along, GIs blasted houses, knolls, sheds, and ditches—anyplace Japanese could be hiding.

Haskett Conner kept glancing at his timepiece. He had been ordered to rescue thirty-seven hundred inmates at Santo Tomás and he intended to do it. But every minute counted. Any delay increased the chances that the inmates would be massacred. Periodically, the lieutenant in the lead tank would look over his shoulder, and each time Colonel Conner would give him a clenched fist jerked up and down—the signal to speed up.

It was nearly midnight on February 2 when Conner's exhausted cavalrymen were given a chance to coil up for a few hours of sleep. That night General Bill Chase set up his CP in a house in Baliuag, twelve miles from the objective. He learned that the house had gained a measure of fame a month earlier: General Tomoyuki Yamashita had spent the night there after pulling out of Manila and heading northward for Baguio.

At dawn on February 3, several thousand emaciated American civilians and military prisoners in Manila awoke with an intense mixture of hope and fear. There was ample evidence that General MacArthur's troops were just outside the city. Deliverance after three years behind barbed wire might be at hand. But would the Japanese command, facing defeat, massacre them?

In the Santo Tomás camp on this morning, prisoners were scrambling for garbage, roots, cats (they had found that cats taste like rabbit) —anything to eat that they could get their hands on. Long gone were the diamond rings and watches the inmates had bartered for condensed milk and rice. Some food had been smuggled in the previous day by solemn-faced Filipino morticians coming for bodies. About a mile to the south, a few of the fourteen hundred bony Americans held at Old Bilibid prison had a delicacy for breakfast: worms and a few frogs caught hopping from outdoor latrines.

Long before dawn, Lieutenant Colonel Haskett Conner's column had renewed its dash for Manila. This might be "The Day"—the return of armed Americans to the sprawling capital from which General MacArthur and his bedraggled soldiers had been driven ignominiously at Christmastime in 1941. In the minds of the men in the flying column was the image of a tall, rawboned, haggard soldier. None of these bronzed fighting men had ever seen this man, but General Jonathan Wainwright would be with them in spirit—he was one of them, having once been a brigade commander in the 1st Cavalry Division.

Nearly an hour before daylight, pilots of the 24th and 32nd Marine Air Groups lifted off from a hastily built strip on top of a paddy field near Magaldan, fifteen miles east of Lingayen Gulf. All during the 1st Cavalry's sixty-mile dash to Manila, the Leatherneck flyers had provided dawn-to-dusk air cover, and now they were reconnoitering the key Novaliches Bridge eight miles north of the capital.

General Chase was worried about this bridge, which afforded a crossing over a stream that had banks too high and too steep to permit fording. If the span was blown, it could hold up Chase's columns indefinitely. But word came back from the Marine pilots: Novaliches Bridge was still standing. Chase, greatly relieved, sent a signal to Lieutenant Colonel Conner: grab the bridge.

Just as Conner's leading tanks approached the bridge, the American column was raked by fire from in front and both sides of the approach. Tank hatches snapped shut, brakes squealed, and cavalrymen leaped out and scattered for cover. Foot soldiers tangled with clusters of Japanese on both sides of the road; up front the tanks fired their 75s into likely hiding places.

Navy Lieutenant James P. Sutton, a bomb-disposal officer from Lawrenceburg, Tennessee, attached to the 1st Cavalry Division, was lying in a ditch, blasting away with a carbine. Major James C. Gerhart of Santa Fe, New Mexico, executive officer of the squadron, rushed up to Sutton and shouted, "Come with me quick, the bridge is mined and the fuse is burning!" The Navy officer jumped to his feet and ran after Gerhart.

Reaching the head of the span, Lieutenant Sutton quickly sized up the situation. Indeed the fuse was burning briskly. With Japanese machine-gun bullets zipping past him, the bomb-disposal officer raced onto the bridge and cut the flaming fuse just before it reached the explosives. The gateway to Manila had been narrowly saved. Later Sutton would find that there had been enough explosives to have blown him halfway to Tokyo: four hundred pounds of TNT and three thousand pounds of picric acid.

Conner's cavalrymen scrambled back onto their vehicles and the column started across the Novaliches Bridge. Major Gerhart's jeep was moving when he hurled himself into it, having just spotted a Japanese soldier running at full speed fifty yards away. As the jeep kept rolling, Gerhart put the stock of his carbine against his stomach and squeezed the trigger. The running man toppled over. Pleased with his marksmanship, the major turned to a GI and said, "Hell, I've been teaching my boys to shoot from the waist for three years. Now I had to show them that I could do it myself."

Conner's mechanized column pushed past burning houses and dead Japanese on the far side of Novaliches Bridge. At 6:35 P.M., with dusk settling over the Philippines, troopers wearing the over-sized shoulder patch of the 1st Cavalry Division crossed the city limits of Manila, the first armed Americans to reach the capital. But it was a precarious toe-hold, for the division was strung out to the rear for nearly forty miles.

About two hours earlier, at 4:45 P.M., anxious internees in the Santo Tomás camp heard the throbbing roar of low-flying airplanes; less feeble inmates hobbled outside to gaze skyward. Nine American fighter-bombers swooped in so low that they almost knocked two Japanese from a guard tower. To save face, the camp guards refused to look up, allowing the inmates to notice something their keepers had not: a small bundle dropped into the main courtyard of the former university. Stealthily, a prisoner recovered the object—pilot's goggles. Attached was a note in scrawled handwriting: *Roll out the barrel. Santa Clause is coming Monday or Tuesday!*

The note electrified the prisoners in the main building. But it was dark before the news could be spread to inmates living in shacks and other structures. On the eve of deliverance, anxious anticipation hung over the camp.

15

The Pacific War's Strangest Episode

In the darkness and bewildering maze of Manila streets, Lieutenant Colonel Haskett Conner's flying column had become a crawling one. Riding with the lead tanks were two natives who had been Philippine Scouts in the American army. As the 1st Cav neared Manila, the Filipinos had offered to guide the Americans to the Santo Tomás prison camp. Skeptical, Conner had put many sharp questions to the volunteers until all doubts were allayed that they were genuine patriots.

Conner's column passed a convoy of Japanese military trucks loaded with supplies that was parked along a black and deserted street. The vehicles had clearly just been abandoned, for the motors in some were still idling. The veteran cavalrymen knew that Nipponese who had been in the convoy were close by, probably in some of the houses lining the street. Word was passed down the American column: "Be alert! Be alert!" Every rifle and machine gun in the convoy was pointed to the side, with fingers on the triggers.

Suddenly, a shadowy figure leaped from a ditch and flagged down Haskett Conner's jeep. Miraculously, it was not riddled with gunfire. He turned out to be a Chinese boy, who pointed to a small cemetery right beside the street. "Jap-nese in cem-tery!" Moments later a Japanese force opened fire from among the tombstones, and the march turned into a running gun battle. The mechanized cavalry column continued to roll past as troopers returned the fire, but several of Conner's men were hit running the gauntlet.

Inside blacked-out Santo Tomás, inmates could hear shooting to the north. They listened anxiously as the firing drew closer; starved and wrinkled faces stole glances out the windows of buildings, but no one could see anything. Soon the rattle of gunfire seemed to be just outside the compound. The prisoners could hear Filipino cheers: "*Mabuhay! Mabuhay!*" (Victory! victory!) Then there was the roar of powerful engines and the clank of steel treads on concrete. "American tanks! American tanks!" a shaky voice called out in the main building. But *were* they American—or Japanese?

Suddenly, an eerie hush fell over the entire camp. What did this silence mean? It was 8:50 P.M.

Moments later an obviously American voice outside boomed, "Where in hell is the goddamned front gate?" Elation swept through the thirty-seven hundred brutalized prisoners[1] as a Sherman tank with its nickname, Battling Basic, painted on its turret crashed through the main gate. Others followed. Santa Claus, in the form of filthy, perspiring young soldiers of the 1st Cavalry Division, had indeed arrived as promised. Among the first to bolt into the compound were the two Philippine Scouts who had led Conner's column through the maze of black streets to the Santo Tomás gate.

As *Life* photographer Carl Mydans neared Santo Tomás and saw its ugly fences, he felt a momentary surge of nausea. Fires were burning in much of Manila, and the hazy, red sky, and tension and emotion of the scene made him shake so badly that his camera bag slapped against him. After three years he was returning to the prison camp where he, too, had been an inmate early in 1942 before being exchanged for Japanese newsmen.

Next to Mydans along the outside of the fence was Frank Hewitt of United Press International. Hewitt had been on Corregidor and Bataan when they had fallen, but had escaped. Now he had come for his wife Virginia, who had been stranded in Manila and been in Santo Tomás ever since.

Mydans grew impatient to get inside, and whispered to Hewitt, "The gate's half open and I'm sure the Japs are gone. Let's slip in." Hewitt nodded and followed. Moments later a Japanese soldier leaped from behind a bunker five feet away, shrieked wildly, and fired at the two newsmen. Blinded momentarily by blue flame, Mydans and Hewitt hit the ground. Then the pair of Americans began crawling toward the fence. When they paused briefly Hewitt said, "There *are* Japs in there!"

Moving in the functional daze well known to combat men in tight situations, Mydans walked over to where Lieutenant Colonel Conner was directing operations. Just then someone shouted "Grenade!" Mydans, Conner, and others flopped to their faces in the gutter. There was a blinding explosion and several GIs nearby were wounded.[2]

The camp was bright now with the light from flares overhead. Dismounted cavalrymen were fanning out into the buildings. Tanks and a few jeeps had turned on their headlights, the better to root out enemy soldiers. Firing erupted sporadically, followed by silence. The voices of American officers shouting commands penetrated the eerie setting.

In the meantime, a company of the 8th Cavalry Regiment under Captain Emery M. Hickman of Burbank, Oklahoma, had rushed to Malacanan Palace, the Philippine equivalent of the White House. Hickman and his men dashed onto the palace grounds, wiping out isolated snipers and a machine-gun position. That night a Japanese force would try to seize the palace back, and in a bitter firefight would be driven off. Dawn would reveal forty dead Japanese sprawled about the premises.

Elements of the 8th Cavalry had set out for the Legislative Building on the south side of the wide and swift-flowing Pasig River. This was the same stream that General Yamashita had often gazed at from his office-building headquarters. Rolling down Quezon Boulevard toward Quezon Bridge, the only remaining span over the Pasig, troopers in the rear vehicle, a communications wire jeep, noticed that four trucks had crawled out from a cross street and attached themselves to the tail of the closely formed American convoy. One man in the jeep stared intently at the newcomers; the trucks didn't look right to him. Suddenly, he called out in a stage whisper to his companions, "Those're Japs behind us!"

With that, the GI let loose with a burst from the jeep's 150-caliber machine gun into the nearest truck, which careened crazily off the broad boulevard. A wild shootout ensued. The vehicles of both sides continued rolling as their occupants blazed away at each other. Then it ended as quickly as it had begun. Two GIs were killed, but the opposing force in the four trucks was wiped out.

Continuing southward along Quezon Boulevard toward the Pasig River, the 8th Cavalry column came to the intersection of Azcarraga Street. On the left rose the modern, three-story buildings of Far Eastern University. On the right sat the stone hulk of Old Bilibid prison. It seemed deserted; there were no sentries in the towers nor any sign of life. Unbeknownst to the cavalrymen, behind its massive walls cringed emaciated American civilians along with military survivors of Bataan and Corregidor, some fourteen hundred in all.

As the motorized column continued to roll, the silence was suddenly shattered. Japanese machine gunners and riflemen barricaded inside the Far Eastern University buildings opened up with a murderous fire at almost point-blank range. The troopers scrambled from vehicles, sought cover, and began returning the fire. Frantic American drivers began hastily turning their vehicles around to escape the fusillade, but now other 8th Cavalry vehicles had closed up from the rear. Fortunately, chaos was narrowly averted, and the entire force beat a hasty retreat from the ambush site, returning to Santo Tomás.

There, a major crisis had developed. While some thirty-five hundred inmates wept and shouted with joy, Colonel Toshio Hayashi, the prison commandant, and sixty of his soldiers had herded 267 inmates, mostly women and children, into the steel-and-concrete Education Building, where they were holding them hostage on the third floor. All night the GIs tried to break into the building, but finally had to call off their efforts out of fear for the hostages' safety.

General Bill Chase had arrived on the Santo Tomás grounds an hour after the Battling Basic had crashed through the front gate. Chase had no alternative: the only hope for saving the hostages was through negotiations. But would the men holed up in the Education Building negotiate? In the savage war in the Pacific, such parlays were unheard of.

Lieutenant Colonel Charles E. Brady of West Orange, New Jersey, executive officer of the 1st Cavalry Brigade, was named to try to negotiate with Colonel Hayashi. After dawn on February 4, Brady and Hayashi deliberated through intermediaries, with little success. That night, Colonel Brady, with only an interpreter, entered the Education Building. There he was kept waiting for fifteen minutes until Colonel Hayashi, neatly dressed in shiny boots and with medals on his tunic, entered the room. Hayashi had a pistol on each hip and was accompanied by six armed soldiers. Brady had no weapon.

There was discomfort and fear in the air. Both Brady and Hayashi were ill at ease in such an unusual situation. Colonel Hayashi, aware that he was holding the aces, promptly set down his demands for the release of the hostages: he and his sixty men, carrying their rifles, automatic weapons, and grenades, would be allowed to march unmolested out of the Santo Tomás grounds. An intense and lengthy discussion followed, and it was agreed that if the hostages were left behind unharmed, the Japanese force in the Education Building would be permitted to depart carrying only personal arms, and then be escorted through American "lines" and released.

Later that night, Colonel Brady gave final instructions to the troopers who would conduct the Japanese out of Santo Tomás. "I want each man to carry his rifle with a cartridge in the chamber," he said. "Each man is to cover a Jap. At a certain point agreed between the Japs and me, we will halt and they will continue. Under no condition is any man to get trigger happy. But if they shoot first, let the bastards have it!"

At dawn on February 5, one of the strangest scenarios of the Pacific war began to unfold. Colonel Hayashi, wearing his samurai saber, walked out of the Education Building, followed by officers and then his men. As they appeared, Americans outside tensed and fingers played across triggers. None could remember seeing an armed enemy soldier without shooting at him and being shot at in turn.

The Japanese quickly formed up three abreast, and Hayashi took his place at their head. In rapid order, men of E Troop, 5th Cavalry, also with loaded weapons, moved into single files, one on each side of the Japanese. Colonel Brady then walked to the head of the combined American-Japanese group, alongside Hayashi, and the bitter enemies marched out through the front gate.

As the column headed down side streets, Brady had to warn bug-eyed Filipinos rushing out of buildings to stay back. There were numerous interruptions in the column's progress as Brady and Hayashi argued bitterly over how far the Americans would escort the Santo Tomás guards. Hayashi kept insisting that Colonel Brady and his men conduct them farther and farther.

Finally, Brady called a halt. "This is as far as we're going," he told Hayashi. "This is the front line. This is where we leave you." Actually, the "front" at this time was anyone's guess. The Nipponese colonel again asked for further safe conduct. "This is where we part company," Brady declared firmly.

For the first time, Colonel Hayashi appeared nervous. But he called out a command, turned to Brady, and saluted smartly. The action caught the American by surprise; he paused briefly, then returned the salute. The Japanese column fell in step and marched forward. As each man passed he either bowed to or saluted Lieutenant Colonel Brady.

While hostage-release parlays had been in progress at Santo Tomás, General Bob Beightler's 37th Infantry Division was battling its way into Manila after the bitter and bloody fighting among the fortified caves guarding the Clark Field complex. The Buckeye outfit's 148th Infantry Regiment marched through the Tondo and Santa Cruz districts west of Santo Tomás internment camp, and about ten o'clock on the night of February 4 the 2nd Battalion reached the northwest corner of silent, hulking Bilibid prison. Colonel Lawrence K. "Red" White, 148th Infantry commander, ordered his men to break in. Tough and veteran fighting men, they were shaken by the scene that greeted them.

In the section holding six hundred civilian men, women, and children, filth was everywhere. Floors and entryways were littered with old clothing, bottles, tin cans—once prized possessions. Dazed inmates, ravaged by starvation and unable to speak, could only utter gurgling sounds. None seemed able to comprehend what was happening. Children, their pinched faces white with fear, huddled behind the tattered skirts of their mothers.

In the wing holding the American survivors of Corregidor and Bataan, there was the same human devastation, the same scars of suffering.

Tears welled in the eyes of some of Colonel White's soldiers, many of whom had been carefree participants at high school proms at the time these Battling Bastards of Bataan had been overwhelmed.

For the time being, military prisoners and internees remained in Bilibid; with fighting raging outside and around Far Eastern University, there was no place safer for them to go. At dawn the inmates were hastily removed to quarters at Grace Park when out-of-control fires threatened the prison and it appeared that the Japanese were forming up to recapture it. All departed so quickly that they left behind their few pitiful belongings. When they returned two days later, looters had stolen everything.

Between February 5 and 7, the main bodies of both Mudge's 1st Cavalry and Beightler's 37th Infantry divisions poured into northern Manila. Shootouts erupted at scores of places and, while carrying out planned demolitions, the Japanese set fires that covered the urban area north of the Pasig River with thick clouds of black smoke. Into this maelstrom on the morning of February 7 rode General MacArthur, accompanied only by bodyguards with Tommy guns. On the north side of the city founded in 1571 by Spanish explorer Miguel Lopez de Legaspi, his jeep, flying a five-star pennant, pulled up in front of a regimental CP. Within minutes word had seeped down to the lowest ranks: "MacArthur's here!"

Douglas MacArthur had lost no time getting back to the capital he had evacuated on Christmas Eve 1941, after declaring Manila an open city to prevent its destruction by the invading Japanese. Now, surveying the areas already taken by his men, MacArthur could see that Manila had suffered and foresaw that it was going to suffer more. His repeated calls to the Japanese commander in the capital to surrender had gone unanswered; now MacArthur knew it would be a fight to the death.

He hopped into his jeep and raced off for the Santo Tomás internment camp. Driving through the gate battered down by the Sherman tanks, MacArthur received rousing cheers from the gaunt and sickly survivors. Occasional shells from enemy artillery exploded in the compound as the general strode inside a building. He poked through corridors and rooms jammed with humanity, talking emotionally with Theodore Stevenson, a Presbyterian medical missionary who had been the camp doctor. Dr. Stevenson had been jailed by the Japanese because he refused to change death certificates on which he had boldly scrawled: *The contributing cause of death is malnutrition.*

As Douglas MacArthur left Santo Tomás, maimed veterans hobbled toward him, trying to raise enfeebled hands in salutes and reaching out to touch his uniform. Women embraced him; many tried to kiss his cheek.

Then it was on to Old Bilibid prison. As he walked into the civilian section, pandemonium erupted as scarecrow figures tried to embrace him or just touch his sleeve. Weeping women threw scrawny arms around MacArthur and had to be gently pried loose.

In the military section of Bilibid, in contrast to the turmoil in the civilian side, the supreme commander came upon lines of ragged soldiers—bearded, soiled, unkempt, little more than skin and bones—each standing silently at attention by his cot, ready for inspection by the supreme commander. A lump rose in Douglas MacArthur's throat and he fought back tears. These were his "boys"—the gaunt, grim, ghostly legion of Bataan and Corregidor.

The eerie silence was broken only by the occasional sob of someone who could no longer fight back the tears. MacArthur passed slowly, down the lines of long-suffering men, through the debris of dirty tin cans they had eaten from, the bug-infested bottles they had drunk from. As he stopped before each filthy cot, a soldier would whisper weakly, "God bless you, General" or "Thank God you're back." His voice choked in emotion, MacArthur could only mumble, "I'm a little late, but we finally made it."[3]

MacArthur took his leave from the prison and walked the block to where a group of GIs were crouched behind a low wall. Up ahead a Japanese machine gun began firing, and a lieutenant furiously signaled the general to take cover. MacArthur paused for a minute, remaining upright, then slowly walked away to return to his headquarters in a sugar refinery north of Manila.

Elsewhere in central Manila, there was bitter fighting. At 8:00 A.M. on February 9, Captain George West and his men of Company G, 129th Infantry, 37th Division, were poised across the water from Provisor Island, a plot of ground some four hundred by one hundred yards in the Pasig River. Almost every foot of the tiny island was covered by five large concrete buildings and smaller shedlike structures—a power plant. It was hoped the complex could be seized intact to provide Manila with electricity, and it was Company G's task to take it from the Japanese force holding it.

Captain West planned to seize a boiler plant first. After an artillery plastering, a platoon set out in two assault boats. One craft reached the island safely. The other was sunk, killing two men; the remainder were able to swim to the island. Fifteen of West's men bolted into the boiler plant, and another heavy firefight broke out, with West's GIs finally being driven out. They took refuge behind a coal pile and were pinned down by machine-gun bursts. Two men tried to swim back but were killed midstream.

Unable to move, the Americans remained behind the coal pile all day. After dark, Captain West swam to the island, dragging an engineer assault boat behind him. He was struck by a bullet, but kept swimming. Reaching the island, West loaded seven men into the boat and went with it back to the far shore. Then the Company G commander returned to pick up the remaining men. At midnight, West took a nose count: of the eighteen men who had first reached Provisor Island, all but one had been killed or wounded.

Hastily, another attempt was organized to seize the island. At 2:30 A.M., after a sixty-minute artillery pounding, ninety Company E men shoved off in six assault boats. The night had been dark, but as two of the craft reached the island the moon came out from behind a cloud. A hail of Japanese machine-gun and mortar fire sank three trailing boats.

Periodic machine-gun bursts pinned the Company E men behind the coal pile, but when the moon finally set, at 5:00 A.M., they bolted into the bullet-scarred boiler plant. A final firefight broke out amid the machinery, and at dawn the Americans were in control of the eastern half of the boiler plant, while the Japanese held the western half.

Later that morning, Company E methodically cleared out the other half of the boiler plant and gained control of the eastern part of Provisor Island. As usual, the Japanese troops fought to the death. After 37th Division artillery and mortars, along with direct fire by tanks and tank destroyers, pounded the Japanese-held half of the industrial fortress, American soldiers wiped out the remaining resistance.

Seizing postage-stamp-sized Provisor Island had been costly: the 2nd Battalion, 129th Infantry, suffered casualties of a hundred men—all of them in vain. The power plant had been pulverized by American artillery and mortars, along with Japanese demolitions, and was of no use to anyone.

The bloody affair at Provisor Island gave a bitter foretaste of the savagery that would rage in Manila, where the fighting had taken on a new complexion. For the first (and only) time in the Pacific, GIs were engaged in street-to-street, building-to-building, and room-to-room death struggles. American advances were often measured in yards, or by the bloody seizure of a few rooms in a fortified building. Japanese soldiers, looking forward to dying for the emperor, had to be rooted out by bayonets, rifles, grenades, flamethrowers, dynamite, and point-blank tank fire.

General MacArthur had forbidden the use of artillery in order to save Filipino lives. But American casualties became so heavy in the fierce street fighting that the supreme commander was finally forced to approve the use of artillery against "anything holding up progress or costing American lives." Artillery would not be aimed, however, at structures, such as churches and hospitals, known to contain Filipino civilians. But even that restriction was soon lifted when it became obvious that the Japanese were firing 5-inch naval guns from the second and third stories of the Philippine General Hospital, and had set up machine guns in churches.

Manila's misery would drag on and on. Two weeks after the 1st Cav had dashed across the northern city limits, the capital shuddered almost constantly from the convulsive roaring of "Long Toms" (155-millimeter guns) shelling the Japanese inside Manila, as well as on its outskirts. The Filipinos would pay an enormous price for liberation. The Pearl of the Orient, with its host of magnificent buildings and churches, was doomed to utter destruction. And American fighting men would be reluctant parties to its demise.

16

Assault on the Genko Line

While two American divisions had been fighting Japanese and liberating prisoners in northern Manila, Swing's 11th Airborne Division had advanced northward from Tagatay Ridge to the Parañaque River, three miles south of the capital's outskirts. Along the Parañaque the airborne men butted up against the Genko Line, a fortified belt of reinforced concrete pillboxes and bunkers, and the strongest defensive position in the Manila region. The Genko Line included the strongpoints of Nichols Field and old Fort William McKinley and reached clear back to suburban Manila, where pillboxes abounded at street intersections.

Late on the night of February 4, at his headquarters in an ornate structure called Garcia Mansion fronting on Manila Bay, General Joe Swing ordered Colonel Hardrock Haugen's 511th Parachute Infantry to launch an attack after daybreak at the Genko Line. A few hours later, Colonel Irvin R. Schimmelpfenning, the division's thirty-six-year-old chief of staff, went forward to reconnoiter the terrain they would have to cross in a few hours. Suddenly, a Japanese machine gun chattered in the blackness and Colonel Schimmelpfenning toppled over dead.

The popular young colonel's death left many in the 11th Airborne shaken. Was this a harbinger of disaster for the attack against the Genko

Line? One of those devastated by Colonel Schimmelpfenning's death was Colonel Haugen: the two had been close friends since their days as classmates at West Point. But Haugen was determined to fight on, and shortly after dawn his 511th Parachute Infantry forced a crossing of the Parañaque River and battled their way northward along the shore of Manila Bay against dug-in Japanese machine gunners and riflemen. It was a savage struggle, and the American paratroopers rooted out stubborn Japanese defenders, house by house, pillbox by pillbox, with rifles, bayonets, mortars, and flamethrowers. It took two days for Haugen's men to hack out a hole two thousand yards deep into the Genko Line.

On the morning of February 11, the 511th Parachute Infantry jumped off less than one mile below the Manila city limits. Typically, the thirty-six-year old Colonel Haugen was out in front. His staff had long been concerned about that. Hardrock Haugen always took too many personal risks, seeming determined to prove he was the toughest man in the regiment. And following the death of Colonel Schimmelpfenning, those around Haugen had overheard him musing that he might soon be sharing his friend's fate.

Haugen and a group of troopers were advancing toward a street intersection when a machine gun in a pillbox began spitting lead. The colonel and several others were cut down. Medics rushed forward, turned Haugen over, and saw blood spurting from a gaping wound in his chest. Barely conscious, the colonel, along with the other wounded troopers, was hurried to an aid station.

The 511th Parachute Infantry pressed its attack into Manila and reached Liberated Street, where the regimental CP was set up in an abandoned building. Shortly after 3:00 p.m., General Joe Swing strode through the doorway and up to Lieutenant Colonel Edward H. Lahti, the 511th's executive officer. "Haugen's been shot and evacuated," Swing stated. "Lahti, you're in command." The general swung around, retraced his steps, and left the building.

Colonel Lahti's military career had begun at age sixteen as a corporal in the Oregon National Guard. Later, he had joined the regular Army, and after several years as an enlisted man received an appointment to and graduated from West Point. At age thirty-one, Lahti would be one of the youngest regimental commanders in the Army.

Colonel Lahti received an order to hold the regiment at Liberated

Street and to send a patrol northward to contact a patrol of Mudge's 1st Cavalry Division working its way southward. Lahti decided to go himself. Climbing into a jeep with a driver and two troopers wielding Tommy guns, the colonel drove through streets that were ominously deserted. This was no-man's-land. Periodically, the jeep was fired on by snipers, and had to dodge mines planted at intersections, but Lahti finally managed to locate a patrol from the 5th Cavalry Regiment. American divisions from north and south of the city had linked up.

That night a weary Private First Class Jerard Vlaminck, a machine gunner in Company A of the 511th Parachute Infantry, and his comrades were in position along Manila Bay. Vlaminck had been trudging along all day carrying the machine-gun tripod, two boxes of ammunition, seven grenades, and his M-1 rifle. Such was the burden of a paratrooper, who seldom had the luxury of riding even part of the way. Orders had been received to dig in, but the parachutists were so exhausted they merely propped their backs against trees or buildings and fell asleep.

Vlaminck chose to lie on the sandy beach alongside a little fishing boat. He hugged his rifle to his chest and tried to sleep. But sleep would not come—he was too drained, physically and emotionally. The night was unsettlingly quiet. Off toward the north Vlaminck could see a yellow haze: Manila was burning. The exhausted private glanced southward through the blackness and saw a lightning bug. It reminded Vlaminck of his home in Minnesota.

Suddenly, the trooper sat upright, wide awake. This lightning bug had a peculiar glow; it would get bright and then dim. All the time it came closer. Then Vlaminck heard strange voices near the lightning bug. Probably Filipinos. Private Vlaminck grew tense; he had spotted silhouettes near the lightning bug and they were coming directly toward him. The hush grew oppressive. Vlaminck lay motionless.

By the glow of the flames consuming Manila, the parachutist caught a glimpse of a saber at the side of one figure. When the pair of intruders were twenty-five feet from Vlaminck he aimed his rifle and squeezed the trigger. A bullet tore into the shoulder of one man. As he howled and grabbed his shoulder with one hand, the other figure raised a saber and charged toward the American. As the figure made a lunge, Vlaminck fired again. The razor-sharp blade, glinting in the reflection of the yellow Manila haze, slashed into the sand a foot from the paratrooper. The Japanese officer fell dead at Vlaminck's feet. The "lightning bug" lay beside the corpse: the officer had been smoking a cigarette.

Then Vlaminck heard a splashing noise and turned to find the enemy soldier he had shot struggling in the shallow water. The trooper fired twice more, and the splashing ceased. An investigation revealed that both of the dead men were high-ranking officers. They were loaded with grenades and apparently had been cut off in the 511th Parachute Infantry's advance that day.

While Swing's paratroopers were hacking through the center of the Genko Line, the 188th Glider Infantry Regiment and an attached battalion of the 187th Glider Infantry had been pressing forward on the right flank in an effort to capture Nichols Field, the strongest point in the fortified enemy defenses around Manila. The flat terrain around Nichols Field bristled with anti-aircraft guns, concrete bunkers, and pillboxes. All the Japanese positions were camouflaged by vegetation that had grown up around them over the years. Each of the concrete structures housed machine gunners and riflemen. Around the perimeter of and at points within Nichols Field the Japanese had erected sturdy barbed-wire fences that were covered by men manning automatic weapons. In the hills beyond the airport, the Japanese had emplaced 5-inch naval guns salvaged from ships sunk in Manila Bay. These weapons had poured such heavy fire onto the airborne men as they sought to overrun the field that a company commander had radioed higher headquarters: "Tell [Admiral] Halsey to stop looking for the Jap fleet. It's dug in here at Nichols Field!"

On the morning of February 12, American artillery and mortars, along with Marine Corps planes based near Lingayen Gulf, pounded Japanese bunkers and gun emplacements on and around Nichols Field. Then grim glidermen, expecting to be raked by a torrent of fire, began advancing from two sides to dig out members of the 3rd Naval Battalion. The heavy bombardment had done its job: Nipponese fire lessened significantly, and by dusk the airborne troopers had wiped out the sailors on most of the field. But the new landlords of Nichols Field were shelled by large-caliber guns from Fort William McKinley, northeast of the airfield. Until that Japanese strongpoint in the Genko Line was captured, Nichols Field could not be used as a base for American warplanes.

Elements of Lahti's 511th Parachute Infantry were ordered to seize Fort McKinley, which was defended by the 4th Naval Battalion. On February 13, a paratrooper platoon, led by Lieutenant Ted Baughn, formed up along a railroad embankment outside Fort McKinley to attack the big-gun emplacements several hundred yards away. On the way to the tracks, a few of Baughn's men had discovered a case of booze, and before jumping off in the attack each member took a long drink. Then the troopers crawled through a fence and out into open rice paddies. Soon there was the sound of shells screaming toward them, and the parachutists flopped face downward. The ground was rocked by explosions, and shrapnel hissed past just overhead.

A young Filipino who had been accompanying Baughn's platoon (the troopers called him "Minnow" due to his size) leaped to his feet, shouted "Advance! advance!," and ran forward. As if on cue, Lieutenant Baughn and his entire platoon jumped up and charged ahead, all the time yelling "*Banzai! Banzai!*" They continued their mad dash as Japanese machine guns opened up and mortar shells exploded around them.

Out of breath and with the enemy fire growing stronger, the airborne men began searching for cover. Lieutenant Baughn saw a large shellhole ahead and sailed into it. He found he was so hoarse from shouting *Banzai!* that he could only speak in a whisper.

After everyone had taken cover, Corporal Claude Hillman was hit by a bullet that glanced off his helmet and stunned him. Both scared and angry, Hillman scrambled to his feet and started racing over an open rice paddy toward the Japanese positions. A trooper, sizing up the situation, brought Hillman down with a flying tackle and got him to a relatively safe position. Except for a king-sized headache, the corporal had not been injured.

A short time later, the pinned-down troopers heard a call for help. In his shellhole, Lieutenant Baughn recognized the voice; it was that of Private First Class Jerard Vlaminck, the trooper who had shot the two Japanese officers on the Manila Bay beach a few nights earlier. Vlaminck was badly wounded. Without regard for enemy bullets, one of Baughn's squad leaders, Sergeant Richard Sibio of Columbus, Ohio, leaped from cover and raced to the prostrate Vlaminck. Picking up his bleeding comrade and placing him over his shoulder, Sibio headed back with his burden until he had found a relatively safe position. Then Sergeant Sibio rejoined his comrades in the advance.[1]

One of the troopers in Lieutenant Baughn's platoon was twenty-one-year-old Private First Class Manuel Perez, Jr. Quiet, unassuming, with a perpetual smile on his boyish face, Perez had been alternating with Private First Class Ancel J. Upton as lead scout, and this was Perez's day for that perilous task. Being lead scout never held out the promise of longevity.

Private Perez had nearly washed out of the paratroopers back at Camp Mackall, North Carolina. A dedicated soldier, Perez had suffered from one crucial shortcoming in basic training: he couldn't shoot accurately. After everyone in the company but Perez had qualified with the rifle, Lieutenant Ted Baughn had been assigned to tutor Perez on the rifle range for a week. At the end of the seven days of intensive practice and instruction, Manual Perez had qualified with a rating of marksman—the lowest of the three designations in riflery.

Now, outside Luzon's frowning Fort William McKinley, Manuel Perez was well out in front of his advancing company in his role of lead scout. His pal Ancel Upton had been worried about Perez's depressed frame of mind: that morning the youth from Chicago, Illinois, had confided to Upton, "Ancel, I'm tired of all this fighting and killing. Today I will be killed or wounded—one way or the other, I'm going back to the States."

As Lieutenant Baughn's platoon edged nearer to the fort, Japanese fire grew more intense. Up ahead Perez spotted a concrete bunker from which a pair of .50-caliber machine guns was blazing away. There was virtually no cover, and the paratroopers were lying face down as streams of bullets went over their heads. Sergeant Max Polick, a squad leader from Medina, New York, saw Perez scramble to his feet and, crouching and weaving, head for the chattering machine guns. Baughn's platoon covered their lead scout as best they could by peppering the bunker with rifle fire.

Perez crawled up to the bunker and tossed a couple of grenades in through the embrasure. There was a loud blast. Then Perez climbed on top and dropped two phosphorous grenades into a vent. His comrades saw the scout flatten out and then the flash from the explosion. A plume of white smoke poured out the vent. The machine guns fell silent. Perez was sitting in a cloud of smoke looking back at his comrades and grinning. Sergeant Polick, Sergeant Sibio, and others saw him hold up his hand and form a circle with his thumb and first finger.

Manny Perez's work was unfinished. There were ten more concrete pillboxes in the string defending the approach to Fort McKinley. The trooper returned to his platoon's position and loaded up with grenades. Dodging and weaving his way back through the field, Perez edged up to a pillbox next to the knocked-out bunker. He fired his rifle four times into a port, and Japanese sailors started pouring out the rear door. Perez shot and killed eight of them. One Japanese rushed toward the American screaming *"Banzai!"* and hurled his rifle with fixed bayonet at Perez. The paratrooper parried the flying rifle, but the jolt knocked away his own. Perez snatched up the other man's rifle and bayoneted him with it.

Four more men came out the rear door. Perez clubbed two of them to death and bayoneted the others. Then he scrambled into the pillbox, where he encountered the sole surviving defender. A hand-to-hand struggle erupted, and Perez killed his adversary with a Japanese bayonet.

The 11th Airborne's one-man army continued to knock out nearby bunkers, returning periodically for fresh supplies of grenades. At one point, a Japanese sailor charged toward the unsuspecting Perez with his bayonet raised, but one of Perez's comrades shot him in the head.

When Manny Perez's rampage was over, enemy dead in large numbers were sprawled around and in the eleven pillboxes he had assaulted. Perez's earlier premonition that he would be killed or wounded that day and returned to the States "one way or another" failed to come true. But thirty days later, Manuel Perez would be dead—killed by a sniper's bullet while out in front of his attacking company.[2]

Unbeknownst to the Americans, Admiral Sanji Iwabuchi, who had ignored General Yamashita's order declaring Manila an open city, was in Fort McKinley, having moved there on February 14 after the 37th Infantry and 1st Cavalry divisions had closed in on his Manila headquarters. Aware that Fort McKinley would soon be overrun, Iwabuchi ordered its defenders to abandon the strongpoint after first blowing up the fort's facilities and ammunition. The Japanese would depart on the night of February 17.

On February 16, elements of the 511th Parachute Infantry had clawed their way to the last ridge overlooking Fort McKinley. At 3:00 P.M. Colonel Ed Lahti and his battalion commanders, Major Frank "Hacksaw" Holcombe and Major Henry Burgess, were gathered on the ridge discussing positions for the night accompanied by a background of explosions: Fort McKinley's garrison was blowing up its ammunition before evacuating. Suddenly, they heard an eerie whirring sound drawing closer, and moments later Lahti was struck by a powerful blow and knocked over backward as though he had been kicked by a mule. Lying beside him was a large chunk of iron that had been catapulted from Fort McKinley. Holcombe and Burgess escaped unscathed.

Dazed and bleeding, Ed Lahti glanced at his upper arm where the loaf-of-bread-sized chunk had struck him. Doesn't look too bad, he told the others. What he couldn't see, Holcombe and Burgess could: Lahti had suffered a deep slash reaching entirely around his arm and back to his shoulder. The majors insisted that Lahti wait for an ambulance. Lahti growled, "Hell, no. I'll get back [to an aid station] on my own."

The colonel located a small scooter (the type dropped from aircraft to provide an extra measure of mobility on the battlefield) and drove away in a cloud of dust. Reaching a CP, Lahti contacted General Swing by radio: "I got a little flesh wound. I'll get the doc to sew me up and get right back on the job."

Within hours a battalion surgeon, Captain W. L. Chambers, had performed extensive embroidery work on Colonel Lahti and told him, "A hundred years from now you'll never know you've been hit!" A few days later Captain Chambers himself would be seriously wounded.

As a grudging concession to the large amount of blood he had lost, Lahti rested for two hours, then, with his arm in a black sling, went back to the front line. With him went thirty-two surgical stitches.

Meanwhile, fighting inside Manila proper had grown more brutal.

Long gone was Douglas MacArthur's dream of taking the beautiful city intact. On February 16, elements of the 5th Cavalry regiment were ordered to dig out a Japanese force entrenched in Rizal Stadium, a baseball facility comparable to a major-league park in the United States. The cavalrymen were pinned down by machine guns in bunkers on the playing surface, most of them located in left field, and by riflemen in sandbagged positions under the grandstand. Two dead Japanese lay sprawled on the pitcher's mound. Suddenly, three Sherman tanks battered through the cement wall surrounding the outfield and began firing at positions on the field. Flamethrowers and satchel charges (bundles of explosives) wiped out the remaining defenders, and by 6:30 P.M. the stadium was under new ownership.

On the following day, February 17, some two thousand soldiers and Imperial Marines entrenched themselves in the ancient walled city known as Intramuros, where they were determined to make a last stand. Built by the Spaniards in the sixteenth century, with walls that were nearly forty feet thick and fifteen feet high in places, Intramuros was an imposing fortress. Along with many closely built houses, the *Kempei Tai* station and the dreaded Santiago prison (where thousands of Filipinos had suffered and died) were located within its massive walls. Inside, the Japanese held five thousand Filipino civilians as hostages.

Over a loudspeaker, General Oscar Griswold pleaded with the commander to surrender, or at least free the hostages. There was no reply. Griswold had no choice: he ordered a bombardment of Intramuros. Then tanks, followed by foot soldiers, punched their way inside. The fighting was savage. But after six days and nights of rooting out tenacious Japanese, a pulverized Intramuros was in American hands. Thousands of Japanese and Filipino corpses, many immolated by flamethrowers, littered the hundred and sixty acres.

Meanwhile, General MacArthur had learned that an assault was being planned against the red-roofed Manila Hotel, where he, his wife Jean, and son Arthur had spent many happy hours before having to flee their six-room, air-conditioned penthouse on Christmas Eve 1941. That ornate penthouse, with its multitude of red drapes and French mirrors, held memories for Douglas MacArthur. From a balcony off the dining room he had regularly taken in the spectacular view of Corregidor in

Manila Bay and the purplish mass of Bataan. The penthouse had been filled with countless memorabilia and personal belongings gained over a lifetime—hundreds of his father's priceless books, autographed pictures of General Pershing, Marshal Foch, and other famed military leaders. As far as MacArthur knew, these belongings were still there, even though it had been occupied by a series of Japanese dignitaries.

MacArthur decided to join the assault on the Manila Hotel. The hotel would be a tough nut to crack. Like other major buildings in the capital, it featured a number of easily defensible strongpoints, especially the tunnels that ran beneath the sturdy, five-story structure.

During the night before the dawn attack, the 82nd Field Artillery Battalion periodically shelled the hotel. At daybreak, Douglas MacArthur, assuming the role of rifleman, joined cavalry troops ready to charge the hotel. Before the jump-off, flames were seen leaping from the penthouse; the Japanese had set it afire.

Minutes later the cavalrymen charged the front door and got inside, where a gun duel erupted that left four or five Japanese dead on the thick carpet. Then the Americans, with the unarmed five-star General MacArthur on their heels, headed up the stairs. At each level there was a shootout. The route to the upper floors was strewn with Japanese corpses, raising fears among some officers that one might be shamming and could suddenly gun down MacArthur.

When the general reached his old penthouse home it was little more than smouldering ashes. A dead Japanese colonel was stretched out across the threshold of the open doorway. MacArthur stepped over the body and edged inside. A young cavalry lieutenant, his face blackened by a mixture of smoke and perspiration, and clutching a Tommy gun in one hand, entered, looked down at the bloody corpse of the colonel, and called out to MacArthur, "Nice going, chief!"[3]

17
Angels From Heaven

Twenty-year-old Lieutenant George E. Skau of Connecticut, leader of the 11th Airborne's reconnaissance platoon, and eight of his men were concealed in a mountainside jungle thicket overlooking the Los Baños internment camp, twenty-five miles below Manila near the southern shore of a large lake called Laguna de Bay. It was Sunday, February 18.

Four days earlier Skau and his troopers had slipped into Japanese-controlled territory to watch the comings and goings in the prison camp. They observed during the day; at night they would edge down from the mountain and steal up to the six-foot fence surrounding the enclosure. Before dawn they would return to the mountainside perch and make detailed sketches of the location of watchtowers, guard posts, pillboxes, machine guns, entrances, and buildings.

In the prison camp, located on the grounds of the University of the Philippines agricultural college, were more than two thousand emaciated prisoners, mainly American civilians who had been living in Manila when it was captured by the Japanese in January 1942. There were large numbers of Roman Catholic nuns and priests, Protestant missionaries, doctors, lawyers, engineers, business executives, and several hundred wives and children. Since the Americans had invaded Luzon the previous month a haunting specter had hovered over the bleak enclosure: Rather than allow the inmates's liberation by American troops, would the Japanese guards commit mass murder?

On this Sunday morning, Sister Patricia Marie Callan, an American, was walking to the makeshift chapel where each day mass was offered by one of the sixty-five Catholic priests with sufficient strength to stand long enough for the ritual. Sister Patricia Marie felt blessed by God. She had survived the ordeal of nearly three years of brutal imprisonment and, along with other Maryknoll Sisters, had been given quarters in the pig shed, a more desirable lodging than the decrepit straw huts that housed most of the inmates.

Even as she prayed fervently for the Los Baños prisoners' liberation, Sister Patricia Marie knew that such a thing would require little short of a divine miracle. The nun and a few others knew that the Japanese had placed some sixty-five drums of gasoline throughout the barbed-wire enclosure, and had set up machine guns above the camp on Mount Makiling. On the approach of American soldiers, guards had been ordered to hastily saturate the straw huts and other structures with gasoline and set them ablaze. As terrified inmates fled outside, they would be mowed down by machine-gun fire.

Early on Sunday morning, February 18, the 511th Parachute Infantry's 1st Battalion, led by Major Henry Burgess, the Wyoming rancher, was pulled out of the Fort McKinley fight and brought into Manila for what they were told would be a rest. Burgess reported to 11th Airborne Division headquarters and learned that several days earlier, General MacArthur had told General Swing, "Joe, I want you to rescue the civilian prisoners at Los Baños as soon as you can." How the feat would be accomplished was left up to Swing.

Major Burgess was told that his battalion would conduct the raid. It was a sobering revelation, and Burgess was struck by the enormous obstacles to success. How could a force of four hundred and twelve paratroopers slip undetected deep into Japanese-controlled territory, wipe out a large number of enemy soldiers, and bring back to safety more than two thousand men, women, and children, many of whom were unable to walk? Then Burgess got another jolt: Some eight thousand men of the Japanese 8th Division were located only eight miles southwest of the Los Baños prison camp.

Burgess spent the remainder of that day and all of the next discussing the rescue mission with General Swing, Lieutenant Colonel Henry J. "Butch" Muller, the division's twenty-six-year-old G-2, Lieutenant Colonel Douglas N. Quandt, the operations officer, and their staffs. Their plans were drawn up in the strictest secrecy. The element of surprise would be crucial. Should the Japanese get word of the mission, Los Baños could run red with American blood—prisoners' as well as paratroopers'.

On Monday morning, the 1st Battalion's "rest" came to an abrupt halt. Burgess instructed his number two man, twenty-seven-year-old Captain Nathaniel "Bud" Ewing, another Wyoming rancher, to start marching the battalion southward in order to shorten the distance to the Los Baños camp. Burgess and Ewing were longtime friends, having served together in the Wyoming National Guard.

As planning for the raid continued, nagging problems surfaced faster than did answers. Some would have to remain unanswered; time was running out. Due to the many imponderables, no formal written plan could be drawn up. Los Baños would be an operation in which there would be a number of options. Once the operation began to unfold, it would be up to Major Burgess to make on-the-spot decisions. In overall charge of the mission would be the commander of the 188th Glider Infantry, Colonel Robert "Shorty" Soule. L-Day (Liberation Day) was set for Friday, February 23.

At noon on Monday, Joe Swing and his planners received an unexpected intelligence bonanza. Peter Miles, a handsome engineer who had once been a saloon bouncer and snake charmer, walked into 11th Airborne headquarters after having escaped from Los Baños the day before. Miles, sharp and articulate, provided a wealth of information about the camp, relating in detail the daily routine in Los Baños, including the revelation that only those Japanese actually on guard duty were armed.

"Those Japs not on duty arise just before dawn and take calisthenics in an open area near their barracks," Miles stated. "At this time their weapons are locked in a rack in a short connecting room between two long barracks where the Nips sleep."[1]

By Wednesday, February 21, the Los Baños rescue plan was finalized. The mission would be launched by Lieutenant Skau and thirty one of his recon troopers (who called themselves the "Killer Platoon"). Skau's men would paddle over Laguna de Bay in *bancas* (native canoes) that night, slip ashore at Mayondon Point two miles north of the prison camp, and make contact with a guerrilla force. In the early Friday morning (L-Day) hours of darkness, loaded with grenades and carrying Tommy guns, the Killer Platoon would crawl up to guard posts and pillboxes and wait for the 7:00 A.M. signal to attack. Skau and his troopers, along with a group of Filipino guerrillas, would then kill the on-duty guards.

Help would be needed immediately to wipe out the off-duty soldiers and secure the sixty-acre complex. That help would come from the sky. At the minute that Skau's Killer Platoon started shooting and grenading guards, Lieutenant John B. Ringler of suburban Buffalo, New York, and his Company B would bail out of nine C-47s and land next to the compound. Jumping with Ringler would be Lieutenant Bill Hettinger's machine-gun platoon. The drop zone—a small field hemmed in by the barbed wire of the camp, a high voltage electric transmission line, and a railroad track—was a major headache for the mission's planners. The potential for disaster was great, but John Ringler remained undaunted. "It'll be a tight fit, but we can do it." he said.[2]

Once on the ground, Lieutenant Ringler and his parachutists would race across camp to the weapons rack where the arms of the off-duty guards were kept. It was hoped that those guards would still be engaged in calisthenics, but no one doubted they would race for their weapons. The side who reached the arms rack first could well determine the outcome of the rescue mission.

In the meantime, Major Burgess would rejoin his battalion (less Ringler's company), which Captain Bud Ewing would have marched southward for fifteen miles along the road from Manila to Los Baños. The paratroop force would bivouac on the western shore of Laguna de Bay near the town of Mamatid. At 4:00 A.M. on L-Day, the paratroopers would load onto fifty four amphibious tractors, known as "amtracs" and "alligators," which would then slip into Laguna de Bay and head for Mayondon Point, two miles north of the prison camp. With Burgess's

LAGUNA DE BAY

MAMATID

San Cristobal River

675

San Juan River

CALAMBA ISLAND

CALAMBA

LINGA

472

MAYONDON PT.

1 ☒ 511(-)

D ◎ 45T

GT2 AMTRAC

SAN ANTONIO

LAKE ALLIGATOR

Los Baños

Manila R.R.

INTERNEE CAMP

MT. BIJANG

MT. CAMOTES

511th B CO

MT. MAIBARARA

MT. MAPINGGON

infantry troopers would be one hundred men and four guns of Captain Louis Burris's Battery D of the 457th Field Artillery Battalion.

Burgess's amtracs were to rumble onto the Mayondon Point beach at 7:00 A.M., the same time that Skau's Killer Platoon would be opening fire and Ringler's parachutists would be jumping. Designated men would fan out to protect the Mayondon Point beachhead, while the remaining troopers would roll on to the prison camp in the amtracs.

A diversion would be mounted to draw the nearby Japanese 8th Division away from Los Baños. Colonel Shorty Soule would lead a force in a headlong plunge down the road from Manila toward Japanese 8th Division positions at the east-west flowing San Juan River near Mamatid. Soule would have Lieutenant Colonel Ernest LaFlamme's 1st Battalion, Company B of the 637th Tank Destroyer Battalion, and elements of the 472nd and 675th Field Artillery Battalions.

Shortly after dark on Thursday night, there was a roar of powerful motors and a line of fifty-four amphibious tractors crashed through the underbrush and into the Laguna de Bay shoreline bivouac of Major Burgess's battalion. The "alligators" were awesome to see—large, noisy, each one armed with machine guns. But they were vulnerable in combat because they were slow, thin-skinned, and lacking in maneuverability.

Out of one hopped Lieutenant Colonel Joseph W. Biggs, commander of the 672nd Amphibious Tractor Battalion. Biggs reported to Major Burgess and was informed of his mission. He was jolted. His amtracs would have to navigate course changes in blackness with only hand compasses, keep the column closed to avoid chaos, and hit a pinpoint target on shore at a precise time after a journey of some twenty miles.

At just past midnight, with the tension over the dark bivuoac along Laguna de Bay almost tangible, a Filipino man of about forty emerged from out of the underbrush and was promptly collared by sentries, who brought him before Henry Burgess. In fractured English, the intruder's first words were: "What time are you going to attack Los Baños camp?"

Burgess glared at the man, who was now deeply alarmed. So was the major. Was this native a Japanese spy? How did he know the target of the raiders? Questioned sharply, the Filipino grew hysterical and protested that he merely lived nearby and was out for a walk. "I think he's a goddamned spy!" a trooper called out. "Yeah, shoot the bastard!" said another.

Finally, Major Burgess told the frightened Filipino, "You're coming along with us—and you're riding in my amtrac."

Twelve miles to the southeast, sleep was coming fitfully for inmates of the Los Baños camp. Earlier that evening they had been told that the camp's food had been exhausted and that no more was coming. All day Japanese soldiers had been digging a long, deep ditch outside the barbed wire. Many prisoners were convinced that they would be buried in this excavation in the morning, after being bayoneted or machine-gunned.

Before dawn on L-Day, February 23, some one hundred and thirty of Lieutenant John Ringler's paratroopers were at bomb-pocked Nichols Field outside Manila. In effect, they had been "freed" after having been locked up in a prison for several days in order to assure secrecy. "We've been sprung!" a GI exclaimed. Breakfast was served. Then there were shouts of "load 'em up!" and the troopers, burdened with heavy combat gear, waddled up short ladders and into nine C-47s of the 65th Troop Carrier Squadron. With Major Don Anderson piloting the first aircraft, the transport planes, one after the other, zoomed down the rubble-strewn runway and lifted off for the short hop to Los Baños. Lieutenant Ringler would be the first to jump, after shoving out an equipment bundle of automatic weapons and ammunition. "If the Japs shoot at the first parachute out," Ringler had quipped, "they'll hit the bundle and not me."

Ringler stood in the C-47 door as the wind rushed in. Already the sky was starting to lighten. Off in the distance, perhaps five miles, he spotted colored smoke. That was a good sign: George Skau and his recon men were marking the DZ.

Down below in the hot, fearful prison camp, Sister Patricia Marie Callan was walking to the chapel for 7:00 A.M. mass. It well might be her last one, she reminded herself. Suddenly, she heard the roar of motors. She squinted skyward and saw a low-flying formation of airplanes nearing the camp. Moments later, billowing white canopies filled the air, and the Maryknoll nun called out in joyous excitement, "*Parachutes! Parachutes! Americans!*"

All hell broke loose. Lieutenant Skau and his Killer Platoon pounced on the Japanese guards, gunning them down and hurling grenades. Confused and panicked, guards surviving the first assault ran around aimlessly until they too were cut down.

Meanwhile, Lieutenant Ringler's parachutists had made an almost textbook-perfect landing: one man was injured when his head struck the railroad track. Moving like cogs in a well-oiled machine, Ringler's men rushed the barbed-wire fence and were soon inside. Startled by the sudden assault from the blue, the Nipponese off-duty guards milled about in confusion, then, sizing up the situation, dashed for the structure holding their weapons. It was too late: Ringler's jackrabbits had already won the race.

Sister Patricia Marie, in the meantime, had reached the chapel. Those inside heard a sharp grenade explosion: an American had killed the guards on a corner just outside the chapel. Inside the ramshackle structure the sister and others flung themselves face-down onto the dirt floor. The Catholics among them began reciting the rosary out loud. Overhead, the constant roar of American fighter-bombers added to the noisy din.

As Sister Patricia Marie poked her head through the open window to look skyward, bullets began ripping through the thin walls. The Maryknoll nun flopped to the floor, but periodically got to her feet and went to the window to give those stretched out flat a play-by-play account of the action raging over the prison grounds. At one point the sounds of exploding grenades punctuated her commentary. "For God's sake," shouted a Jesuit priest who had taken refuge under a makeshift altar, "get down, Sister, get down—before you get yourself and all of us killed!" His plea was followed by more grenade detonations.

Suddenly, an American paratrooper carrying a Tommy gun rushed through the door. From their prone positions on the floor, the internees glanced up anxiously. To these servants of God who had never seen an American soldier in combat gear, with steel helmet, jump boots, and baggy pants, this warrior seemed like Superman. With the American were several young Filipino guerrillas, barefoot and wearing shorts and large straw hats with turned-up brims. "Where are the Japs?" the lanky paratrooper called out. "There's none in here," a shaky voice responded. The American turned and dashed back out the door, followed by the Filipinos.

Meanwhile, Major Henry Burgess's fifty-four amtracs had crawled out of the surf near Mayondon Point, and began clanking inland. A Japanese officer near the Los Baños camp, no doubt roused from sleep, staggered out of a house along the road. With one hand he clutched his coveted samurai saber, while with the other he was trying frantically to pull on his trousers. An amtrac machine gun chattered, and the Japanese crumbled to the ground in a bloody heap, still clutching his saber.

Reaching the compound, the driver of the lead alligator saw that the front gate was closed and asked Henry Burgess what to do. "Crash through it!" the major exclaimed. Revving the motor, the driver charged at the barrier. Bits and pieces of wood, metal, and wire flew in all directions as the ponderous vehicles smashed into the gate. Other amtracs followed.

Inside, Lieutenant Tom Mesereau, a former all-American football lineman at West Point, was forming up his Company C. The tall, beefy Meserau and his seventy-five troopers had a crucial mission: intercept the advance guard of the Japanese 8th Division toward the southwest. All Mesereau and his little band of lightly armed paratroopers could hope to do was slow down the enemy forces long enough to allow the evacuation of the internees.

"When you make contact with it [the advance guard], shoot hell out of them and force them to deploy," Burgess reminded Meserau. "That should take up at least an hour." Mesereau and his troopers hurried off.

Inside the barbed wire enclosure bedlam had erupted. A swirling mass of hysterical, frightened, and alternately euphoric interness milled about. The paratroopers continued to flush out Japanese soldiers hiding in and just outside the camp. Isolated clashes broke out and bullets whistled over paratroopers and internees alike. Each new fusillade brought eerie screams from terrified female prisoners.

Lieutenant Ringler, shaking his head, came up to Major Burgess. "My men can't get the people to head for the loading area," he complained in frustration. "Most of them are cowering in their shacks and barracks." Ringler added the obvious: "it's chaos!"

Burgess also felt frustrated. He had no loud-speaker with which to communicate with the milling prisoners. An hour had gone by since the Americans had first stormed the camp, and little seemed to have been accomplished except the killing of scores of guards and the chasing off others. During the firefights, a few buildings and shacks had caught fire, and the blaze, fanned by the wind, was spreading toward Burgess and Ringler, who were standing at the spot designated as the amtrac-loading area. Thick black clouds of smoke rolled over the camp. Internees, terrorized and bewildered by the flames, now poured out of their lodgings and headed for the loading area where the alligators were lined up. The camp burned faster and hotter with each passing minute.

Perspiring paratroopers dashed into the shack that served as a hospital and carried out a hundred and thirty patients. For some internees, the

Angels from Heaven had arrived too late: several corpses lay on filthy hospital cots. The troopers brought out these dead bodies as well; they would be returned for burial.

The tough, battle-hardened paratroopers acted with tenderness in loading the hundred and thirty ailing internees into the amtracs. Other men, women, and children climbed into the remaining vehicles. Crammed with internees, the long line of amphibious vehicles crawled off toward Laguna de Bay. They would cross the bay, deposit their charges, then make a return trip to pick up the rest of the internees and paratroopers.

The raging fires crept closer. Shouting to be heard, Major Burgess told the people remaining, "The Japs are probably closing in on us. So we want to get you out quickly. You'll have to walk to the beach. Take only essential items. The Army will supply you with clothes."

Sister Patricia Marie turned to other nuns and whispered, "Oh, my! Can't you just see us wearing khaki pants and shirts and black veils?"

Lines of dazed prisoners shuffled out of the camp. Mingling among them, for protection and to offer assistance, were paratroopers. But they were hungry, having given away their rations. Two priests were carrying their precious belongings—chalices and ciboriums—in bundles over their shoulders. Men, women, and children toted their pitiful belongings in cloth wrappings dangling from sticks. The column was soon strung out for nearly a mile, and progress was so slow that Major Burgess feared it would take days to cover the two miles to Laguna de Bay. Some people fell, unable to continue; they were picked up and carried by paratroopers. Two amtracs that had broken down that morning and been repaired were used to haul the weaker inmates. A group of nuns and priests was carried in one alligator. As it ambled past, American soldiers erupted in laughter. In large letters on the side of the amtrac was painted its nickname: *The Impatient Virgin*.

Finally reaching the Laguna de Bay shoreline at the tail of the column, Major Burgess received alarming news. Captain Tom Meserau had returned from his mission designed to intercept and slow down the point of any Japanese force heading for the prison camp. Now he was telling Burgess that he and his men had clashed with an enemy company, and there were indications that a much larger body of Japanese was heading toward Los Baños. If the amtracs did not return soon, some twelve hundred civilians and paratroopers might be trapped.

During the afternoon, an occasional mortar shell would explode near the beach where the fearful internees were huddled. At one point a burst of small-arms fire hissed in. Loud cheers were raised when someone spotted Colonel Bigg's amphibious trucks. Internees and paratroopers scrambled aboard. Major Burgess was with the last group of six amtracs to shove off. Mortar shells began splashing around the departing vehicles, but their drivers took evasive action and none was hit.

By the time Major Burgess had reached the relative safety of the beach at Mamatid, everyone had been evacuated. But he was greeted by a high-priced one-man reception committee: General Oscar Griswold, commander of XIV Corps. Burgess and his Angels from Heaven, as the 11th Airborne Division came to be called, had beaten the odds with the aid of Filipino guerrillas. All 2,147 internees and 412 paratroopers, along with several Los Baños corpses, had been brought out from under the noses of the Japanese. The only casualty had been a woman inmate grazed by a bullet.

Now General MacArthur's focus turned to a huge rock perched in the mouth of Manila Bay—Corregidor. MacArthur had first seen Corregidor in 1903 when he had arrived in the Philippines for duty as a "shavetail," or second lieutenant. For nearly three years now, Corregidor had been a fixation with MacArthur. It had significant military value, for the harbor at Manila could not be used until "The Rock" was captured. But it had a spiritual value, too. MacArthur considered Corregidor hallowed ground, for it had been there that America's flag had been ground into the dust. Until Old Glory was raised on Corregidor again, Douglas MacArthur would have no rest.

18

"We're Jumping on Corregidor!"

Colonel George M. Jones, the thirty-three-year-old leader of the 503rd Parachute Infantry Regiment, strode into the tent hospital on southern Mindoro island and up to the bedside of an old pal, Colonel Orin "Hardrock" Haugen. Jones, tall, lean, and bronzed, tried to conceal the concern he felt over the condition of Haugen, who a few days earlier had been cut down by a 20-millimeter bullet in the chest at a Manila street intersection while leading his 11th Airborne Division paratroop regiment in an attack. After an exchange of greetings and small talk, Colonel Jones remarked offhandedly, "We're jumping on Corregidor in a few days."

Prior to the war, Haugen had been stationed on the craggy, steep-sided rock and knew that there was no suitable drop zone for a parachute force. He was aware that the island was heavily fortified and that brisk winds could carry large numbers of paratroopers to their deaths in Manila Bay. Orin Haugen was silent and then exclaimed, "Corregidor! Oh, no, George, they can't do *that* to you."

Later Colonel Jones clasped his friend's hand and left the hospital. He would never see Haugen again. A few days afterward the wounded officer would die on a medical plane bound for the States.

As George Jones rolled along through the green countryside toward his command post, Hardrock Haugen's haunting remark about the island fortress stayed with him: "They can't do *that* to you . . ." The phrase, coming from such an experienced paratroop officer, did nothing to boost Jones's confidence.

Some ten days earlier, at almost the precise time Verne Mudge's 1st Cavalry Division spearheads were dashing into northern Manila, General MacArthur had given Sixth Army the order: "Attack and seize Corregidor." D-Day had been set for February 16.

General Walter Krueger and his planners formed a combined parachute-seaborne team built around four battalions and named it the "Rock Force." Colonel Jones was appointed overall commander of the operation, and twenty-seven-year-old Lieutenant Colonel John J. Tolson III was appointed his deputy. The main assault units in the operation would be the three battalions of Jones's 503rd Parachute Infantry Regiment, and the 3rd Battalion, 34th Infantry, of the 24th (Taro Leaf) Infantry Division. Supporting units would include the 462nd Parachute Field Artillery Battalion, a company of the 161st Parachute Engineer Battalion, and assorted medical, antitank, signal, and ack-ack units.

Assaulting Corregidor would be a very personal matter for Jones and Tolson, as well as for Lieutenant Colonel Edward M. Postlethwait, leader of the 34th Infantry battalion that would make the seaborne attack. Several of their West Point classmates had been captured by the Japanese in the humiliating American debacle at Bataan and Corregidor. For Postlethwait, the Manila Bay region also held fond memories. After his graduation from West Point in 1939, he had been assigned to the Philippines. The day before he was to depart, he had become engaged to Merace Taralseth of Warren, Minnesota. She had joined the new lieutenant a few weeks later and they were married in Manila.

With the invasion of the Philippines by MacArthur, the Japanese high command had been growing increasingly concerned over Corregidor. Like the Americans, the Japanese knew that the massive rock had a significance to both sides far beyond its military value in controlling shipping into the capital. Douglas MacArthur had sworn to recapture Corregidor, and if he were to do so, the Japanese Empire would lose face in the eyes of the world.

Since its seizure in June of 1942, the Japanese had garrisoned the island fortress with only a caretaker force. Its members had been fond of telling the Filipinos in the bay region that "after the war we will turn Corregidor into a beautiful public park." Since the first of October 1944, with American troops on Leyte, the park concept had lost its luster, and the Japanese had begun reinforcing The Rock with infantry units and Imperial Marines. In mid-October, several *Shinyo* squadrons (suicide boats), under Lieutenant Commander Shoichi Koyameda, had docked at the fortress.

Imperial Navy Captain Akira Itagaki was the commander of the Manila Bay Entrance Force, and had troops on Corregidor and three other tiny islands nearby. For many weeks Itagaki had been warned by the high command in Tokyo to take measures against a parachute assault. But he had stubbornly refused to listen, declaring that Corregidor, where he had his headquarters, was too small and had too many natural obstacles for the Americans to even consider an airborne landing.

In early 1942, the Japanese high command had studied a Corregidor parachute assault and rejected it, invading by sea instead. Now, with an American attack on Corregidor looming, Captain Itagaki concentrated most of his firepower toward the beaches. And when the U.S. fleet arrived, Itagaki was convinced that Koyameda's suicide boats would wreak havoc on it.

Shaped like a tadpole, with its bulbous head pointing west toward the South China Sea, Corregidor is but three and a half miles long and one and a half miles across at its widest point. The tadpole's eastern (tail) section is sandy, wooded, and little more than a hundred and fifty feet above Manila Bay at its highest point. At the center of the island, Malinta Hill rises abruptly to a height of three hundred and fifty feet. It had been in a tunnel burrowed into Malinta Hill that first General MacArthur and later General Jonathan Wainwright had directed the last-ditch stands at Bataan and Corregidor in early 1942.

Just to the west of Malinta Hill the ground falls away sharply to a five-hundred-yard waist rising only a hundred feet above the water. This low area was known as "Bottomside" to American soldiers prior to World War II. Along Bottomside to the north and south are wide

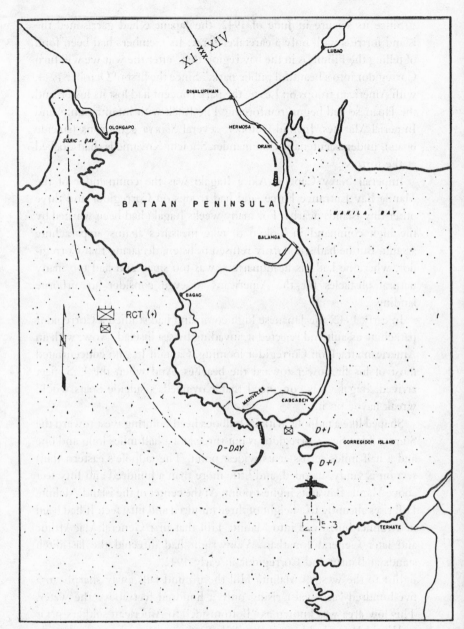

Corregidor

sandy beaches, ideal for amphibious assault. It was here, on the northern beaches, that the Japanese had invaded Corregidor nearly three years earlier.

West of Bottomside lies a gradually rising area called "Middleside," giving way on the west to the steep slopes leading up to "Topside," the tadpole's huge head. Rising some five hundred feet above Manila Bay, Topside drops precipitously to the water on the north, west, and south, and was the key terrain feature on Corregidor. A Japanese force congregated there could bring any amphibious landing beaches under fire.

On February 6—D-Day minus 10—Rock Force commander Colonel George Jones flew low over Corregidor with a bomber force. He was encouraged by what he saw—or didn't see. There was no sign of Japanese defenders, a fact that seemed to confirm Sixth Army's "Estimate of the Enemy Situation" that had reported there were only six to eight hundred Japanese defending the fortress. This estimate would prove to be grossly inaccurate. Actually, there were nearly six thousand Nipponese living largely underground on The Rock, a mixture of army soldiers and Imperial Marines, both combat and service troops.

Gaining precise intelligence on Japanese strength on Corregidor had proved impossible, despite sophisticated aerial photography techniques and an abundance of guerrilla reports. Prior to earlier MacArthur invasions, a commando-type unit, the Alamo Scouts, some wearing Japanese army uniforms, had slipped ashore, moved about inside enemy positions, and reported back with valuable information. On three occasions in recent nights the Alamo Scouts had tried to sneak onto The Rock, and each time had failed.

Soon after returning from his February 6 flight over Corregidor, Colonel Jones and his staff drew up an operational plan. At 8:30 A.M. on D-Day, approximately one-third of his paratroopers would bail out over the bulbous head of the tadpole—Topside. Included in the initial jump would be Lieutenant Colonel John L. Erickson's 3rd Battalion, artillery, signal, and engineer units. They would aim at two drop zones, the golf course and the parade ground in front of Topside barracks.

Colonel Erickson's mission was to clean out the Japanese defenders on Topside prior to that afternoon's jump by Major Lawrence B. Caskey's 2nd Battalion of the 503rd Parachute Infantry and supporting units, and a mass bailout on D-Day plus 1 by the 503rd's 1st Battalion, led by boyish-faced Major Robert H. "Pug" Woods. Erickson's first-wave paratroopers also were to establish firing positions on Topside to cover the 10:30 A.M. D-Day amphibious assault on Black Beach at Bottomside by Colonel Postlethwait's battalion of the 24th Infantry Division.

It would be difficult to envision a worse locale than Topside for a mass parachute landing. Both DZs were frighteningly tiny, each less than a thousand feet long and four hundred and thirty feet wide. The ground was littered with boulders, deep bomb craters, scrap iron, debris, and razor-sharp sections of tin roofing. The golf course and parade ground were bordered by splintered trees capable of impaling a descending man. Half-demolished barracks and other buildings presented yet another fearsome peril. If the wind was blowing briskly—and it most probably would be—they faced being blown over the towering cliffs or plunging directly into Manila Bay.

Colonel Jones, after inspecting Corregidor from the bomber, concluded that ten to fifty percent of his paratroopers would suffer injuries in the jump. But the risk of heavy jump casualties had to be accepted in order to rapidly establish a strong force on Topside and furnish covering fire for troops coming in by boat. Otherwise, Postlethwait's amphibious assault on Bottomside would be a bloodbath.

Due to the tinniness of the DZs on Topside, the smallness of the entire island fortress, and the steady twenty-five-mile-per-hour winds, the airborne operation would be the most daring and unorthodox of the war. There would be no margin for error: if the mass drop was not carried out with clockwork precision, scores of paratroopers would drown and the entire Corregidor operation end up in disaster.

Aircraft of Colonel John Lackey's veteran 317th Troop Carrier Group would take off from southern Mindoro island (some hundred and sixty miles south of Corregidor) and approach The Rock in two columns. Each aircraft would be over the Topside drop zones only eight seconds, and in that period of time six men were to bail out. The C-47s would then make wide circles and return over the DZ to drop six more parachutists. On a final pass they would discharge the remaining five or six men. This procedure violated American airborne doctrine, which called for dropping all paratroopers in a plane at one time and as close together as possible.

While preparations proceeded for the combined parachute-amphibious assault, B-24s of the 307th Bomb Group continued to pound The Rock with heavy bombs, giving special attention to Topside, as well as Malinta Hill, which was the nerve center of the Japanese command. General George Kenney's heavies had called on Corregidor almost daily since late January, trying to knock out the captured American 12-inch guns that could wreak havoc on the invasion warships and landing craft on D-Day. Since January, they had unloaded a hundred tons of explosives a day, and starting on February 7 they doubled this tonnage. By the time Colonel George Jones's first paratrooper bailed out over Topside, Corregidor would have been hit by 3,128 tons of bombs—the most concentrated pounding any invasion target would receive during the Pacific war.[1]

One day before the assault on Corregidor, a small flotilla of U.S. cruisers and landing craft under Admiral Russell "The Count" Berkey, sailed out of Subic Bay northwest of The Rock. On board were members of the 151st Regimental Combat Team of the 38th Infantry Division. The destination of the landing force was the town of Mariveles on the southern tip of the Bataan peninsula three miles northwest of Corregidor. Reaching The Rock just after daylight, Berkey's cruisers began pounding the cliffsides of the fortress where large-caliber guns were known to be concealed by vegetation that had grown over cave mouths.

Corregidor's gunners responded with only two rounds. But one of them scored a bull's-eye on an LSM (landing ship medium) as it entered Mariveles Harbor. That was the only resistance; the 38th Division assault troops waded ashore without a shot being fired at them.

On The Rock, Imperial Navy Captain Itagaki decided to play his trump card: he would unleash thirty of his suicide boats, based on Corregidor, against the American ships in Mariveles Harbor that night. Some eighteen of these *Shinyo* boats loaded with dynamite either lost their way in the blackness, developed engine trouble or were swamped, but the remaining twelve were able to attack the invading vessels. Six *Shinyos* exploded against three gunboats patrolling the entrance to Mariveles Harbor, sinking them immediately. Alerted by the explosions, other American ships opened fire against the suicide boats, blasting several of them out of the water. One exploded at such short range that it heavily damaged an LCS 27.

As a handful of the surviving suicide boats were limping back across Manila Bay to their roosts on Corregidor just before dawn on D-Day, a hundred and sixty miles to the south there was activity on the airstrips along the lower coast of Mindoro, where grim-faced warriors of the 503rd Parachute Infantry Regiment had been awakened to face one of the most trying ordeals of their young lives: a drop onto heavily-defended Corregidor.

Few had been able to sleep during the night. Most of those who said they had were lying, comrades knew. As the dark sky began to show streaks of gray, many gazed upward and wondered if they would ever see another dawn. Breakfast was served, but most troopers only pecked at their food. One youth called out to his comrades, "This is the U.S. Army's version of the Last Supper." Only a few chuckled. For now, the humor had gone out of their lives.

Colonel George Jones's 503rd Parachute Infantry Regiment was an extremely close-knit fighting machine. Its members were fiercely proud, keenly loyal to each other and to the regiment. They were members in good standing of the world's most exclusive clique—the paratrooper fraternity. Membership could not be purchased, and it could not be bestowed due to political or social connections. Rather, entry through the portals of the paratrooper fraternity could be earned only by the candidate enduring the most arduous training program its officers and sergeants could conceive—and then by measuring up on the field of battle.

Paratroopers in the 503rd came from a wide spectrum of American society. There were the wealthy and the destitute, and those in between. There were law enforcement officers and ex-convicts, white collar and blue collar workers, school teachers and grave diggers, cowboys and boxers. Regardless of their civilian background, all men were "equal" here, judged on their combat merits. All were volunteers for hazardous duty. Each was a tough, resourceful fighter.

Although some replacements would be seeing their first action on this day, the 503rd Parachute Infantry was a veteran outfit that had been

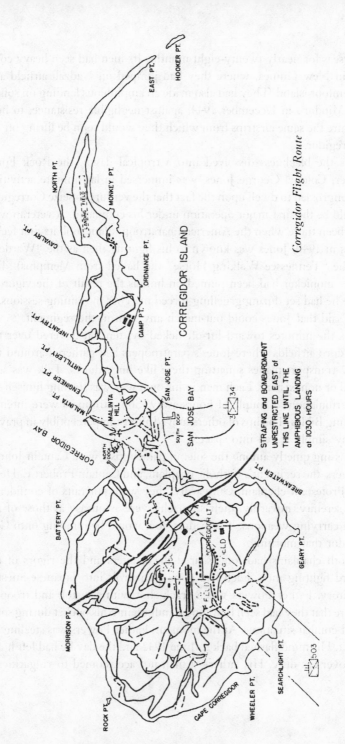

Corregidor Flight Route

CORREGIDOR ISLAND

HOOKER PT.

EAST PT.

NORTH PT.

MONKEY PT.

LANDING FIELD

ORDNANCE PT.

CAVALRY PT.

CAMP PT.

INFANTRY PT.

ARTILLERY PT.

SAN JOSE PT.

ENGINEER PT.

MALINTA PT.

MALINTA HILL

SAN JOSE BAY

SOUTH DOCK

3 × 34

NORTH DOCK

CORREGIDOR BAY

BREAKWATER PT.

BATTERY PT.

STRAFING and BOMBARDMENT
UNRESTRICTED EAST of
THIS LINE UNTIL THE
AMPHIBIOUS LANDING
at 1030 HOURS

CORREGIDOR LT. H.

"CORREGIDOR"

F FLD

G FLD

GEARY PT.

MORRISON PT.

ROCK PT.

WHEELER PT.

SEARCHLIGHT PT.

CAPE CORREGIDOR

111 × 503

overseas for nearly twenty-eight months. Its men had seen heavy combat in New Guinea, where they had jumped on Nadzab airfield and Noemfoor island. They had also made an amphibious landing on southern Mindoro in December 1944, against negligible resistance, to help capture the same airstrips from which they would soon be lifting off for Corregidor.

As the blackness dissolved into a tropical dawn, the Rock Force leader, Colonel George Jones, was immersed in last-minute activities, too engrossed to dwell upon the fact that the venture to seize Corregidor would be the first major operation under his command. A veteran who had been there when the American paratroop infant took its first feeble steps in 1940, Jones was known to his fighting men as the "Warden" or the "Tennessee Walking Horse" (he hailed from Memphis). The latter monicker had been pinned on him as the result of the vigorous pace he had set during gruelling forced marches in training sessions. It was said that Jones could out-march any man in the regiment.

As the minutes toward lift-off ticked by, tension hovered over the Mindoro airfields where Jones's paratroopers had gathered around the C-47 transport planes squatting there like huge ducks. Talk was subdued or nonexistent. Each man in his own way was steeling himself for the tribulations a couple of hours away. Some troopers were intently reading Bibles. The lips of others moved almost imperceptibly in prayer. Many simply stared into space.

Passing quietly among the solemn parachutists were Captain John J. Powers, the regiment's Catholic chaplain, and Captain Probert E. Herb, the Protestant chaplain. Outwardly, they were portraits of confidence and serenity; inwardly, their stomachs were as queasy as those of the men carrying weapons. The padres, too, would be jumping onto Corregidor that morning.

Both chaplains had long shared the dangers and the rigors of the 503rd fighting men. Each had gone on patrols into Japanese-infested territory. Father Powers was a crack shot with a pistol, and troopers swore that they had seen him slip a handgun into his pocket during some tight combat situations. At the moment, Father Powers was steeling his spirit. His mind flashed back to June 1942 and the day he had left home for overseas duty. His father—a man not accustomed to vulgarities—

had walked him to the station and, as Captain Powers stepped up to board his train, had whispered in his ear, "John, don't get shot in the ass." It was the elder Powers's way of telling his son that if his destiny was to be wounded or killed, he should meet it while facing the enemy.

Standing beside one C-47, Sergeant John Phillips, his face a mask of determination, was checking and rechecking his Tommy gun. He could hardly wait to get to Corregidor to settle a personal vendetta with the Japanese. For many months, Phillips had been trying to contact his brother, who was in the 32nd Infantry Division, a veteran Pacific unit. When the paratrooper had finally caught up with the 32nd and inquired of his brother, he received the reply, "Oh, he was killed two days ago." Since then Sergeant Phillips had constantly volunteered for perilous patrols and exposed himself to enemy fire.

Going along on the Corregidor jump would be a civilian, Harold Templeman, an American Red Cross field director. Despite his non-military status, Templeman had long before earned the 503rd paratroopers' highest accolade: "Harold is one of us." Once a star athlete at the University of Wyoming, the Red Cross director had been with assault elements on all 503rd operations, including the parachute jump onto Noemfoor and the amphibious invasion of Mindoro.

Now, minutes before taking off for Corregidor, Templeman was busily supervising the loading of scores of Red Cross bundles containing cigarettes, tobacco, candy bars, and toilet articles. These would be parachuted onto The Rock, and if all went well, Templeman intended to have a canteen open for the fighting men within three hours after landing.

Elsewhere on the field, Private First Class Frank D. Ruotolo was gripped by a haunting premonition. He edged up to a pal, Corporal Walter Gonko, a native of Kansas who had been a coal miner, hobo, and wheat harvester. "Walt, I think I'm going to be killed on Corregidor," Ruotolo said. "If it happens, will you contact my girl friend in New Haven, Connecticut, and tell her I loved her?"

Seeking to shake Ruotolo from his blue mood, Gonko laughed and replied, "Hell, Frank, I'll do better than that. I'll ask her to marry me."

Lifting off with Colonel Jones's paratroopers would be a Signal Corps Photo Group led by Lieutenant Dick Williams and including Sergeant

Frank J. Goetzheimer, Corporal Wilbur B. Goen, Corporal George W. Woodruff, and Corporal Robert C. Lautman. But there was something unique about these cameramen: none had ever parachuted before. Their training in parachute jumping had been gained only a few days earlier and had lasted twenty minutes. The instructions began with, "This is a parachute . . ."

Soon shouts rang out over the hot airfields: "Load 'em up! Load 'em up!" The order sent chills through most troopers: the moment of truth had arrived. Heavily burdened with combat gear (some would jump with loads weighing ninety pounds), they began filing into fifty-one C-47s—"Gooney Birds," as the men called them—and took their places in bucket seats along both sides of the aircraft. In the lead C-47 was Lieutenant Colonel John Erickson, lanky, tough, and something of a medical miracle. Erickson, leader of the 3rd Battalion, would be the first armed American to set foot on Corregidor since Wainwright's garrison was overwhelmed there in June 1942. Erickson had been so seriously wounded during bitter fighting in New Guinea that doctors had doubted he would survive.

At the controls of Erickson's Gooney Bird was Colonel John Lackey, commander of the 317th Troop Carrier Group. Lackey's sky armada would fly over the DZ at only a thousand feet, which would allow paratroopers to bail out five hundred feet above towering Topside.

Waiting for the order to lift off, these American paratroopers were going into battle with vengeance in their hearts. There were no flamboyant exhortations to "Remember Bataan!" or "Avenge Corregidor!" There was no need. All knew of the suffering, starvation, and humiliation endured in the Philippines by their brothers in arms, of the infamous Death March in which thousands of American soldiers had perished. Colonel George Jones—the Warden—had set the tone: "The Jap wants to die for his emperor. Do your best to accommodate him."

There was a deafening revving up of powerful motors, and at 7:00 A.M. Colonel Lackey's leading Gooney Bird accelerated down a runway and lifted off, the other C-47s following. The armada circled once, then headed for Corregidor.

Shortly after the Gooney Birds had taken off from Mindoro, fireworks erupted anew on and around Corregidor. At 7:15 A.M. a force of cruisers and destroyers under Admiral Berkey opened a terrific bombardment of Topside, the caves along the cliffsides, and other critical points. The naval gunfire halted at 7:55 A.M., and then a flight of B-24 Liberators flew over and pounded Topside with hundreds of fragmentation bombs, a measure intended to send Japanese defenders scurrying for cliffside caves and to clear the decks for the imminent arrival of American paratroopers.

As the final bomber dropped its load and headed back to its base, thirty-one A-20s—"Grim Reapers"—and twelve twin-engined B-25 attack bombers zoomed low over Topside and let loose with their explosive cargos. Then the attack bombers banked and returned, pouring streams of .50-caliber bullets into the mouths of caves along the Topside cliffs.

Just offshore on the light cruiser *Montpelier*, Seaman James H. Fahey, a teenager from Waltham, Massachusetts, and his shipmates were staring with open mouths at the savagery of the bombing. As with other ships in Berkey's force, the *Montpelier* was holding its fire for fear of hitting the American warplanes swarming all over The Rock. The concussion from the chain of bomb explosions was so intense Fahey could feel the light cruiser quivering. Then an exhilarating thought flashed through Seaman Fahey's mind: "Our guys who were on Corregidor when it fell in 1942 would sure enjoy seeing this extravaganza!"

Fahey turned away from the rocking The Rock was absorbing and looked skyward. In the distance on this warm, clear morning he saw two lengthy columns of airplanes approaching from the south. At first they were only specks, flying low—Fahey judged about a thousand feet—and at that distance seemed to be hanging in space. Knowing they carried American paratroopers returning to Corregidor, he felt a thrill.

Unseen by the sailors in Berkey's bombardment force, Colonel John Erickson—the medical miracle—was standing in the doorway of the leading Gooney Bird. In each of the other C-47s crouched other jumpmasters, ready to spring when green "Go!" lights flashed on.

Minutes earlier calls of "stand up and hook up!" had rung through the cabins of the Gooney Birds. It took an effort to stand. The paratroopers felt awkward in their burdensome combat gear as they staggered into position, one behind the other. The stress from waiting returned—worse than ever. Suddenly, the planes seemed to lurch. It would only be seconds now. Thoughts of avenging Corregidor vanished momentarily, replaced in each man's mind by the question: Will I still be alive five minutes from now?

At the controls of one Gooney Bird, twenty-two-year-old Lieutenant Donald Lundy of Esterville, Iowa, gazed at smoke-shrouded Corregidor as it drew steadily toward him. Lundy, who had flown many C-47 missions, recalled the briefing officer's remarks: "You'll receive virtually no ground fire." But how did the briefer know that? Moments later Lundy was glad he had put on his Mae West (inflatable life preserver), uncomfortable as it was in the oppressive heat of the cockpit. Bullets from The Rock zipped skyward in search of Gooney Birds. Two men standing hooked up and ready to jump from one C-47 were hit.

Now Colonel Lackey's lead C-47 was nearly over the drop zone. Crouched in the doorway, Lieutenant Colonel Erickson spotted his target, the parade ground. Next to the doorway the green light flashed on, and a crew member gave Erickson a sharp rap across the back of his calf. "Let's go!" Erickson shouted, and was out. Leaping after him were Corporal Arthur O. Smithback of Stoughton, Wisconsin, and Private First Class Stanley J. Grochala of Trenton, New Jersey, the first two armed American enlisted men to return to the Rock.

It was 8:33 A.M. The death struggle for what General Douglas MacArthur called the "Holy Grail of Corregidor" was on.

Pfc. Manuel Perez, Jr., the one-man army of the 11th Airborne Division. (Sketch by Lou Varrone)

Key figures in Cabanatuan internment camp rescue. Captain Robert W. Prince (left) led infantry Rangers. Lieutenant Colonel Henry A. Mucci (center) commanded operation. Sergeant Theodore R. Richardson opened prison gate. (Courtesy Robert W. Prince)

One of the Pacific war's strangest episodes. Armed men of the U.S. 1st Cavalry Division (in files to either side) provide an escort from Santo Tomás prison camp for armed Japanese (in center). (U.S. Army)

A few Rangers who freed Bataan vets at Cabanatuan. Lieutenant John F. Murphy in center foreground. (Courtesy Robert W. Prince)

Men of the U.S. 1st Cavalry Division stand guard outside Santo Tomás against expected attack. In the street is a dead Japanese soldier. (U.S. Army)

A vicious battle with flamethrowers, tanks, and machine guns took place inside Rizal Stadium in Manila before the Japanese were wiped out. (Courtesy Rocco Narcise)

Not a single bomb fell on Manila, but bitter street fighting rendered the Pearl of the Orient one of the most thoroughly destroyed cities in the Pacific. (Courtesy Rocco Narcise)

Fortress Corregidor.

Lieutenant Colonel John J. Tolson, III, Deputy Rock Force Commander. (U.S. Army)

Private Lloyd G. McCarter, one-man army of The Rock. (Sketch by Lou Varrone)

Faces reflect tension as a stick of paratroopers, led by Sergeant Albert Baldwin, prepares to bail out over Corregidor. (U.S. Army)

Heading for Black Beach on Corregidor's Bottomside are landing craft carrying men of Lieutenant Colonel Edward Postlethwait's battalion of the 24th Infantry Division. Members of the 503rd Parachute Infantry Regiment landed a few hours earlier on Topside, in the background. (U.S. Navy)

ABOVE: American paratroopers landing on Corregidor's Topside. Other troopers have already shucked their chutes. (U.S. Army)

BELOW: American naval shells explode on Topside while paratroopers were still descending. (U.S. Army)

Landing craft carrying Postlethwait's infantry battalion head for Black Beach on Bottomside. Topside is in foreground. (U.S. Army)

Parachutes litter parade ground on Corregidor's Topside, but hundreds more para-troopers were still jumping. (Colonel Henry Gibson)

Lieutenant Colonel Edward Postlethwait, 24th Infantry Division, led Corregidor amphibious assault. (Linda Donnelly)

Mortally wounded and isolated, parachute doctor Captain Emmet R. Spicer calmly filled out his own death certificate. (Logan W. Hovis, M.D.)

Parachute Lieutenant William E. Blake and his demolitionists sealed hundreds of Japanese into, or drove them out of, scores of Corregidor caves. (Author's collection)

Among the first to jump on The Rock were two combat doctors, Captain Robert McKnight (left) and Captain Logan W. Hovis. McKnight was badly injured. (Logan W. Hovis, M.D.)

Postlethwait's men stalk the enemy on Malinta Hill. (U.S. Army)

General MacArthur is accompanied by Colonel George M. Jones, Rock Force commander, in a tour of Corregidor. Some armed Japanese were still in caves and tunnels. (Author's collection.)

Shortly after jumping onto The Rock, paratroop Sergeant Frank Arrige and Private First Class Clyde Bates shinny up flagpole to hoist Old Glory. (U.S. Army)

Twenty-fourth Infantry Division machine gunners fire into enemy-held cave. (U.S. Army)

One of World War II's most dramatic events. General MacArthur at Corregidor flag raising. (U.S. Army)

A few hours after Corregidor was secured, Colonel George M. Jones stands on bomb-battered barracks. Bataan is in background. (Author's collection)

General Yomoyuki Yamashita, the Japanese commander in the Philippines, at his postwar trial in Manila. Accused of war crimes, Yamashita was tried under procedures that many Americans thought made a mockery of the United States judicial system. He was executed. (U.S. Army)

WAR DEPARTMENT

OFFICE OF THE CHIEF OF STAFF
WASHINGTON 25, D. C.

25 July 1945

TO: General Carl Spaatz
Commanding General
United States Army Strategic Air Forces

    1. The 509 Composite Group, 20th Air Force will
deliver its first special bomb as soon as weather will
permit visual bombing after about 3 August 1945 on one of the
targets: Hiroshima, Kokura, Niigata and Nagasaki. To
carry military and civilian scientific personnel from the
War Department to observe and record the effects of the
explosion of the bomb, additional aircraft will accompany
the airplane carrying the bomb. The observing planes will
stay several miles distant from the point of impact of the
bomb.

    2. Additional bombs will be delivered on the above
targets as soon as made ready by the project staff. Further
instructions will be issued concerning targets other than
those listed above.

    3. Dissemination of any and all information concerning
the use of the weapon against Japan is reserved to the
Secretary of War and the President of the United States.
No communiques on the subject or releases of information
will be issued by Commanders in the field without specific
prior authority. Any news stories will be sent to the War
Department for special clearance.

    4. The foregoing directive is issued to you by direc-
tion and with the approval of the Secretary of War and of
the Chief of Staff, USA. It is desired that you personally
deliver one copy of this directive to General MacArthur and
one copy to Admiral Nimitz for their information.

THOS. T. HANDY
General, G.S.C.
Acting Chief of Staff

Official order given to drop "special bomb" on any one of four Japanese cities.
(U.S. Air Force)

19

Onslaught From the Sky

Lieutenant Colonel John Erickson had jumped from five hundred feet, and the twenty-four-mile-per-hour wind had carried him far from his parade ground DZ. He hit jarringly near Battery Wheeler, one of the prewar American gun positions that guarded Manila Bay, southwest of his target. Cut and bruised, Erickson shucked his chute, climbed over the ramparts of Battery Wheeler, and trudged off toward the parade ground to assemble his battalion. Only later would he learn that recesses under the big-gun positions had been filled with Japanese soldiers.

The smoky blue sky over Corregidor was awash with billowing white parachutes as troopers plunged through jagged roofs of wrecked concrete and steel buildings and into deep bomb craters. Others slammed into the sides of cliffs and were left dangling when their chutes caught on trees. One stick of eight men landed in front of a cave filled with Japanese, and they were cut down with grenades and automatic-weapons fire before they could get out of their harnesses. Some troopers were impaled on splintered trees and steel reinforcement poles, suffering agonizing deaths.

When Corporal Walter Gonko's chute opened he was alarmed to see that he was heading directly toward a bombed-out barracks. Just before he struck the third floor ledge a vision of his brother, Julian "Luke" Gonko, flashed before his eyes. Luke had been a Marine aboard the cruiser *Nashville* and was killed by a *kamikaze*. "Luke, I'm joining you," the paratrooper called out. Then he was engulfed by blackness.

When Sergeant Gonko regained consciousness he was lying at the base of the building. Bullets were splattering against the crumbling wall high over his head. Gonko's harness was so twisted he was unable to move, and he lay motionless for what seemed an eternity until a comrade, Private First Class Ervin "Lip" Lutryzykowsky, came by and cut him loose. Lutrzykowsky continued on his mission, and as Gonko tried to get to his feet excruciating pain jabbed him in the back.

The injured trooper crawled arduously onto the parade ground and lay there as bullets occasionally zipped past until a medic found him. The medic relieved the worst of Gonko's suffering with a morphine shot, then told him he had a "broken back." The sergeant lay helpless for two more hours until stretcherbearers, under sporadic fire, arrived and carried him to a first aid station in a bomb-damaged building. As the pain became unbearable, Gonko received more morphine injections.

"We're going to evacuate you as soon as a hospital ship lands," a medic told him.

"When will that be?"

"In four or five days."

In the meantime, Lieutenant Donald E. Abbott, executive officer (second in command) of Company E, 2nd Battalion, had crashed down into a large pile of rubble near Battery Wheeler. (Executive officers of Caskey's 2nd Battalion, which was to jump that afternoon, were sent in with the initial drop.) The brisk wind caught Abbott's billowing chute and dragged him across the rocky terrain. To his horror, he saw that he was being whisked directly toward the nearby cliffs. With the help of two troopers, the lieutenant was able to control his chute just before it pulled him over the edge of the precipice.

Corporal George Woodruff, one of the Signal Corps' instant-paratroopers who was making his first jump after twenty minutes of instruction, struck with terrific impact and badly sprained an ankle. Undaunted, Woodruff was snapping pictures of landing parachutists within seconds. His fellow photographer, Corporal Wilbur Goen, injured a knee on slamming into the rocky ground, and was unable to move. But he pulled himself to a sitting position and began photographing the violence unfolding around him.

In the meantime, Captain Logan W. Hovis of Parkersburg, West Virginia, one of two 3rd Battalion surgeons, landed in a heap in the center of his DZ, the rubble-strewn remains of a small golf course. Weighing just over a hundred and twenty pounds and lugging some forty pounds of medical equipment, Hovis was dragged across the rocky ground as the wind caught his chute. Fearing injury to his two most valuable military assets—his surgeon's hands—he made no effort to collapse it. Eventually, the twenty-seven-year-old doctor's chute halted when it caught in some bomb-splintered trees, but he was so twisted in cord that he was unable to move his battered and bruised body. There he remained until Lieutenant William Ziler happened by and cut him free.

As planned, Captain Hovis hustled to the old lighthouse, located on the highest point of Corregidor, and rapidly organized an aid station. It was not done a minute too soon. Medical soldiers were soon streaming in with jump and battle casualties. Getting the mangled men to the lighthouse was difficult. Most of the equipment parachutes loaded with litters had been carried by the wind into Manila Bay. The medics quickly improvised, and brought in casualties on blown-out doors, on blankets attached to long poles, and in their arms or over their shoulders.

Logan Hovis's fellow surgeon, Captain Robert McKnight, suffered a severe fracture of the ankle on landing. He was immediately brought under fire by Japanese machine gunners and, while in great pain, was pinned down behind a fallen tree trunk for twenty minutes. Much to his distress, Doc McKnight would have to be evacuated. This left the medical burden for the 3rd Battalion on the shoulders of Captain Hovis and his aid men.

Hovis received word that the regiment's Protestant chaplain, Captain Probert Herb, was in an exposed position on the golf course DZ, in severe pain and unable to move, and under fire. Gathering a few medical soldiers, Hovis went looking for Chaplain Herb and upon finding him saw that both his legs had been shattered in a jarring landing. Hovis splinted the chaplain's fractured legs as best as he could under the conditions, and helped carry Herb to the aid station on a door.

The other regimental chaplain, Father John Powers, was having equally bad luck. While descending in his chute, he had been hit in the rear upper leg by a Japanese bullet. Moments later Powers ricocheted off an artillery piece near the edge of a cliff and struck his head on the rock surface. Dazed and reeling but still conscious, Father Powers stumbled about the battlefield in a totally confused state of mind.

The Catholic chaplain's clerk, Corporal James Fraser, who had jumped with Powers, launched a search for the padre. Fraser feared that Powers had missed Topside and plummeted into Manila Bay. He finally located the chaplain sitting on the ground directly in front of a cave filled with Japanese soldiers. Fraser could hear them chattering inside, and saw that Father Powers was displaying a total lack of concern over his perilous predicament. The chaplain even wore a fixed grin.

Corporal Fraser maneuvered the wounded Powers away from the cave's mouth and behind a large clump of earth, where they found a few paratroopers hugging the ground. It looked to Fraser like a reasonably safe place to take temporary refuge. But moments later Japanese on the other side of the hillock began hurling grenades in the direction of the Americans.

All the while Jim Fraser had nearly been driven out of his mind by his boss, who had been jarred temporarily out of his own mind and kept asking the same questions over and over again. "Where are we, Jimmy?" Told repeatedly that they were on Corregidor, the padre always wanted to know, "Where is Corregidor?" Relentlessly, the chaplain kept saying, "Give me my [trench] knife, Jimmy, and let's get going!"[1]

Eventually, the Japanese hurling the grenades slipped away and Captain Powers was helped to an aid station. Later a paratroop patrol would kill twenty-one armed Japanese in the cave.

Sergeant Major Karl H. Landes (known to comrades as "Doc") bailed out from the second C-47. At age thirty-eight the Hungarian-born Doc Landes was five years older than regimental commander George Jones and old enough to have been the father of the unit's teenaged troopers. But he had taken part in all previous 503rd actions and more than held his own.

As soon as Sergeant Landes's chute popped open he saw that he was going to land directly onto a bombed-out barracks. He gritted his teeth for the expected crunch but, to his surprise, it never came—his canopy had caught on a roof beam and he came to a halt dangling with his feet only four feet above the ground. Stopping only long enough to aid a trooper who had nearly bitten off his tongue in a jarring landing and was bleeding profusely, Landes hurried off to set up 3rd Battalion headquarters in an old watch tower.[2]

Another parachutist was not as fortunate as Landes. Major Arliss E. Kline, commander of the 462nd Parachute Field Artillery Battalion, also found himself plunging toward a barracks. He slammed onto its roof, rolled off, and fell three stories into bombed rubble. Knocked senseless, Kline received numerous broken bones in his face and body and had to be evacuated. The battalion executive officer, Major Melvin R. Knudson, assumed command.

Out on the parachute-strewn parade ground a few minutes after landing, nineteen-year-old Private First Class Thomas J. Smith of Hinesville, Georgia, was clinging to the bottom of a bomb crater, trying desperately to reach someone on a field radio. With him was Lieutenant B. H. Stone, Sergeant C. C. Morris, and two other sergeants. They could not budge because of the small-arms fire whistling just overhead. Finally, the firing slackened and Lieutenant Stone, trying to improve transmission, placed the radio on the rim of the crater and crawled up after it. Moments later a shell exploded. Tom Smith pressed his face against the bottom of the hole and felt a flash of relief that the projectile had missed. Then a heavy object struck the back of his leg. It was the riddled body of Lieutenant Stone, who had rolled back down into the crater. On both sides of Smith lay two dead sergeants, their jump suits saturated with blood, eyes staring sightlessly toward the sky. Only Smith and Sergeant Morris had been spared.

There was another explosion. Four chunks of shrapnel ripped into Tom Smith's back. The teenager was bleeding badly and went into shock. Sergeant Morris, who had again escaped unscathed, injected him with morphine. An undetermined amount of time later Smith was hazily aware that he was being carried on a litter by two medical soldiers. Suddenly, a fierce firefight broke out, and the carriers hastily stuck Smith in a clump of bushes. In his morphine-induced euphoria, Trooper Smith was not unduly concerned that bullets were zipping past and that dead and wounded American and Japanese were falling on all sides. He fell asleep in the center of the violence and did not receive another scratch.

High overhead in his circling Gooney Bird control plane, Colonel George Jones saw that the gusty winds were blowing his troopers far from the parade ground and golf course DZs. The Rock Force commander promptly radioed all pilots: "Drop remainder of paratroopers at four hundred feet." This was a hundred feet lower than Long John Erickson and his first sticks had jumped from. Colonel Jones knew that this decision could entail added risk. Parachutes would barely have time to open before troopers slammed into the ground. But it would also result in more men landing on the DZ instead of in Manila Bay or onto Japanese positions.

The Rock Force commander was one of the first to bail out from the lower altitude. Hardly had he left the plane than a gust of wind carried him toward Battery Wheeler, the same area where Lieutenant Colonel Erickson had landed a short time earlier. In a split-second, Jones saw that he was going to miss Topside and fall into Manila Bay. Desperate, he tugged on the risers to change his course away from the cliff's edge. Then he crashed into a tree, one so splintered by the bombardment that it incongruously reminded him of the trick cigars that used to explode in the faces of vaudeville comics. The Warden felt a stab of pain; a needle-like five-inch piece of tree had pierced the fleshy inside of his thigh and lodged there. In excruciating pain, Colonel Jones managed to pull out the splinter.[3]

With his leg throbbing convulsively, Jones scrambled from the tree, tended to his nearby orderly, who had broken his ankle, and hobbled across the parachute-strewn parade ground toward a long, battered troop barracks that had been selected as Rock Force headquarters.

While the Tennessee Walking Horse was limping toward his CP, a short distance away his opponent on Corregidor, Imperial Navy Captain Akira Itagaki, was huddled in a cave with a few staff officers and trying to bring some form of order to the chaos around him. Itagaki had been taken by total surprise when American paratroops began spilling out of C-47s over Topside. A parachute attack on Corregidor was impossible, Itagaki had repeatedly assured worried subordinates.

Shortly after the airborne assault got underway, several troopers landed near Wheeler Point, not far from the old lighthouse, and some three to four hundred yards southwest of the DZ. The parachutists spotted Japanese soldiers in a nearby cave and hurled grenades inside. There were piercing screams from the caves, then silence. The troopers carefully probed into the opening and found eight mangled and dead enemy officers. Among them was Captain Akira Itagaki, commander of the Manila Bay Entrance Force. At the moment the defenders needed him most, they had been deprived of their leader.

Some fifty minutes after the first American had landed, Captain Emmet R. Spicer of Goldsboro, North Carolina, surgeon of the 462nd Parachute Field Artillery Battalion, was bending over two troopers who were writhing in agony from jump injuries. Before being called into the service, Spicer had served a short time as superintendent of a state hospital in Raleigh. He had become bored with his Army job and volunteered for the paratroops. Dedicated and energetic, the free-spirited Emmet Spicer found the excitement of jumping from the sky more to his liking.

Now, on the bleak, pock-marked stone in Manila Bay, Captain Spicer was nearly finished with the aid for the pair of injured men when a trooper dashed up to him: "Doc, McKee's been hit bad and he's out there in Jap positions."

The surgeon prepared to go out to tend to the wounded McKee, but his medics pleaded with him not to try. "Japs are popping up from holes like gophers all over the place," they exclaimed.

"I'm going," Spicer said firmly. "There's wounded troopers out there and I'm going to them."

Doctor Spicer walked off toward the locale where Trooper McKee, and possibly other comrades, were lying wounded. Days later Spicer would be found—dead. The combat surgeon had apparently been shot by a sniper as he walked alone. Knowing that his wound was a fatal one, he had sat down on the ground, injected himself with morphine, filled out his own death certificate, and lain back to await his end.[4]

While Emmet Spicer's life was ebbing away, Corporal Frank Arrigo and Private First Class Clyde I. Bates were dashing across the parade ground with a folded American flag tucked under the arm of one of them. It was approximately 9:45 A.M. Enemy bullets hissed past the pair of troopers as they shinnied up the tallest pole left standing. Working quickly as Japanese snipers tried to pick them off, Arrigo and Bates then scampered back down. For a few moments they gazed proudly at their handiwork: the Stars and Stripes was fluttering majestically in the breeze. America had returned to Corregidor.

While the fireworks and dramatics were unfolding on The Rock, Lieutenant William E. Blake, chief demolitions officer of the 503rd Parachute Infantry Regiment, and the troopers in his stick were fighting for their lives in mid-air. Just seven minutes away from the DZ, the left engine of Blake's Gooney Bird had caught fire. As he looked out the open door, hot oil, burning carbon, and pieces of the engine flew past. Lieutenant Blake, of Ronceverte, West Virginia, rushed to the cockpit, where the pilot was laboring to keep the wobbling plane on an even keel. "Head for the DZ, make one pass, and let us bail out of this firetrap," Blake exclaimed.

"Can't do it," was the reply. "I won't be able to keep the plane up long enough." The pilot said he was going to drop out of formation and head for an airstrip on Bataan.

The Gooney Bird steadily lost altitude. At one point the order to throw out all equipment bundles came from the cockpit. Out went two flame-throwers, various radios, and machine guns. "Pitch out more stuff!" the pilot called out. The troopers began ripping up the C-47 with a vengeance. Out went the radar, door, steps, litters, brooms, and ration cartons. "Heave out everything that's not nailed down!" Lieutenant Blake shouted above the roar of air rushing through the open doorway.

Still the C-47 lost altitude, and the water loomed closer. "More stuff! More stuff!" the pilot ordered. Blake told his men to hurl out their personal gear: weapons, ammunition, and steel helmets.

Now the other engine began smoking. Blake looked down from the other door and saw that he and his troopers had been bombarding a convoy. The lieutenant swore that a case of rations had made a direct hit on a PT boat. Blake ordered reserve chutes pitched out, leaving the paratroopers with just their Mae Wests and main parachutes.

200

The plane continued to lose altitude. Bill Blake felt that the only hope was for the paratroopers to bail out—over water. He had spotted a few small vessels along the route and hoped that crewmen would be able to fish out the paratroopers before they drowned. It was an agonizing decision; secretly, Blake questioned how many troopers would make it. But he was convinced that the odds for survival were better than they would be if the troopers rode the Gooney Bird to a crash landing on water.

A grim Bill Blake went to the cockpit to advise the pilots of his decision. Up ahead he spotted land. Noah had never been more exhilarated to see land than he was at that moment, Blake told himself. Drawing closer, Blake saw a likely DZ off in the distance between two mountains. It was Bataan.

"Head for those rice paddies," the parachute officer said.

"We'll crash land," the pilot said.

"Like hell, we will. Head for those rice paddies. That's where you and us are going to part company."

With one engine an idle, black chunk of metal and the other engine smoking, the Gooney Bird was down to five hundred feet. Blake ordered his men to stand up and hook static lines to the overhead cable. The customary order for an equipment check was not given—there was no equipment to check.

Bill Blake looked down the line at the faces of his standing troopers. He felt a surge of pride. There had been no undue excitement or hysteria during the entire ordeal. And each man knew the peril was still very real: they would have to jump from a low altitude, and their reserve chutes had been pitched into the water.

Now the C-47 was over the rice paddy. "Go!" Lieutenant Blake screamed above the wind, and thumped the first man on the rump. Out they went in staccato fashion. Blake jumped last. He saw the enormous rectangle of sky and felt the angry hurricane blasts ripping at his body. Moments later there was the white flash of exultation—his parachute had popped open.

Bill Blake let out the most fervent exclamation of his life: "Thank God!"[5]

Through out the parachute operation, American PT boats cruised back and forth some hundred and fifty yards off-shore from The Rock. At that short distance the little craft were enticing targets for enemy gunners hidden in caves on the face of the cliffs, but the PT boats were there for one purpose: to fish paratroopers out of Manila Bay. The PTs had to move in a hurry; a paratrooper, loaded with between forty and ninety pounds of gear and ensnarled in his chute harness, was usually dragged under in seconds.

The wind catching the chutes of landed troopers pulled many of them over the sides of the cliffs, but few men plunged directly into the water. Now a PT boat was racing toward two parachutists who had landed in the bay within a few yards of each other. The first to be pulled out of the water was Private First Class Ammizon B. Impson, Jr. of the 462nd Parachute Field Artillery Battalion.

The rescued trooper had an identical twin, Private First Class Jack N. Impson, who was also a member of the 462nd Parachute Artillery and jumping in this same mission. Ammizon and Jack Impson had been inseparable during their nineteen years. They had joined the Army together and had volunteered together for paratroops. As Ammizon Impson lay gasping for breath on the PT boat deck, his first thought was of his twin. Had Jack Impson hit the DZ safely? The crew of the rescue vessel was hauling the second paratrooper from the bay. In a curious twist of fate, it was Jack Impson.

For an hour and twenty minutes Colonel Lackey's Goonies dropped paratroopers, then made a beeline back to the airstrips on southern Mindoro to pick up Major Lawrence Caskey's battalion for the second mass jump.

On The Rock late that morning, Colonel Jones took a quick nose count. Of the 1,000 men who had jumped, 750 were fighting or ready for action. Nearly all had received broken bones, cuts, bruises, or sprains. Almost fourteen percent had been injured in the jump. At this point, the Warden felt good about the situation. His 750 able-bodied troopers matched in numbers the 600 to 800 enemy troops Sixth Army intelligence had said were on Corregidor. Jones had no way of knowing that his men were outnumbered seven to one at this point.

20

Ape-Like Climb Up Malinta Hill

At mid-morning twenty-five LSMs (landing ship, medium) crammed with solemn men of Lieutenant Colonel Ed Postlethwait's battalion of the 34th Infantry Regiment were churning through Manila Bay toward Black Beach, a two-hundred-yard-wide strip on the south shore of Bottomside in front of the demolished hamlet of San Jose. Postlethwait's men had been ordered to charge up four-hundred-foot-high Malinta Hill and seize it, thereby cutting the Japanese force at Corregidor's narrow waist in two.

The twenty-eight-year-old Postlethwait, a tall, lean officer from Bloomington, Illinois, was beset by concerns. His battalion had been engaged in vicious fighting on Bataan at a place called Zig-Zag Pass, and he had only learned of the present operation four days earlier. To make matters worse, fighter-bombers were supposed to have pounded Black Beach, setting off land mines in the process, but the air strikes had never come off. Then the battalion ordnance officer had declared that his mine-detection and disposal equipment would have to be carried in a truck, but since there was no room in the vehicle, the equipment had been left behind.

One of those crouched low in the assault craft was Lieutenant Patrick D. O'Connell of Grand Forks, North Dakota. A veteran of months of heavy fighting as a member of the 24th Infantry Division, O'Connell was none too sure that he would survive the attack on the big rock in Manila Bay. His thoughts flashed back briefly to the previous evening on Bataan when a solemn Ed Postlethwait had gathered his officers and told them: "Once on Corregidor, there will be no place to go but forward. Our mission is simple: we are to take Malinta Hill at all costs and stay there until we kill all the Japs—or they kill us."

Huddled next to Lieutenant O'Connell in the assault boat was the battalion bugler, Robert F. Todd of Columbus, Ohio. Folded under Todd's arm was an American flag: it was his job to plant Old Glory on some elevated object within minutes of the first wave storming ashore.

At 10:28 A.M.—two minutes ahead of schedule—the first five LSMs of the 592nd Engineer Boat and Shore Regiment scrunched onto the churned up sands of Black Beach. The ramps creaked in protest as they were lowered and men of Captain Frank Centenni's K Company and Lieutenant Lewis Stearns's L Company scrambled ashore. They were greeted only by sporadic small-arms fire—and the largest, bluest, most hostile swarms of flies yet encountered in the Pacific.

A curious silence had gripped the hulking gray mass of The Rock. But Postlethwait's first-wave GIs didn't stop to count their blessings. Dashing across the sand while dodging mines and shell holes, they picked their way through endless mounds of rubble that had once been buildings and began clawing their way up Malinta Hill. It was an arduous, exhausting climb up a steep, rugged slope, and the GIs had to pull themselves up it "like gung-ho apes," in the words of one soldier. Once on top of the barren hill, men of K and L companies lay on the ground, gasping for breath, hardly able to believe their good fortune: expecting a bloodbath, they had reached the top of the towering objective without the loss of a man.

From an observation post in the East Defense Officer's Station, Captain Centenni could see readily why Malinta Hill was so crucial to the Corregidor assault: spread out before his eyes was all of Bottomside, Middleside, and the entire two-mile tail of the rocky tadpole. But where was the enemy? Unbeknownst to the Taro Leaf division GIs, a Japanese force of some two thousand men had taken refuge from the massive air and naval bombardment in Malinta Tunnel, eight hundred and thirty feet long, as well as in scores of offshoots and recesses.

In the meantime, succeeding waves of LSMs had been heading through choppy waters for Black Beach. In one third-wave landing craft, Lieutenant Colonel Postlethwait was sitting calmly on a truckload of ammunition. As the craft neared shore, Japanese gunners—who had pulled back into deep caves while the destroyers were firing at them, then returned to set up their guns—opened up from Ramsey Ravine and Breakwater Point. Bullets ripped through Postlethwait's boat, and everybody on board but the battalion commander fell to their faces in the slime, trying to put as much distance as possible between themselves and the ammo truck.

One of those lying flat was Homer Bigart, a correspondent for the *New York Herald-Tribune.* Bigart heard a loud grunt and looked up to see a baby-faced soldier next to him raise a bloody stump where his hand had been. An instant later there was a sickening, squishing sound: a machine-gun slug had ripped into the back of another soldier and come out his chest, leaving a gaping red gash. The man toppled over dead into a pool of his own blood.

For nearly two minutes—it seemed like an eternity to those aboard —machine-gun bullets pinged and ricocheted off the sides of Postlethwait's craft. A 20-millimeter shell zipped past the battalion commander's head and through the conning tower, killing the coxswain. A sailor leaped to the coxswain's post and minutes later beached the landing craft.

All hell had broken loose on Black Beach. Now fully recovered from the naval bombardment, Japanese gunners were pouring mortar, machine-gun, and rifle fire into the landing area. Cries of "Medic! Medic!" added to the confusion. One tank had been knocked out by mines, and GIs huddled behind it for protection as bullets sang against its blackened hulk. Two jeeps loaded with mortar shells were struck by antitank guns; the mortarmen were killed or wounded. A jeep pulling an antitank gun and crammed with its crew was blown to bits. Within thirty minutes, Colonel Postlethwait had lost half of his vehicles to mines and to antitank fire from cliffside caves.

Sergeant Jerry Rostell of New Jersey, was hobbling about the fire-swept beach in excruciating pain, his leg mangled by a shell explosion, blood dripping onto the sand with each step. Still, Rostell somehow managed to get to knocked-out jeeps and trucks and pull out wounded GIs before the vehicles exploded. Furious over seeing his comrades cut down without a chance to retaliate, Lieutenant Pete Slavinsky of Pennsylvania, set up a machine gun along the beach and, ignoring the hail of bullets zipping past him, raked the caves on the cliffside. Lieutenant Bill Skobolewsky of Naticoke, Pennsylvania, was also angry, as one vehicle after the other was blown up by mines. Ignoring the fact that machine-gun bullets could detonate the explosives, Skobolewsky began slithering and crawling along the beach, marking each mine with short twigs, and then a path through the minefield with white tape. Later, it would be found that the lieutenant had marked two hundred sixteen mines.

Meanwhile, Lieutenant Colonel Postlethwait had set up his CP in a large shell hole near the beach. His radio operator, Corporal Joe Princiotti of New York City, was trying desperately to contact the paratroopers on Topside. Finally, he looked at Postlethwait and grinned. "I got 'em!" A linkup, of sorts, had been made between parachute and water-borne forces.

Up on Malinta Hill, men of Centenni's K Company and Stearns's L Company were puzzled by their curious isolation from the action. Looking down at the turmoil, destruction, and death raging on Black Beach, smoke seemed to cover every foot of the island—except for the top of Malinta Hill. But these veterans held no illusions that they were home free; they knew their time would come—and soon.

About an hour and a half after K and L companies had reported Malinta Hill secure, Air Corps Colonel John Lackey and his Gooney Birds were approaching The Rock for their second visit of the day. On board were men of Major Caskey's 2nd Parachute Battalion. For one of those hooked up and waiting to jump, twenty-seven-year-old Captain Henry W. Gibson, this would be a curious kind of homecoming. Gibson, leader of Battery B, 462nd Parachute Field Artillery Battalion, had been born in Tacloban, the site of MacArthur's headquarters at the beginning of the present campaign. Years before his birth, Gibson's father had been sent to the Philippines with a group of American teachers to establish the commonwealth's public school system. While a boy in the Philippines, the future parachute officer had often visited Corregidor to participate in swimming meets.

Standing in the open door of one C-47 was Captain Hudson C. Hill, commander of Company E. As was the case with the other paratroopers, Hill's "butterflies" were furiously flapping their wings. Having recovered from the morning's torrential rain of bombs, shells, and rockets, Japanese gunners had opened a heavy fire on the slow-moving C-47s (which had reduced their speed to only eighty-five miles-per-hour in order to minimize the chances of parachutists being blown by the gusty wind into Manila Bay). But Captain Hill had concerns other than the heavy anti-aircraft fire: his flight was coming in at just three hundred and fifty feet over Topside. A veteran jumper, Hill knew that at that altitude a parachute, after popping open, would only have time to oscillate once, before the trooper smacked into solid rock.

At precisely 12:40 P.M. Hill, followed at split-second intervals by his stick, bailed out. Heavy ground fire hissed past him. Then he crashed into an old artillery barracks—hard—and on through a bomb-created hole to the basement. His head was awhirl; brightly colored stars danced before his eyes. Nineteen of Hill's teeth had been shattered. Somehow he pulled himself to his feet, struggled out of the basement, and went in search of his company.

As twenty-one-year-old Private First Class John E. Bartlett of Pleasant Hill, Illinois, was coming down in his chute he was appalled to see his squad leader, Sergeant Chris Johnson, miss Topside altogether and disappear over the side of the cliff, apparently plunging to his death. Two hours later Sergeant Johnson rejoined his squad. His chute had caught on a tree protruding from the face of the cliff, and he had managed to cut himself loose and reach solid ground.

In the C-47 directly behind Bartlett's a bullet plowed through a K-ration package in the baggy jump pants of trooper James McLain while he was preparing to bail out, saturating his leg with chopped eggs and blood.

Private First Class Roy Hollingsworth of Cincinnati, Ohio, was making his first combat jump and seeing his first action. The eighteen-year-old machine-gunner landed on a tin roof, which created a noise something like that of a hundred metal cymbals. Enemy bullets, alerted to his presence, were soon zinging through the tin roof around him. In a puzzled tone, the green youngster called out to two veterans who had landed nearby, "Who in the hell are they shooting at?" Despite the peril of their situation, the experienced combat men broke out in guffaws. Only then did Hollingsworth realize that *he* was the one being shot at.

As the C-47 carrying Lieutenant Edward T. Flash, of Cleveland, Ohio, and his stick was making its first pass over the DZ, bullets riddled the floor and wounded three men, all of whom were hit in the legs. Despite the intense pain, two of the wounded troopers insisted on jumping. The third was bleeding so profusely he could not stand. On the second run, Flash's plane was again punctured by bullets, and splinters were sent flying through the cabin.

On the third pass, the twenty-four-year-old Flash bailed out. He had jumped from such a low altitude that his chute barely had time to open before he hit beside the large, empty swimming pool on the edge of the golf course. Lieutenant Flash was still trying to shake the cobwebs from his head moments later when he spotted a blurry object plunging from the sky—a trooper with a "streamer," or parachute that had failed to open. With a sickening thud the unlucky soldier splattered onto the bottom of the concrete pool. Blood shot up in small geysers. Lieutenant Flash felt like vomiting.

Due to the low jump, nearly all of Flash's platoon landed on the golf course and incurred a variety of severe sprains and broken legs or ankles. Flash quickly assembled his able-bodied men, and after an exchange of fire with an enemy band, rushed the platoon to assigned positions on Topside, near Wheeler Point. After getting settled, Lieutenant Flash and his men noticed a bright red American roadster with a rumble seat piled high with Japanese soldiers coasting from Topside down toward Bottomside. Surprised by the sight of a moving, fire-engine-red sports car in the center of a pitched battle, the paratroopers gawked in amazement for several moments. Then two machine guns opened fire and riddled the fleeing vehicle, sending it spinning off the narrow road. Four or five men scrambled from the wrecked car and tried to run, but were picked off by Flash's riflemen.

Within minutes of landing, Private First Class Park A. Hodak of Spring Creek, Pennsylvania, and his gun crew of the 462nd Parachute Artillery had assembled their 75-millimeter pack howitzer. Almost at once they began blasting away at Japanese positions, firing so rapidly that soon the shell casings were not coming clear when the breach block was opened. Hodak instinctively reached in to pull out a stuck casing and the white-hot piece of metal scorched the skin off his entire hand. But he continued to service the howitzer.

Hodak later saw a lone paratrooper with a flamethrower pouring streams of fire into a cave in which Japanese were holed up. A flamethrower always reminded Hodak of a dragon belching fire from its nostrils. The trooper at the cave suddenly let out a piercing shriek, then fell dead. The artillerymen were astonished to see an American sailor dash to the site and flop down alongside the dead parachutist. The sailor, who probably had never seen a flamethrower, picked it up and resumed sending its fiery death into the cave. When the flamethrower was apparently out of fuel, the sailor calmly pitched it aside and disappeared over a hillock.

After all of Major Lawson Caskey's lift had landed, Colonel George Jones again took stock of the situation. He found that of 2,019 paratroopers who had jumped in the morning and afternoon operations, 279 had been seriously injured, wounded, or killed. With Topside and Malinta Hill in American control, the Warden was so encouraged that he contacted General Chink Hall, XI Corps commander, and requested a change in plans. Major Pug Woods's 1st Battalion was to bail out over Topside at 8:30 A.M. the following morning. But in order to avoid heavy casualties in a jump onto The Rock, Jones recommended that Woods's battalion come in by assault boat. General Hall approved. Woods's paratroopers would fly from Mindoro to San Marcelino airfield on northern Bataan in the morning, then head for Black Beach in landing craft.

Seated in the headquarters of the 503rd Regiment that evening was a disgusted Lieutenant Colonel John "Smiling Jack" Tolson, deputy commander of Rock Force. The New Bern, North Carolina, native had broken a foot on landing earlier in the afternoon and his mobility was limited. Medics had placed the injured foot in a cast and Tolson, who had been involved in the Corregidor planning from the beginning, would stay on The Rock and carry out his duties.[1]

As night drew a curtain over the Philippines, Captain Frank Centenni of Postlethwait's battalion peered northeastward from Malinta Hill into the distance and saw a yellow glow on the horizon: Manila was ablaze. Perched tensely on Topside and on Malinta Hill and huddled down on Bottomside near Black Beach were almost twenty-five hundred Americans. Burrowed into tunnels, caves, and spider holes were nearly six thousand Japanese soldiers and Imperial Marines ready to die for their emperor. A ghostly hush had fallen over The Rock, but it was a huge powder keg ready to explode.

21

No Quarter Asked or Given

With the arrival of D-Day night, Japanese soldiers and Marines, alone, in pairs, and in tiny groups, began emerging from the maze of tunnels, caves, pillboxes, and ammunition magazines that catacombed Corregidor. Most of the underground cavities were connected by a network of corridors and passageways. Already this night, Japanese had been popping up like gophers in front of and behind the American paratroopers on Topside and Postlethwait's infantrymen on Malinta Hill.

At about 9:00 P.M. parachute Corporal Walter Gonko was lying on the floor of a Topside aid station in a wrecked barracks. The only sound was from crickets outside. Suddenly, explosions rocked the far end of the building. Japanese were pitching in hand grenades. Medics dashed outside, where the weapons of their patients had been stacked, and gave each wounded man a rifle or Tommy gun. Corporal Gonko, who had been diagnosed as having a broken back, called out to a medic, "Help me to a standing position so I can shoot." As the medic struggled to get Gonko to his feet, searing pain shot through the corporal's body. But grim-faced and propped up against a post, he continued to hold his rifle at the ready for the expected charge through the door. Around him, other wounded men were doing likewise.

Soon the explosions ceased; the Japanese had apparently slipped back into their underground lairs. But Gonko remained upright and leaning against the post all night. Feeling much relieved in a standing position, he decided that his back was not broken after all or he would not have been able to stand.

Elsewhere on Topside, Sergeant Thomas L. Shutt, a section chief, Private First Class Park Hodak, and other men of B Battery, 462nd Parachute Field Artillery, were sprawled around a room on the first floor of a battered building. Suddenly, there were loud shouts from adjoining rooms and several rifles were fired inside the structure. Out in the dark hall, a voice shouted, "A goddamned Nip just ran through our room! He's headed outside!"

Shutt, Hodak, and other artillerymen grabbed their weapons and raced outside in search of the intruder. But the enemy soldier had vanished. Only after dawn would he be found: hit by a bullet, he had climbed into a garbage can outside the building, put the lid over himself, and died.

In the blackness atop Malinta Hill, men of Captain Centenni's K Company had formed a "covered wagon" perimeter and were peering intently in all directions. They could not dig foxholes in the solid rock and hardly dared move a muscle, knowing that the Japanese thrived on night action. Should any American as much as rise up to relieve himself, he risked being riddled by fire from his jittery comrades.

Shortly after midnight Japanese mortar shells began exploding on Malinta Hill. Then bursts of automatic-weapons and rifle fire split the night from the direction of two K Company outposts below known as "Little Knob" and "Goal Post Ridge." Minutes later an eerie silence descended. Nervous men on the hill heard a crunch of footsteps; someone was coming up the steep incline. The GIs tensed, ready to open fire.

The grunting and huffing noises grew louder, as the unidentified intruder drew closer. Sobbing sounds were heard. Struggling up from Little Knob was Private Rivers P. Bourque of Delcambre, Louisiana. In one hand he clutched his rifle, while over his shoulder he carried a badly mutilated, half-conscious comrade. He was dragging along a third man whose arm had been peeled of much of its skin and was dripping blood with each step.

"What the hell's going on down there?" someone asked Bourque in a stage whisper. With a mixture of anger and frustration the soldier sputtered out a few sentences about how the Japanese had suddenly burst from the blackness and virtually wiped out his squad on Little Knob. Only Bourque and Private Cassie, of Detroit, Michigan, had escaped the grenade onslaught. Cassie had volunteered to remain at the outpost with two badly wounded comrades.

A few minutes later two men from Goal Post Ridge scrambled to the top of Malinta and had an identical story to tell. Out of the blackness had come a shower of grenades that killed or wounded all but two of the their squad. Private Clarence Baumea, of Michigan, had agreed to stay behind and defend the wounded at the isolated outpost halfway down Malinta Hill. Captain Centenni was faced with an agonizing decision. His heart told him to take his company, edge down the hill, and rescue the wounded men. But his orders had been specific: hold Malinta Hill to the last man if need be.

Hardly had the pair of survivors gasped out their report than the top of Malinta Hill erupted with small-arms fire and the explosions of grenade. Imperial Marines had slipped out of Malinta Tunnel and were scrambling up the steep northeast side of the hill. Centenni's men held their fire until the attackers were almost upon them, then loosed a fusillade of rifle and machine-gun fire and peppered the oncoming Japanese with grenades. Silhouetted by the light of blue flares, rifles grasped in one hand and grenades in the other, the Japanese soldiers swarmed up the barren hill. At times they lunged to within ten feet of the Americans' smoking weapons. As they were blasted by grenades or riddled at point-blank range by bullets, the Imperial Marines tumbled down the almost vertical incline, landing with thuds far below.

One Japanese charged Private Adolph Neamend, of Bethlehem, Pennsylvania, who emptied his rifle clip into him. From ten feet away another Japanese pitched a grenade at Private Ray Crenshaw, of Clinton, Oklahoma, who quickly located it in the blackness, pitched it back at the enemy soldier, then killed the man with his rifle. For ninety minutes the fight raged atop Malinta Hill, with the casualties piling up on both sides. With the arrival of dawn, the Japanese, carrying some of their dead and wounded, broke off the attack.

The bodies of some forty Imperial Marines hanging on the rocks below the hilltop began to smell once the hot sun rose. Elsewhere, wounded Japanese sprawled across the hillside, their faces covered with flies, could be heard groaning. Insects had swarmed over their ghastly wounds, causing such pitiful cries of torment that GIs pumped bullets into the most severely wounded.

Throughout the uproar atop Malinta Hill, the Japanese had been going after Lieutenant Colonel Postlethwait's men along the beaches on Bottomside. At one point, near A Company's positions, a loud blast echoed through the night. Japanese engineers had set charges in a cliff above the company with the intention of burying the Americans. But too much TNT had been used, and instead of rock and dirt covering A Company, the side of the cliff had catapulted outward into the dark waters of Manila Bay.

Shortly afterward, the tense men of A Company heard splashes in the water just offshore from Black Beach. The GIs raked the surf with small-arms fire and heard screams. The Company A men kept shooting until the screaming had stopped, and with dawn found the dead bodies of twenty-three Japanese soldiers. Closer inspection revealed TNT charges in waterproof packages tied around their waists; they had apparently intended to hurl themselves as human bombs into American positions on Bottomside.

At about the same time that the suicide swimmers had been heading for Black Beach, about thirty Japanese soldiers slipped out of a side entrance to Malinta Tunnel and crept to a trolley underpass, where they assembled for a charge on Black Beach. Staff Sergeant Eugene Plantdon, of New Hampshire, and Private First Class Robert Taylor, of, Long Island, New York, were standing watch at the tunnel's main entrance just above the underpass. The two GIs heard shouts of "*Banzai!*" as the band emerged from cover and began charging across a two-hundred-yard strip toward Black Beach. Plantdon and Taylor opened fire, and moments later the sound of American rifles and machine guns erupted from the shore. The Imperial Marine lieutenant leading the charge was gunned down along with several others, and a large group leaped into two shell holes. There they stayed as GIs pitched grenade after grenade in after them, eventually killing all. Some of the tunnel force, however, infiltrated to within fifty yards of small medical tents tucked in among the sand dunes; they were finally detected and wiped out.

At dawn an American tank crawled up to the main mouth of Malinta Tunnel and fired a round into the long, dark corridor. Near the opposite end of the tunnel, at the east slope of Malinta Hill, several American machine gunners were waiting. Thirty-five Japanese charged out of the rear entrance to escape the tank fire and ran right into the blazing guns of the Americans.

That same morning—D-Day plus 1—Lieutenant Colonel Ed Postlethwait ordered Captain Frank Centenni to send patrols down from Malinta Hill to Little Knob and Goal Post Ridge to see if there were any wounded survivors of the previous night's Japanese assault. One soldier was found alive—barely—on Goal Post Ridge, but when the patrol tried to edge onto Little Knob it was greeted by a hail of small-arms fire. Four men were cut down.

Captain Centenni decided to lead another patrol in an effort to reach Little Knob. Stalking along through the thick vegetation, Centenni and his men walked into an ambush. A heavy fusillade of machine-gun fire raked the little column, followed by a shower of grenades. Centenni, who had been out in front, bore the brunt of three grenades. His men tried desperately to reach him, but the Japanese fire was so heavy they had to withdraw without their leader's dead body.

Earlier that morning, up on Topside, Lieutenant Edward Flash and his platoon of paratroopers lay exhausted after a tense night. They had been constantly on the alert, as shadowy figures crawled through the dark night trying to infiltrate their position. The troopers were ravaged by thirst; mouths felt as though they were filled with cotton; lips and tongues were starting to puff up. Long before, each man had consumed his two canteens of water; resupply containers had parachuted into Manila Bay. Suddenly, a pitiful cry for help rang out from near a railroad track down below. The voice was laced with anguish. But was it from a badly wounded paratrooper, or an enemy trick to get Americans out in the open where they could be cut down by machine-gun bursts? It was a chance Lieutenant Flash would have to take.

Covered by an artillery piece that fired point-blank at a pillbox overlooking the railroad tracks, the platoon leader and three men began crawling toward the source of the pleading voice. When they got there, Flash and his men found an ashen-faced paratrooper sprawled near the tracks. His jump suit was saturated with blood, and flies swarmed over a ghastly stomach wound. Flash scooped off handfuls of the insects, but they were quickly replaced by swarms of others.

Placing the wounded trooper on a cot spring they had brought with them, the rescue party began the arduous trek back to their positions. All the while, Flash's platoon on the higher ground had been blasting away with rifles and machine guns at pillboxes and into vegetation from where Japanese might riddle the rescuers. But, undaunted, enemy marksmen fired at Flash and his three troopers as they struggled along with their heavy burden.

It seemed to Ed Flash, a keenly conditioned man who had been a star baseball and basketball player at Otterbein College in Ohio, that he had just finished climbing Pike's Peak when he and his gasping men finally reached their platoon and gently lowered the cot spring with the semi-conscious trooper. Immediately, others rushed the wounded man to an aid station. Only then did Lieutenant Flash and his fellow rescuers realize that they had all been hit by Japanese bullets while trudging back with their burden. The four troopers walked back to the regimental aid station without assistance. On the way, Flash became aware that he had no control over his left arm, which had been hit just above the elbow. Unbeknownst to him at the time, Flash's arm had been broken and a radial nerve severed by the impact of the bullet.

Elsewhere on Topside, a squad from F Company of Caskey's parachute battalion was probing catlike along the side of a hill. Out in front —as usual—was Sergeant John Phillips, whose war had turned into a personal vendetta against the Japanese after his brother with the 32nd Infantry Division had been killed. The patrol came to a small hillock, and Phillips scrambled around one side of it. Sergeant Chris Johnson took the other side. Following in file was Private First Class John Bartlett.

Suddenly, like a jack-in-the-box, a dome-helmeted Japanese Marine popped up fifteen feet in front of Bartlett, who had never seen a live enemy soldier. A curious sensation surged through the GI. This was the situation he had heard about constantly in training: kill or be killed.

Bartlett's mind was awhirl. He was aware that the enemy Marine was pointing his rifle toward him, but was powerless to act.

The sharp crack of a rifle split the air. Then another. Sergeants Phillips and Johnson had spun around just in time to see the Imperial Marine drawing a bead on Bartlett and had cut loose with their weapons. In a fraction of a second, Bartlett's instinct and training took over, and he whipped up his rifle to shoot back. The three paratroopers fired one slug after the other into the Marine, and he finally collapsed in a heap.[1]

In the meantime, Corporal Walter Gonko had torn up the emergency medical tag that stated "suspected broken back." As long as he could remain standing, he could endure the pain. After grabbing a quick cup of coffee at Harold Templeman's Red Cross canteen in a bombed-out building, the former coal miner and itinerant wheat harvester hobbled off in search of his squad, a part of Battery D, 462nd Parachute Field Artillery.

Gonko soon became lost, then alarmed; there was not a single American to be seen. Rounding a small hillock, he was greeted by a horrifying sight: four Japanese soldiers, each burned to a crisp, were standing upright, just as they had been before being showered with napalm. The sight sickened Gonko, but he could not take his eyes off the cadavers' hideous faces. Their teeth protruding against the black background of incinerated flesh gave them the appearance of having macabre fixed grins. They seemed to be mocking the American, as if to say: *Our ordeal is over, but you, you poor bastard, will have to go on. And sooner or later you'll end up just like us—mutilated and dead.*

Far south of flaming Corregidor that day, Major Pug Woods hastily assembled his parachute battalion and supporting troops at a Mindoro airstrip at dawn and briefed them on their change of orders. Instead of jumping on The Rock, they would fly over it, parachute equipment bundles onto Topside, and continue on to the San Marcelino airstrip on Bataan. From San Marcelino, Wood's paratroopers would be shuttled to Corregidor by sea.

Colonel John Lackey's C-47s, carrying Woods's paratroopers, had just begun their run over Topside at 8:32 A.M. when it became clear that

Colonel George Jones had made a wise decision. Now recovered from the massive D-Day bombardment and the surprise of the parachute assault, Japanese gunners loosed a murderous anti-aircraft fire. Of the forty-four planes in the flight, sixteen were hit by gunfire and five C-47 crewman were wounded. Had Woods's men jumped, the heavy ack-ack fire would have been turned on them as they descended.

After landing at San Marcelino, Woods's troopers were rushed by truck to nearby Subic Bay, where they boarded World War I vintage destroyers and sailed southward to Mariveles. There they transferred to Higgins boats.

Robert "Pug" Woods had only recently been appointed to command the 1st Battalion. As with new COs in any army, he was the subject of much discussion and analysis by his troopers. To his men, Woods seemed to be a good, cool soldier. But he hardly lived up to the Hollywood image of the tough, fire-eating, hard-cussing paratrooper. Slight of build and with a choir-boy's face, Pug Woods would prove, in the few days left in his young life, that he was indeed a cool, courageous fighting man.

After knifing through Manila Bay on the four-mile trek from Mariveles to Corregidor, Woods's assault craft were nearing Black Beach when Japanese in overlooking caves suddenly opened up with heavy bursts of machine-gun fire. Then mortar rounds began to explode around the little boats. In one of the leading landing craft, Lieutenant Jesse B. Gandee, of Winter Park, Florida, leader of a 150-caliber machine-gun platoon, was trying to flatten out below the waterline but finding it impossible due to the shallow draft of the Higgins boat. Gandee could hear the *rat-a-tat-tat* of bullets striking the side, and glanced upward from under the rim of his helmet to see splinters flying past just overhead. Then he heard a yelp from Corporal Maurice Abrigon in front of him and saw him collapse to the deck with a bullet in the knee.

Gandee became aware of the grating chatter of automatic weapons just behind him, and looked around to see a pink-faced sailor, who looked no more than eighteen, standing upright and manning twin .30-caliber machine guns. The youth was pouring streams of bullets into the caves, and stopped only after he was cut down by a Japanese slug.

Moments later a mortar shell exploded at the waterline of Lieutenant Gandee's boat, blowing a hole in the port side. Flying splinters and shrapnel struck the platoon leader in the lower back. A surge of alarm shot through Gandee's head: he was paralyzed from the waist down. The boat went dead in the water, but it was now close to shore; men scrambled out of the craft, jumped into water up to their necks, and waded to the beach. Corporal Abrigon and Lieutenant Gandee were left lying helpless in the riddled Higgins boat, which was taking on water. After an interminable period of time, another Higgins boat stopped and evacuated Gandee and Abregon to a destroyer.

All the while, Nipponese in cliffside caves continued to pour ma-chine-gun fire into paratroopers dashing onto Black Beach. Large num-bers of them were pinned down flat on their faces in the wet sand as the destroyer *Claxton* edged in close to shore and began firing its 5-inchers point-blank into the caves. Finally, the Japanese machine guns fell silent. Major Woods quickly assembled his units and led them up to Topside. Now all of Colonel Jones's three parachute battalions had congregated on the rocky head of the tadpole.

That same afternoon of the seventeenth, Lieutenant William T. Bai-ley's F Company of Caskey's battalion received a bloody nose when it tried to seize Battery Wheeler. Flamethrowers and grenades were used against the Japanese in underground ammunition magazines, but F Company was finally driven back. Three of its six officers were lost.

As F Company retired to lick its wounds, Lieutenant Joseph A. Turinsky, leader of D Company, received word that he was to launch another frontal assault against Battery Wheeler. Turinsky and his men were apprehensive; human flesh and bone were being sent over open ground to attack a miniature concrete fortress behind which enemy machine gunners were lying in wait.

Twenty-two-year-old Private Paul A. Hughart, of Morgantown, West Virginia, who had been a scrappy amateur boxer, and his waiting D Company comrades looked on glumly as medical soldiers filed past carrying bloody and mutilated F Company troopers who had been gunned down in the first assault on Battery Wheeler. Then a voice barked out "Let's go!" and the men of D Company got to their feet and began edging down a long embankment that led to the coastal battery.

Almost at once several Japanese machine guns raked the advancing paratroopers, who returned the fire and pitched smoke grenades at the concrete ramparts. An enemy bullet pierced the front of the helmet of Sergeant Amelio Pucci, who had been moving forward next to Hughart when he went down. A fleeting thought raced through Hughart's mind: Sergeant Pucci will never get to fulfill his wartime ambition—to kill a Japanese soldier barehanded.

Pucci, a neat hole in his helmet, fell beside a bomb crater. Hughart leaped into the cavity and was joined moments later by Sergeant Nelson Stowe and Corporal Robert Nagy.

"Where's Pucci?" Stowe gasped, out of breath.

"He's dead," Hughart replied. "Shot through the head. He's lying beside the crater."

Stowe and Nagy reached up and dragged Pucci into the crater, and noticed that he was breathing. Minutes later the "dead" man opened his eyes. The bullet had plowed into his helmet, caromed around it, and come out the back, knocking Pucci cold in the process. The following day he would be back in the thick of the fighting.

As Japanese bullets hissed past, Lieutenant Turinsky's men reached the gun battery and scrambled up onto its ramparts, where a hand-to-hand fight erupted. By late afternoon Battery Wheeler was under American control. Sprawled about the concrete emplacement were the dead bodies of sixty-four Japanese. But Major Caskey's F and D companies had also paid a price—some twenty killed or wounded.

Elsewhere on Topside late that afternoon, Lieutenant Daniel J. Doherty, leader of D Battery of the 462nd Parachute Artillery Battalion, received good news. Twelve of his men who had been reported missing and were presumed dead traipsed into Doherty's CP wearing wide grins. They had been blown over a cliff the previous day and landed in a ravine near the narrow beach at the bottom. Japanese in caves on the face of the cliff had promptly raked the parachutists with machine-gun fire, and the artillerymen had responded with rifles and Tommy guns in an effort to fight their way back up to Topside. But the Japanese fire had been too heavy, and they had crawled down instead.

Finally, the little band reached the beach, five hundred feet below Topside's plateau, and signaled a PT boat, which dashed in and picked them up. They were taken to an offshore destroyer, then delivered to an escort vessel of Lieutenant Colonel Postlethwait's 34th Regiment amphibious assault force. Under Staff Sergeant William Ellis, the D Battery men made the landing with Postlethwait's troops. In so doing, Ellis and his troopers gained a unique distinction: they were the only Americans to make *both* an airborne and an amphibious assault on Corregidor.

In the meantime, a sharp fight had erupted along the road leading from Black Beach on Bottomside up to Topside. Colonel Jones considered this a crucial operation, for it was vital to clear the road if waterborne supplies were going to reach the paratroopers. One company of Postlethwait's infantry battalion was attacking up the road from the east, and a company of parachutists was pushing down the road from Topside on the west.

Halfway down the hill, the 503rd troopers were raked by machine-gun fire from Japanese soldiers perched in a series of caves overlooking the road. The Americans were forced to scatter for cover. A hurried call was put in for Lieutenant Bill Blake, the parachute regiment's demolitions expert who, along with his men, had arrived on Corregidor by boat after having bailed out over Bataan.

Rapidly taking stock of the situation, Blake saw that there were six cave openings. While riflemen peppered them with small-arms fire, Lieutenant Blake, Corporal Delbert L. Parsons, and Private First Class Willie J. "Andy" Anderson edged to within five yards of the entrances. Moments later grenades flew out of a cave and exploded ten feet from the three demolitions men, wounding Anderson in the legs.

Bill Blake pitched a WP (white phosphorous) grenade—whose particles could burn through human flesh—into one cave opening, then hurled another that missed the target. It bounced off the bank and detonated in front of the troopers, showering them with phosphorous and inflicting light burns. Under cover of the smoke from the WP grenade, Anderson, disregarding the shrapnel in his legs, slipped up to the cave mouths and attacked them with a flamethrower.

Nine screaming men bolted out of the caves, burning from head to foot, and nearly trampling Blake, Anderson, and Parsons in their agony. Flaming napalm fell off the Japanese as they ran; paratroopers shot them with rifles.

Sealing up three of the caves with explosives, Lieutenant Blake and his two demolitions men turned to the three remaining caves. But before they could turn a flamethrower on them, a Japanese soldier appeared in the mouth of one waving a piece of white cloth. It was a rare sight: a Bushido warrior trying to surrender. Itchy-fingered paratroopers opened fire and drove the lone soldier back into the cave. Twice more he ventured out, only to be greeted with more bursts of gunfire.

Lieutenant Blake, pressed against the hillside just outside the cave, could hear angry voices and scuffling sounds inside. Apparently, the Japanese soldier was trying to get out of the cave and his comrades were trying to hold him back. By now, Blake had gotten the troopers to cease firing, and the enemy soldier ventured out once again and was taken prisoner. It became immediately obvious that he was totally deaf, and bleeding from the eyes, ears, nose, and mouth. Blake concluded that the six caves were entrances to a single large underground chamber, and the concussions from the explosions at the first three caves had inflicted the injuries on the enemy soldier.

The demolitions men began blasting around the entrances to the three remaining caves. Not a peep was heard from the Japanese huddled inside as Blake and his two troopers proceeded to systematically bury them alive by sealing the openings. In the next few days, Corporal Parsons and a few demolitionists would seal forty-three caves on that one hillside.

In the meantime, another section of Lieutenant Blake's team under Sergeant Donald V. Broniman had been called to a Japanese position confronting Captain Joseph M. Conway's H Company. It was an old American gun site with a large double steel door protecting the entrance to its underground chamber. The 503rd's intelligence officer had declared that the cavity might be a powder magazine, in which case Conway's troopers could be blown clear back to Luzon if they tried to assault the position.

Sergeant Broniman and his men blasted open the first steel door with bazookas and, after the smoke had cleared, slipped inside. They found themselves in a tiny chamber. Before they could open the second steel door, Japanese soldiers tried to pitch grenades through small air vents. Broniman and the others beat a strategic retreat in order to draw up a new operational plan.

As nightfall descended over embattled Corregidor, so too did an uneasy calm. Up on Malinta Hill just before midnight Lieutenant Albert S. "Tex" Barham, of Texas, who had won a battlefield commission on Leyte, was peering into the blackness, listening intently for telltale sounds. Suddenly the K Company officer tensed. There were shadowy figures moving in the darkness. Barham launched flares that silhouetted perhaps two hundred crawling shapes only thirty feet down the slope.

K Company opened fire at point-blank range and pitched so many grenades that they nearly ran out of the explosives. Tex Barham was hit in the face by grenade fragments, the blood nearly blinding him. But he had to get grenades. Scrambling on all fours to L Company positions a hundred yards away, Barham and Sergeant Herman Taylor loaded up with grenades and made the rapid return crawl—only to find that the Japanese had vanished down the hill.

The sharp fight in the blackness had cost K Company twenty-two casualties. One of these was Lieutenant Henry G. Gitnick, of Pennsylvania, who had replaced the dead Captain Frank Centenni as company commander. Now, as a bright yellow moon bathed barren Malinta Hill in its rays, Gitnik was lying wounded, having been hit by grenade fragments in the head and arm. Lieutenant Robert J. Fugitti, of Philadelphia, Pennsylvania, replaced Gitnik, becoming the third K Company leader in forty-eight hours.

In the moonlight, Lieutenant Fugitti counted noses—there were only two officers, including the bandaged Tex Barham, and thirty-six men left in K Company. They waited through interminable minutes; the enemy would be back, that they knew. They had no water. Mouths were parched. A few canteens of water had been brought up the hill that afternoon and been given to the wounded.

At 3:05 A.M. Japanese mortar shells began exploding on top of Malinta Hill. "There come the bastards again!" someone shouted. Flares were fired, again illuminating the dark shapes clawing up the steep incline. Then came the frantic shouts of "*Banzai!*" followed by a charge against K Company positions. Bullets flew and grenades exploded in fiery orange balls. The night was pierced by shrieks and screams. After an hour, the Nipponese force scrambled back down the hill.

A second nose count revealed only thirty-three able-bodied GIs on the elevation. Would dawn ever come? When it finally arrived, K Company men looked down on one hundred-fifty Japanese cadavers—their faces and wounds covered by flies—sprawled about the rocky slope.

Down near Black Beach during that long night, a lone Japanese soldier, a mine strapped to his body, had sneaked through American positions and was slithering along on his stomach looking for a likely target. The intruder passed up several trucks loaded with ammunition and crucial supplies and crawled under a Red Cross wagon. Seconds later a fiery explosion rent the night, as the suicide soldier blew up cigarettes, soap, soft drinks, toothpaste, shaving cream—and himself.

While the fighting had been raging on Malinta Hill, paratrooper Paul Hughart, the West Virginia mountaineer, and his D Company comrades were lying exhausted on Battery Wheeler on Topside. But sleep would not come for most, knowing as they did that directly below them were Japanese soldiers in an underground powder magazine that might be blown at any moment. At about 1:15 A.M. Hughart snapped out of a fitful sleep. Below he could hear intermittent clicking noises that sounded like a firing mechanism being set. Hughart nudged a comrade next to him. "That's got to be Nips down there," he whispered.

The minutes passed slowly. Just before 2:00 A.M. Hughart heard faint footsteps from the concrete stairs below. Then a dim figure could be discerned at the top of the stairway. Next to Hughart a rifle barked from the blackness, no more than ten feet from the silhouette. The bullet caught the shadowy figure squarely in the face, and it tumbled back down the steps.

Minutes later another figure bolted up the steps. Trooper Hughart saw the flash of a nearby rifle and heard a sickening thud as the bullet tore into the enemy soldier. He too was knocked over backward and rolled to the bottom of the stairs, his body halting against a steel door that led into the underground powder magazine. Later investigation would reveal that the pair had been dead Nipponese officers that were naked except for white socks. Each had been hideously burned, probably by flamethrowers in the savage fighting of the previous afternoon.

At about 3:00 A.M. an enormous blast rocked the western end of Topside. The terrain and the seascape hundreds of feet below were illuminated as though it were noontime. The Japanese under Battery Wheeler had ignited the main powder magazine, and the entire gun position erupted with angry flames. D Company paratroopers dashed madly off the parapet—and right into the sights of a band of Japanese soldiers that had infiltrated American lines and was crouching in the darkness to one side of Battery Wheeler. Trooper Hughart leaped into a bomb crater and, by the light from the flames, saw that it was occupied by several Japanese. There was no time for him to fire, so Hughart grabbed his rifle by the barrel and bashed two of the enemy soldiers across the face. There were crunching sounds as the heavy rifle butt ground facial bone into pulp. The trooper scrambled out of the crater before the other Nipponese could react.

All around Battery Wheeler a wild melee erupted. There were grunts, groans and shouts. Eerie shadows cast by the raging fire danced about. Rifle shots rang out and grenades exploded. One American was shot through both arms and both legs; another received six flesh wounds to his legs. Two Japanese were gunned down as they tried to climb onto the concrete parapet of the gun position. But surprisingly few were killed on either side in this Pier Six brawl, due mainly to the darkness and the chaos that made it difficult to detect friend from foe.

With all of Colonel George Jones's Rock Force on Corregidor by the end of D-Day plus 1, the pattern for the death struggle had been established. Due to the small size of the island fortress, the rocky terrain, and the rabbit warren of connecting tunnels, caves, underground powder magazines, and pillboxes, it would be impossible to conduct actions by regiment or battalion. Instead, American patrols would have to fan out from Topside at daylight and begin digging out the Japanese—who had burrowed like moles into underground lairs—using flamethrowers, grenades, dynamite charges, small-arms, and point-blank howitzer fire. At dusk, the paratroopers would pull back into their covered wagon-style perimeter on Topside. There would be no such thing as a rear area. Medical stations, command posts, and artillery positions would be constantly subjected to surprise attack, particularly at night.

By midnight of D-Day plus 1, Colonel George Jones knew that Sixth Army intelligence reports of only six to eight hundred Japanese on Corregidor had been totally wrong. Already, in two days, more than eight hundred dead Japanese were strewn around The Rock, with large numbers of others buried in sealed caves and underground chambers.

Each American knew that it would be a savage, no-holds-barred fight to the death. The Japanese Bushido code taught the warrior—from private to general—that he was invincible; each soldier was imbued with the sacredness of an honorable death on the battlefield over disgraceful surrender. Each Japanese would resist until killed, no matter how hopeless his situation.

That night, in the dark and dingy tunnels inside The Rock, Japanese warriors sang a battle song, "*Umi Yukaba*":

> Across the sea,
> Crosses in the water;
> Across the mountains,
> Corpses heaped on the field;
> I shall die for the Emperor,
> I shall never look back.

Then they stole out into the blackness to attack the Americans.

22

"Ban-zai!"

By the time the sun rose on the morning of February 18—D-Day plus 2—an overpowering stench hung over Corregidor. Dead Japanese bodies—some eight hundred of them—were strewn about the bleak, rocky landscape, becoming bloated and blackened. Some cadavers had burst open as a result of the heat, spilling intestines over mangled bodies. Sun-seared eyeballs swelled, popped from sockets, and were left dangling by thin cords on faces and necks. The white eyeballs offered a grisly contrast to the dark faces of the dead men.

The smell of decaying corpses made many of the American GIs vomit. Crewmen on destroyers a mile offshore were nauseated by the stench. Bulldozers on The Rock were put to work digging long, shallow trenches. Then the dozers shoved hundreds of corpses into the excavations and covered them with dirt. Paratroopers saw two bulldozers push perhaps fifty cadavers over the cliffs of Topside, plunging some five hundred feet into Manila Bay.

The flies, millions of them, were a constant source of torment. Many GIs stopped trying to eat, for it was impossible to put a bite of food into one's mouth without a dozen flies descending. Flies bred in the rotting cadavers tried relentlessly to get into the eyes, ears, noses, and mouths of the living.

The situation was intolerable and a threat to the Corregidor operation, so Colonel Jones called in his S-4 (supply officer), Captain Robert M. "Cracker" Atkins, of Miami, Florida. "We've got to do something about these goddamned flies," the Rock Force commander declared. "Get on it!"

Jones knew that Cracker Atkins was a get-things-done type, but he had given the captain a tall order. How does one make tens of millions of flies on a tiny island, half of which was held by hostile soldiers, vanish? Atkins had an idea and promptly contacted his opposite number (G-4) at XI Corps headquarters. The parachute officer minced no words in describing the need for wiping out the Corregidor fly menace, even though he was addressing an officer several notches higher on the command totem pole. Then Atkins outlined his plan for Operation Fly.

A few hours later a C-47 with external wing tanks filled with DDT insecticide flew in at a low level and began criss-crossing Corregidor. "Hot damn," Captain Atkins exclaimed to Colonel Jones, "the flies are dropping like flies!" Each day thereafter a DDT plane would fly back and forth just above the rocky island, with the desired results. The fly scourge was eliminated, much to the relief of the American fighting men —and no doubt to the Japanese as well.

Early on D-Day plus 2 Colonel George Jones set out from his CP toward the road leading from Topside down to Bottomside. This was the same locale where Lieutenant Colonel Postlethwait's men and a company of paratroopers had been battling the previous afternoon, and where Lieutenant Bill Blake's demolition troopers were still busily sealing up caves. Striding briskly along in his Tennessee Walking Horse style, Jones and an aide passed near the decomposing body of a Japanese marine. The colonel did a double-take, thinking his eyes were playing tricks on him. The dead cadaver seemed to be moving ever so slightly. Then Jones realized what was happening: maggots on the corpse were so numerous that, collectively, they were stirring the blackened body.

When Colonel Jones finally reached Bottomside, he found that a patrol of his paratroopers were attacking an old ice plant that had been used to store meat and vegetables. On a hill about two hundred feet from the ice plant a band of Japanese had gathered around a box car on a railroad spur and were pouring rifle fire at the 503rd troopers below. Seeing that his parachutists had their hands full at the ice plant, the Rock Force commander decided that he would personally lead an attack against the Nipponese at the box car. Jones secured a squad from Postlethwait's battalion and hurriedly briefed them. "We'll pitch smoke grenades, then when the smoke has cleared we'll charge the Nips at the box car," the colonel explained. "Any questions?"

There were none. But the 24th Division men were far from enthusiastic. Colonel Jones was wearing no insignia of rank, and the GIs had never laid eyes on him before. "Okay, let's go!" Jones exclaimed, as he started trudging up the slope. Smoke grenades were hurled, but there was no charge. The Japanese at the box car opened fire, however, and two of the infantrymen were cut down.

Undaunted, Jones acquired another squad and started up the hill once again. This time better progress was made. When the smoke cleared the colonel had reached the box car. Unfortunately, he looked around and saw that he was alone; the remainder of his squad had bogged down in confusion after two of its men had been hit. Jones edged around the end of the box car and suddenly found himself fifteen feet from an Imperial Marine in a spider hole. One antagonist was as startled as the other. Before the enemy soldier could react, Jones scrambled for cover, and moments later the American commander on Corregidor, playing the role of squad leader, and a Japanese private were blasting away at each other with their weapons. Unbeknownst to the colonel, up on the edge of Topside Lieutenant Dick Williams, leader of the Signal Corps cameramen who had jumped after only twenty minutes of instruction, was recording the two-man shootout with a telescopic lens.

The Warden soon decided that the duel was a draw and that a dead Rock Force commander would be of little use in the operation. So he withdrew back down to Bottomside. There he gave orders to a paratroop officer to "clean out the Nips around that box car."

On the way back to his CP, Colonel Jones remarked to his aide, "I guess one could say that as a squad leader I'm a flop!"

In the meantime, the Japanese in the ice plant had continued to resist stubbornly. Finally, the paratroopers collected several tires and inner tubes, set them on fire, and crammed them down air vents. Minutes later the Japanese, unable to withstand the fumes, dashed outside, where they were shot. None escaped.

On Topside, Sergeant Major Doc Landes, who had been given his nickname by comrades due to his prewar doctorate in chemistry from the University of Berlin, left his 3rd Battalion CP in an old watch tower to try his hand at driving Japanese out of caves. Landes, a former star on the Hungarian national soccer team, had devised a new procedure for getting the job done. The chemical officer for Erickson's 3rd Parachute Battalion tied a long rope to an open five-gallon can of gasoline and lugged it to a cave in which Japanese soldiers were holed up. He then climbed the hillside over the opening, lowered the gasoline can in front of the entrance, and swung it to and fro until, with a mighty heave, it went sailing into the cave. Nearby comrades hurriedly pitched white phosphorous grenades inside, setting the gasoline afire and turning the cave into an inferno. As expected, several men dashed out and were cut down by the guns of waiting troopers.

At the same time, the 503rd Parachute Regiment's peripatetic demolitions expert, Lieutenant Bill Blake, had also concocted a similar device, which he labeled an "infernal machine." It consisted of filling a five-gallon gasoline can with napalm and taping eight white phosphorous grenades to the outside of it. Around this was placed several turns of prima cord and two blocks of dynamite on each side. Black finished off his infernal machine by attaching a fifteen-minute fuse that led to a cap on the prima cord.

Blake planned to drop the lethal apparatus down a ventilator shaft at the old gun position confronting Captain Joe Conway's M Company. The previous afternoon, Japanese holed up in an underground powder magazine protected by two steel doors had thwarted efforts by 503rd demolitionists to blast them out. The problem in dropping the device down the ventilator was that the fifteen-minute fuse, which would allow Blake and his men time to "get the hell out of there in case the whole joint goes up," would allow the Japanese time to disarm the apparatus.

Blake planned to solve this problem by tying the explosive package above the shaft with prima cord and putting a fuse on it three seconds longer than the one on the main charge. When the first fuse reached the prima cord, after fifteen minutes, it would explode the prima cord and let the device drop down the shaft. Three seconds later the main charge would detonate.

Taking Sergeant Roy King, Corporal Charles W. Hill, and two other demolitionists with him, Lieutenant Blake went to the underground chamber. As Blake hovered over the ventilator shaft, he was startled to hear a voice from below speaking in English: "I wouldn't do that if I were you, there is very much dynamite down here."

Blake called down the shaft, "Hi ya, Nip."

"Very much dynamite down here, you will blow us all up."

"Okay, Nip."

"Hokay."

As Lieutenant Blake and his men blew off a lock to get to the shaft opening, he could hear a group of Japanese chattering below. Again came the voice from the underground chamber: "Don't blow us all up."

"Well, come on out then," Blake replied.

"I can't come out."

"How much dynamite down there, Nip?"

"Eighty thousand pounds."

"Okay, Nip, if you won't come up we'll send you to your ancestors."

"Hokay."

The infernal machine was set, and Blake and his men raced for cover. Soon the troopers could hear the faint pop of the prima cord and then an enormous roar followed by a huge black cloud mushrooming skyward. The powder magazine had disintegrated.

Bill Blake turned to his men and remarked drily, "The Nip was right. Eighty thousand pounds *is* a lot of dynamite."

In the torrid heat, thirst became a problem that tormented everyone. Some drinking water had been brought in by boat for the Americans, but not nearly enough. The Japanese soldiers in their tunnels were suffering even more. In the huge Malinta Tunnel they tried to quench their thirst by drinking canned fruit juices and licking the walls for water seepage. *Sake*, a rice wine, was consumed liberally, but only made the men more thirsty.

That night in his CP on Topside, Rock Force commander George Jones was assessing the day's work. It had been productive: some seven hundred Japanese more had been killed. Jones and his operations officer, Major Ernest C. Clark, Jr., considered Corregidor "buttoned down" for the night, so they were relaxing with a few slugs of Santori Scotch. There was nothing Jones and Clark could do but hope that each unit would hold on through the night against Japanese attacks they knew were inevitable.

Colonel Jones's orderly had found the case of Japanese whisky in a barracks shortly after the initial parachute landings on D-Day. Before being evacuated with a broken ankle received in the jump, the sergeant had turned over the liquor to the Rock Force commander. "I proclaimed him a Hero of Corregidor," Jones remarked drily. The two officers then crawled into what was serving as their beds—a pair of salvaged parachutes lying on the concrete floor—for a brief sleep before the next crisis erupted. It would not be long in coming.[1]

As Jones and Clark tried to steal a few hours of sleep, five hundred yards to the southeast, near Breakwater Point, all was quiet in Captain William T. Bossert's A Company CP, located in an old barracks. Bossert and his staff had no inkling that they were sitting directly on top of an underground Japanese ammunition dump. It was shortly after 2:00 A.M. on February 19—D-Day plus 3—when suddenly an enormous blast rocked Topside. Forty Japanese had set off explosives in the underground chamber, killing half of them. But the Bushido warriors had achieved their goal: an equal number of paratroopers died in the blast.

Colonel Jones and Major Clark were jolted awake by the explosion. Twenty seconds later, a rock the size of a football sailed into their room (the barracks was roofless) and landed within a few feet of them. The force of the blast had catapulted it five hundred yards.

Surviving American paratroopers near the blast site were stunned. But they were hazily aware that the surviving Nipponese—about twenty of them—had staggered out of their tunnel, squatted in a circle, chanted slogans, pressed live grenades to their stomachs, and collectively committed *hara-kiri*.

An eerie silence returned once more to the battle-torn Rock. But as the paratroopers began to recover from the jolt of the blast, some five hundred Japanese soldiers and Imperial Marines emerged from caves below and began to stealthily claw their way up the steep cliffs along the southern sector of Topside. Private First Class Paul Hughart and his D Company comrades were peering intently through the darkness near Wheeler Point. Earlier Hughart and a BAR (Browning automatic rifle) man had scooped out shallow trenches in the broken rock and placed sheets of corrugated tin along a narrow road to give advance warning of infiltrating Japanese.

At about 3:00 A.M. Company D troopers heard the tin creaking faintly. They tensed and readied their weapons. By now it was very dark. Suddenly, Hughart discerned four dim silhouettes just ahead. He fired four quick rounds, then squeezed off four more when five other forms popped up to his right. Company D men began pitching grenades, and soon the shadowy forms vanished.

The GIs laid out their grenades and waited . . . and waited some more. The silence was almost suffocating. Stomachs knotted. It was hot and humid but Trooper Harry Drews's teeth were chattering in anxiety. Then, from the dark stillness a singsong voice called out, "Americans, you die! More blood for the emperor!"

A leather-lunged paratrooper shouted back, "Screw the emperor! More blood for Franklin and Eleanor!"

Three hours passed and nothing happened. Trooper Hughart, who had been lying on the hard, broken rock for nearly eight hours, decided to stand up and stretch his aching bones. Suddenly, the silence was shattered. Hughart was knocked down by a concussion grenade. Instinctively, he got to his feet, and a bullet tore through his right hip at the base of the spine and came out his thigh. Hughart fell to the ground, half-conscious and paralyzed in both legs.

Then all hell broke loose. A clutch of hand grenades flew through the darkness and exploded on and around Captain Bossert's A Company, Lieutenant Turinsky's D Company, and Lieutenant Bailey's F Company. The first coordinated Japanese counterattack on Corregidor had begun. An orange signal flare went up and Imperial Marines shouting *Banzai*, their bayonets gleaming in the light of the flares, charged the paratroop positions.

Turinsky's D Company received the heaviest blow. Bodies of Imperial Marines piled up before the paratroopers' rifles and machine guns, but the screaming marines continued to storm D Company positions, and a face-to-face fight with bayonets, rifle butts, trench knives, and fists erupted. Lieutenant Turinsky was on the field telephone at his CP in the plotting room of Battery Wheeler when shouts of *Banzai!* were heard outside. Hand grenades flew into the plotting room and were followed by blinding explosions. Thirteen troopers were cut down. One of those killed was Lieutenant Joe Turinsky.

Along Bailey's F Company sector, an avalanche of shouting, shadowy figures bounded into view and rushed forward. Twenty-seven-year-old Private Lloyd G. McCarter of Tacoma, Washington, immediately began to blast away with his rifle. A free spirit whose antics had often plunged him into hot water when out of combat, McCarter was a terror on the battlefield. The previous afternoon he had tracked down and killed six snipers who had been firing into F Company. Now, in the face of a full-blooded assault, McCarter, who wore no bars or stripes, assumed a leadership role. With his company in danger of being over-whelmed, he shouted encouragement to his comrades and profanity at the enemy. Soon, all the men around him had been killed or wounded. Clutching his Tommy gun, the 2nd Battalion scout crawled to an exposed position, and the Imperial Marines began concentrating on him. Despite the heavy fire, McCarter continually exposed himself in order to locate and fire on enemy soldiers.

When Private McCarter's Tommy gun would no longer operate, he grabbed a BAR from a dead comrade and continued to inflict heavy casualties. But the BAR, in turn, became too hot to fire, and discarding it, McCarter began firing a Garand rifle. Eventually, he was seriously wounded, but not before he had killed at least thirty-seven men and forced the Japanese assault to waver in front of F Company. Bleeding from head to foot and no longer able to stand, Lloyd McCarter resisted efforts to evacuate him. Only when he lost consciousness could he be carried to an aid station. (Private McCarter's grevious wounds deprived him of neither his spirit nor his sense of humor. Surgeons later reported that when this one-man army awoke from the anesthetic, he spotted a military policeman guarding the door. "Good God, what have I done now?" he exclaimed.)[2]

Up and down the sector being assaulted, tiny groups of Japanese broke through the outnumbered Americans and headed for the command posts located in the long barracks fronting the parade ground, as well as for Major Knudson's howitzers nearby. Artillery Private James J. Edgar was reloading his .50-caliber machine gun when a Japanese marine lunged toward him. The two began a fierce struggle for Edgar's gun. The Japanese finally got a tenacious hold on the barrel; Edgar squeezed the trigger and blew a gaping hole in the other man's midriff.

A few Japanese worked their way to a large barracks on Topside and pitched grenades into the space occupied by Captain Cracker Atkins, the regiment's supply officer, and several of his men. Four troopers were wounded by the explosions, but Atkins and his men, wearing only the undershorts in which they had been sleeping, grabbed their weapons and began blasting at the Japanese outside.

In the same barracks was the Rock Force CP. Bullets hissing into the building left no doubt in Colonel George Jones's mind that the Japanese force had broken through what, in conventional operations, would have been the rear area. The Warden grabbed his carbine, dashed out onto a second-floor balcony, and fired at Japanese darting about the parade ground. Shooting at the enemy soldiers alongside Jones was the deputy Rock Force commander, Lieutenant Colonel Jack Tolson, whose broken foot did not interfere with his marksmanship.

All during the Japanese assault, pack howitzers of the 462nd Parachute Field Artillery Battalion had been firing so frequently—often at pointblank range—that their barrels had become red hot. With the arrival of dawn, Captain Henry Gibson, leader of Battery B, received an urgent call for help. A force of Japanese that had broken through the Topside perimeter had holed up in a sturdy concrete building two hundred yards behind (north of) the long barracks housing Rock Force headquarters. Infantry efforts to root out the intruders had been beaten off by heavy fire.

In full view of the infiltrating enemy band, Captain Gibson took two howitzers and crews to an exposed knoll overlooking the bunker. With Gibson standing upright on the incline and directing the fire, several salvos of high explosive and incendiary shells were poured into the building from less than two hundred yards. When the fire lifted the parachute riflemen edged cautiously toward the smoking, silent structure. All eighty-five Japanese inside were dead.

A hush returned to Topside. Strewn about the landscape were the bodies of perhaps five hundred Imperial Marines who had given their all. A hasty check by Colonel Jones revealed that, despite the heavy gunfire and suicide charges, American losses by comparison had been moderate: thirty-three killed and seventy-six wounded. Japanese who had broken through the American permieter during the stampede were now in hiding all over Topside. Colonel Jones ordered patrols to search every building and to probe anew all the spider holes and other underground cavities. As a result, the remainder of the *banzai* force was hunted down and killed.

By mid-morning, Private First Class Park Hodak of the 462nd Parachute Field Artillery Battalion was seated on the parade ground next to his howitzer. A GI truck crawled past. In its bed were some fifteen dead paratroopers, lying face down and stacked like cordwood, one upon the other. Hanging out the rear were the dead youths' feet, clad in jump boots. The sight of his comrades being hauled en masse to a morgue sickened Hodak.

That afternoon, Captain Logan Hovis, surgeon of the 3rd Battalion, was making his daily visit to the morgue, which Captain Cracker Atkins had set up in the Topside theater. Each morgue call was a traumatic experience. As a combat doctor and as a civilian physician, Hovis had constantly been exposed to death and mutilation. But it still disturbed him that he never knew whether or not he would see the cold body of a friend sightlessly staring up at him when he pulled back a parachute shroud in the morgue. On this day he turned back a cover and was jolted by the dead body of Captain Emmet Spicer, surgeon of the 462nd Parachute Artillery and an especially close comrade. It had been Captain Spicer who recruited Hovis into the paratroops.

Shortly after dawn the following morning, a concealed Japanese machine gun began raking the parade-ground drop zone where troopers were gathering parachute supply bundles. Captain Henry Gibson soon detected the machine gun's position on a knoll a short distance south of his B Battery. Gibson ordered a crew to disassemble a howitzer and reassemble it on the porch of a wrecked officers's quarters. When the howitzer was ready to fire, it was found that a parachute canopy was dangling from the roof directly in line with the target. One trooper tried to dislodge the chute but could not. The Japanese machine-gun crew spotted the howitzer and began firing bullets into the building.

Despite the enemy fire, Private First Class John P. Prettyman leaped up on the porch railing, grabbed the dangling chute, and pulled on it with all his strength. Down it came. A split second later a burst of machine-gun fire stitched Prettyman across the stomach and chest. He toppled over the railing, mortally wounded. But his action cleared the way for the firing mission, and the howitzer took on the Japanese machine gun. It was not heard from again.

Once the shooting had slackened on Topside later in the day, Father John Powers celebrated mass on a makeshift altar outside a barracks. The thirty-four-year-old priest had been hit in the back upper thigh by a bullet while parachuting with the first wave on D-Day. Despite the pain, Father Powers had refused to be evacuated. Aware that informal casualty reports involving wounds that were not grievous or fatal were often laced by GI humor, the priest knew that his own entry had read: "Powers, Captain John J., shot in the ass."

One of the mass participants, Staff Sergeant Andrew J. Amaty, a former stevedore from Brooklyn, New York, noticed that Father Powers hesitated momentarily while he was facing the altar with both arms upraised. The priest turned slowly toward the paratroop congregation and, with his arms still upraised, stated, "I didn't get hit where you fellows said I did. It was nine inches below there." The troopers broke out laughing, and Father Powers continued as though the ad lib had been part of the mass.

There were occasional grim mementos of General Wainwright's last terrible days on The Rock in mid-1942. Down along Black Beach that day Corporal Joseph W. Sinclair, of Presque Island, Maine, was digging a foxhole for protection against repeated Japanese sniping. He came upon a heap of human bones and the rusted dogtag of a Philippine scout. Only a day earlier, Sinclair, a professional soldier who had spent three years on Corregidor before the war, had dug up a dogtag of a prewar comrade on The Rock.

That night on Topside, Staff Sergeant Walter F. Geiger, Jr., and Private First Class Francis D. "Whitey" Eggert, both mortarmen in Pug

Woods's battalion, were on guard duty along a road. Because they were to the rear of their infantry, they alternated keeping watch. Eggert discerned two dim figures approaching, but did not alert Geiger, who was half dozing on a parachute pack he was using as a pillow. Eggert thought the oncoming men were comrades and called out "Hi!" in a stage whisper. He realized his error immediately and whipped up his rifle. Geiger, on the ground, emerged from his partial slumber just in time to lunge to one side as his pillow was sliced in two by a saber. Eggert fired and a Japanese officer toppled over dead. His companion continued to hack at Geiger, inflicting deep cuts on his body and face, before he too was dropped by Eggert's rifle.

Daylight arrived a few hours later with the promise of increased violence on Corregidor. The Japanese were growing desperate. The all-out *Banzai* attack had been wiped out; Postlethwait's battalion atop Malinta Hill had cut the Japanese garrison in two; and drinking water was nearly gone, placing the remaining Japanese troops in danger of eventually perishing from thirst.

23
Holocaust at Monkey Point

The men of Rock Force were becoming increasingly nervous about being on top of the world's most enormous powder keg, and Colonel George Jones had just received evidence that their anxieties were fully justified. A captured enemy document revealed that the explosives stored underground were sufficient, if detonated at one time, to blow up most of Corregidor. Cached in tunnels and powder magazines were some 93,000 hand grenades, 80,000 mortar shells, 2,000,000 rounds of small-arms ammunition, 35,000 artillery shells, and hundreds of tons of dynamite. Colonel Jones and his S-2 kept this discovery to themselves.

Suddenly, at 11:30 P.M. on February 21, there was a powerful explosion inside Malinta Hill. Soldiers on the island later said it felt as though a supernatural force had grabbed the tiny island by its tail and shaken it vigorously. Flames rushed out of tunnel entrances, lighting up the horrified, ghostlike faces of exhausted Americans. Rocks and debris landed as far as two miles away. Men on ships ten miles out to sea could feel the concussion. Six of Postlethwait's men were buried alive by a landslide. Hundreds of Americans on Malinta Hill were knocked down and stunned, though they were unhurt.

Apparently, the Japanese had planned a limited explosion (according to a prisoner interrogated later) to confuse and distract the Americans on Malinta Hill and as a signal to many of the estimated two thousand of their number crammed into Malinta Tunnel to emerge and charge Postlethwait's dazed men. The remainder of the tunnel force was to use the confusion to scramble toward Corregidor's tail for a last stand. But things had gotten out of control, and the explosion had been much larger than planned. Several hundred Japanese defenders were blown up, while a small number tried to assault American positions guarding the hill only to be cut down by Postlethwait's men. A few hundred more bolted out of exits and managed to race eastward into the tail of the tadpole-shaped island fortress.

Meanwhile, the paratroopers on Topside had been involved in a continuing series of nasty clashes as they battled their way down cliff-sides, sealing up scores of caves as they went. Often Japanese rushed out of caves, hurled grenades, fired bursts from their rifles, then slipped back inside—where they would remain while men of the 161st Parachute Engineer Battalion buried them alive.

Throughout the struggle on Corregidor, American warplanes and ships had been of enormous help to Rock Force. There was usually at least one flight of P-47 fighter-bombers circling overhead, ready with five-hundred-pound bombs and napalm. The Thunderbolt flights worked in relays, and on those occasions when they were not overhead, a call to Mindoro air bases, one hundred and sixty miles to the south, brought them racing to the scene within ninety minutes.

On February 22, Japanese soldiers holed up in caves down the cliffs on Topside had inflicted several casualties on Big John Erickson's troopers. Advised of the stiff resistance there, Colonel Jones asked an offshore destroyer to fire her big guns into the openings. Then the Warden hurried to the site and stood at the edge of a cliff over the caves, five hundred feet above Manila Bay. Minutes later the destroyer's guns roared and shells screamed into the cave entrances. Jones could not see the explosions some two hundred and fifty feet below, but he did feel the cliff tremble. What a curious situation, the colonel reflected: standing *on top* of a bombardment target.

On the evening of February 23—D-Day plus 7—Colonel Jones was handed a casualty report by the Rock Force intelligence officer, Captain Francis X. Donovan, that disclosed that the Japanese on Corregidor had lost 2,466 men to date, nearly all of them killed. Hordes of others were sealed up in caves and underground chambers. But Rock Force casualties were growing: 118 killed and 314 wounded.

As expected, Japanese prisoners had been few—only six. One of these POWs was being interrogated by Captain Donovan through a nisei interpreter (an American soldier of Japanese descent). The enemy soldier was nearly delirious from thirst. To each question, he would reply, "Give me water! Give me water!"

"You son of a bitch," the nisei shouted in red-faced anger, "answer my questions and then maybe we'll give you a drink."

With the strength of desperation, the Japanese leaped onto the interrogator, threw him to the floor, and began trying to strangle him. Hearing the commotion from his office in the next room, Colonel Jones stepped to the door, saw the wrestling match in progress, and went back into his office. "Go in there and take care of it," he said to 1st Sergeant Carl N. Shaw.

After a while, Sergeant Shaw returned to Jones's office. "What did you do with the Nip?" the colonel inquired.

"I took care of him like you said," Shaw replied.

"What do you mean, you took care of him?"

"I buried him."

That night Colonel Jones was convinced that the western half of the island fortress was secure enough to launch operations that would wipe out the Japanese on the tail, or eastern portion. Pug Woods's 1st Battalion would jump off at 8:30 A.M., spearheading an attack down the narrow tail, with John Erickson's 3rd Battalion following. But there were still plenty of enemy soldiers holed up on the western half of The Rock, so Caskey's 2nd Battalion would mop up Topside, while Postlethwait's outfit would hold Malinta Hill, Middleside, and Bottomside.

Jones was concerned that a large Japanese force still in Malinta Tunnel might emerge to strike the Americans from the rear once the two parachute battalions had pushed on eastward. That concern was short-lived, however. Just before 3:00 A.M. on February 24, only a few hours before the tail assault was scheduled to jump off, a series of explosions again rocked Malinta Hill. The Japanese in the tunnel had committed suicide by blowing themselves up.

Led by Captain William Bossert's Company A, Woods's battalion started forward promptly at H-Hour. Up on Topside's parade ground, Major Knudson's nine pack howitzers, lined up hub to hub, pounded the terrain to the front of Woods's battalion and on both sides of the advancing paratroopers. PT boats and destroyers, anxious to get in their licks, edged in close to shore and poured fire into Japanese-held caves. Thunderbolt fighter-bombers, circling above, made continual strafing runs on the enemy in front of Woods's parachutists.

Advancing steadily against minimal opposition but past the bodies of scores of Japanese killed by artillery and mortar fire, bombs, shells, and napalm, Bossert's company reached Infantry Point on the northern shore of the tail. At the same time, Lieutenant Wirt R. Cates's Company B and Captain John P. Rucker's Company C had pushed forward to Camp Point, on the southern shore of the tail and almost directly below Infantry Point.

Earlier that day, the 2nd Battalion's D Company, decimated by the heavy fighting around Battery Wheeler, had edged down Topside's steep cliffs to the shoreline with orders to wipe out a stubborn band of Japanese in Cheney Ravine. Reaching the bottom, trooper Harry J. Drews and another scout had stumbled onto eight or nine Nipponese in a ditch. Drews and the other trooper had quickly raised their Tommy guns and raked the enemy squad. Moments later, a torrent of small-arms fire aimed at D Company erupted from caves on the side of the cliff just overhead.

With bullets hissing past, Drews was moving forward past the dead enemy soldiers in the ditch when something told him to turn around. He whirled to find himself facing a bleeding Japanese marine who had been feigning death. Drews dropped him with a burst of fire just as the marine hurled an object. Drews looked down and saw a grenade at his feet. Then there was a blinding explosion. Drews knew his right arm was bleeding profusely; his entire body felt extremely warm—no pain, just warmness. He knew he had been badly hurt and shook his head to clear the cobwebs from it. As he recovered from the shock of the explosion he became aware that he was staggering ahead clutching his

Tommy gun. Through his mind rang the phrase heard so many times in basic training by all soldiers: "*Never* lose your weapon in battle."

A short distance along Drews collapsed. He realized hazily that bullets were chipping the rock around his head and that bodies were falling from the cliffside above. While the firefight raged around him, two comrades rushed to Drews's side and dragged him behind a large boulder. He pulled down his trousers with his left hand (his right arm was broken), saw a large amount of bleeding between his legs, and figured (mistakenly) he had lost his genitals. Just before losing consciousness, Drews thought, "I don't mind dying—but not *this* way."[1]

As darkness fell over Corregidor, Colonel George Jones was sitting in a large bomb crater that was serving as the CP for Pug Woods's parachute battalion. In the bomb crater with Jones and Major Woods were a radio operator and a few other troopers. The Rock Force leader had been up front with Woods's men all day observing the progress of the operation to wipe out the remaining Japanese in the tail and was pleased with the day's results: only two thousand yards remained before the top of the tail was reached. Jones and Woods briefly reviewed plans for renewing the attack at dawn, then the Rock Force commander said he had to return to his CP on Topside.

"Why don't you stay here, Colonel?" the young major suggested. "Then you'll be on hand for the jump off."

"No, I've got to get back, Pug," Jones said. "One of General MacArthur's senior aides showed up at my CP unannounced this morning and acted very mysteriously. I've got to see what he wants." (Jones would learn later that Major General William Marquat had been there to prepare for an impending visit by General MacArthur.)

"You may not get back, Colonel," Woods stated. "It's getting dark, and if the Japs don't shoot you, one of our own itchy-fingered guys might do it."

"Well, Pug," Jones responded, "that's a chance I'm going to have to take."

Together with his orderly, Jones scrambled from the bomb crater and headed for Topside. It was a decision that would save the Rock Force commander's life. Unbeknownst to Colonel Jones as he left the crater, enemy mortarmen were about to pound Woods's positions in preparation for a *banzai* do-or-die charge by some six hundred Japanese soldiers congregated on Water Tank Hill that the Japanese commander in the tail hoped would smash through all the way to Topside.

After Jones had departed, Major Woods summoned his company commanders to brief them on the early morning attack. But Captain John Rucker of Company C was the only one who had arrived by 9:00 P.M., when enemy mortars opened fire. A shell plopped into the CP crater, killing Major Woods and wounding Rucker severely in the arm. Two battalion communications men, Private First Class Glen R. Knapp and Private First Class Roy E. Marston, were also killed, and two other men were wounded. Sergeant Matt Dallas, who had been sitting next to Major Woods, survived the blast unscathed.

Hugging the ground nearby during the barrage was Staff Sergeant Andy Amaty, the former New York City stevedore and now 1st Battalion communications chief, and Staff Sergeant Joseph Mills. Two hours previously, Amaty and Mills had been in the crater CP but had been asked to move by Pug Woods to make room for the arrival of the company commanders. Now, on his own initiative, Sergeant Amaty radioed an offshore destroyer and requested that illumination rounds be fired above the tail. (In the unorthodox Corregidor operation, a destroyer was assigned directly to each parachute assault company.) "It's dark as hell and a lot of Nips are forming up out in front of us," Amaty pointed out. The destroyer complied, bathing much of the tadpole tail in brilliant light, then ceased firing.

"Why'd you stop!" Amaty demanded to know.

"The Old Man says we can't fire any more."

"Why not?"

"Because the Old Man wants to save some flares for tomorrow night."

Sergeant Amaty was furious. Since the Navy man on the ship did not know his rank, the paratrooper demanded in an authoritative tone, "Put the Old Man on the radio immediately. We may not be around tomorrow night!"

There was a brief silence, then the same voice returned: "The Old Man says we'll resume firing flares, but will have to space them out more to conserve them."

"Okay," Amaty exclaimed brusquely, "but get on with it!" Despite the peril of their situation, Amaty and Mills broke out laughing over the "order" issued by a paratroop sergeant to an unknown Navy skipper.[2]

Major John N. Davis, Pug Woods's executive officer, took command of the battalion. Aware that the heavy enemy mortar barrage could be the forerunner of a massive *banzai* charge, Davis requested the 462nd Parachute Field Artillery to pound the terrain around Water Tank Hill. Minutes later Major Knudson's howitzers on Topside were raining shells onto the closely packed force of six hundred Japanese, cutting down more than half of them. Despite the slaughter, some two hundred of the survivors charged down Water Tank Hill toward paratrooper positions. A savage fight raged in the darkness for more than ninety minutes, but the Japanese could not penetrate Major Davis's lines, much less reach Topside, their ambitious objective. With dawn approaching, perhaps a hundred of the original six hundred-man *banzai* force pulled back farther into the tail.

Later that morning Davis's 1st Battalion jumped off to seize Water Tank Hill. Despite having lost some four hundred fifty men during the previous night's butchery, the defenders resisted tenaciously and launched several *banzai* charges that were bloodily repulsed by the smoking rifles and machine guns of the paratroopers and Knudson's howitzers. By 5:45 P.M. Davis's troopers had fought their way forward a thousand yards to a craggy ridge overlooking the short airstrip known to Americans as Kindley Field. As night fell, 1st Battalion positions stretched from Cavalry Point on the north shore of the tail southeast for seven hundred yards to the south shore at Monkey Point.

Few of Davis's exhausted troopers were aware of the historical significance of Monkey Point. Shortly before the outbreak of war, the U.S. Navy, strapped for funds, had pried loose enough money to construct a large tunnel under Monkey Point. This became known as the radio intercept tunnel and contained special electronic equipment developed for decoding top-secret Japanese messages. During the bleak early months of 1942, as the doomed Americans on Corregidor came under seige, enemy radio signals from throughout the Pacific were intercepted and decoded in the Monkey Point tunnel. The pirated information had made it possible for a weak American fleet to ambush and decimate a much larger and more powerful Imperial Navy force at Midway Island on June 6, 1942, thereby buying time for America to rearm.

Now, on the night of February 25, 1945, Captain Bill Bossert's Company A, whose CP had been rocked on an earlier occasion when the Japanese detonated an underground ammo dump on Topside, was slumped wearily on Monkey Point. The tunnel below them would be cleaned out in the morning. Most troopers, unaware that they were perched atop tons of explosives crammed into the radio intercept tunnel —the largest cache on Corregidor—fell into a fitful sleep on the hard, rocky surface.

At his blacked-out CP on Topside that night, Colonel George Jones, Major Thomas Stevens, the regimental surgeon, Major Ernie Clark, the Rock Force operations officer, and Captain Francis Donovan, the S-2, were relaxing briefly with a poker session augmented by slugs of "liberated" Japanese whisky. Colonel Jones was breathing a little easier, for it appeared that the worst of the blood-letting was over. Nearly thirty-eight hundred Japanese had been killed, in addition to the large numbers sealed in caves. Major John Davis had radioed in from Monkey Point and reported a significant slackening of enemy fire. Only about a thousand yards remained until Americans reached Hooker Point at the tip of the tail.

Shortly before 11:00 A.M. on February 26, Staff Sergeant Andy Amaty, the 1st Battalion communications chief, and Sergeant Matt Dallas were washing up for what Amaty quipped would be "the Corregidor Victory Parade." From his position on Monkey Point he could see Knudson's howitzer shells exploding on Kindley Field just to the north. Near Amaty a Sherman tank was firing into several caves.

Suddenly, an enormous explosion under Monkey Point rocked Corregidor and shook Bataan three miles to the north. Sergeant Amaty was engulfed by darkness. Scores of bodies, American and Japanese, were tossed into the air like rag dolls. Boulders, dirt, concrete, chunks of metal, and bits and pieces of what had been human torsos rained down from the sky. A mile and a half away, a paratrooper on Topside's parade ground was injured by a flying rock. A good-sized boulder struck a destroyer two thousand yards offshore. The thirty-ton Sherman tank that had been firing into caves was hurled nearly fifty feet, and the enormous heat from the explosion sealed its three-man crew inside.[3] The blast gouged out of mostly solid rock a crater nearly a hundred and fifty feet long, seventy-five feet wide, and thirty-two feet deep.

Lieutenant Rene E. Stievenart, a Company A platoon leader, had been standing directly on Monkey Point conferring by radio with Captain Bill Bossert, who was a hundred yards away. Stievenart was killed instantly. Bossert was knocked flat, covered with dirt, and suffered a broken rib and crushed chest. A few of Bossert's men dug him out before he suffocated. Major John Davis had been standing near the top entrance to the radio intercept tunnel and was tossed some thirty feet by the blast. He landed in a heap, dazed and gasping for breath. Private First Class Charles Burdick, a radioman who had been next to Davis, was also thrown a considerable distance, but only had the wind knocked out of him. Several hundred yards from the blast, 3rd Battalion surgeon Captain Logan Hovis was kneeling next to his ambulance and tending to a medical soldier who had a gaping wound in his chest. The medic was little more than a boy, and his life was ebbing away. Hovis was feeling sad and helpless when the blast shattered the relative calm and filled the air with debris. A falling chunk of rock penetrated the hood of the ambulance and destroyed the motor. Two medics sitting in the ambulance were unscathed.

Captain Hovis and his medics ran to the explosion site. There Hovis was shocked by the carnage. Butchered bodies were strewn about everywhere. Other men lay motionless, dead but with no visible marks on them, victims of concussion. Scattered across the ghastly landscape were arms, legs, heads, unidentifiable pieces of bone and flesh. Captain Hovis joined with the 1st Battalion surgeon, Captain William C. McLain, in tending to wounded paratroopers. It was often difficult to tell the living from the dead. McLain had been but a few feet from the edge of the blast and was nearly buried by dirt and debris. He was badly shaken but carried on with his medical duties.

All over Monkey Point paratroopers were frantically digging out comrades who were covered by dirt landslides but still alive. Meanwhile, Sergeant Andy Amaty, who had been knocked out by the blast, recovered consciousness and had the presence of mind to radio Colonel George Jones and report the disaster. "Put Major [John] Davis on," Jones directed.

"Major Davis is dead," Amaty replied. (Actually, Davis was alive but dazed.)

There was a brief silence, then the Rock Force commander said, "I'm sending Big John to relieve you [the decimated 1st Battalion]." "Big John" was Lieutenant Colonel Erickson, whose 3rd Battalion had been mopping up behind Davis's troopers.

Colonel Jones rushed to Monkey Point. Gazing at the scores of dead and mangled paratroopers, Jones had to fight back tears. Those killed by concussion appeared to be sleeping and, in his anguish, the colonel felt like calling out to them, "Get up, fellows, get up!"[4]

Despite his torment, the Rock Force commander did not allow the Monkey Point disaster to cloud his tactical judgment. He promptly ordered Big John Erickson to pass through the remnants of the 1st Battalion and continue the assault down the tail. Jumping off at once, Erickson's troopers overran Kindley Field against waning opposition and pushed two squads to the tip of the tail at East Point. Die-hard Japanese, holed up in caves on Hooker Point, a tiny sliver of rock less than a football field in length and lying a hundred yards off East Point, exchanged small-arms fire with Erickson's troopers.

In the meantime, Major John Davis had reorganized his shattered 1st Battalion and led it to Water Tank Hill, where it would spend the remainder of the night. The suicide blast had inflicted 196 casualties on the battalion, including 52 killed. Some 200 Japanese had blown themselves to pieces.

It had taken medical men, working at a feverish pace, more than two hours to clear the casualties from the Monkey Point area. Captain Bill McLain, the 1st Battalion surgeon, wrote of the horror: "As soon as I got all the casualties off, I sat down on a rock and burst out crying. I couldn't stop myself and didn't even want to. I had seen more than a man could stand and still stay normal. . . . When I had the cases to care for, that kept me going; but after that it was too much."

24

"Sir, I Present Fortress Corregidor."

The night of February 26 passed unenventfully. A hush had once more fallen over the tortured Rock. Hardly a shot was fired, but the American GIs on the tail were racked with anxiety. The specter of the enormous blast and disaster at Monkey Point was seared into them now. How many more caches of underground explosives were there below them?

Shortly after dawn, Captain Hoot Gibson, leader of Battery B, was atop Malinta Hill serving as a forward observer for the pack howitzers on Topside. Gibson could see for miles in every direction. On this morning, Japanese soldiers, knowing that the end was near on Corregidor, were trying to swim from the tail to Bataan, three miles across Manila Bay. Spotting a Japanese swimmer clinging to a log, Gibson watched as American machine gunners on Malinta Hill fired several bursts at the escapee. But the fugitive continued to paddle furiously, even though the strong current seemed to be holding him in place.

Beset with boredom, Captain Gibson decided to get into the act and ordered two howitzer shells to be fired at the Japanese soldier. The rounds exploded near him, but he kept going. Those at the observation post decided that the struggling enemy soldier was making a valiant effort to flee. "Hell, let the poor bastard go on!" someone suggested. But moments later a P-47 swooped down and riddled the hapless Japanese with its machine guns. Gibson saw the paddler slide off the log and disappear beneath the waves.

Destroyer and PT-boat crews were leery about fishing fleeing Japanese from the bay. Long ago the Americans had learned that a Japanese soldier or sailor often carried a hand grenade into the water and would blow himself up along with those trying to rescue him. So most of the Corregidor escapees were gunned down in the water.

One of those joining in the "Nip hunt" in Manila Bay was Lieutenant James R. Thomas, a pilot of the 462nd Parachute Field Artillery's Cub observation plane. In a paratroop outfit rife with colorful characters, Thomas was one of the most flamboyant. He packed a pair of pearl-handled revolvers and wore white silk laces in his jump boots. He had gone to flight school to be a fighter pilot, but one day couldn't resist the temptation of flying—upside down—under a railroad bridge. He had been booted out of flight school for his efforts, but his venturesome qualities earned him a home in a paratroop outfit, where feats of derring-do—including off-beat ones—were the norm.

Now Jim Thomas was having a field day over Manila Bay. Flying his Cub with one hand and clutching a Tommy gun in the other, he zipped back and forth over swimming Japanese soldiers and, leaning out the window, blasted the escapees with bursts from his machine gun. When a destroyer tried to usurp a swimmer Lieutenant Thomas had ear-marked for himself, he buzzed the ship at mast level, wig-wagging the Cub's wings until the naval gunners ceased firing.

By sundown of February 27, organized resistance on Corregidor had ceased. Rock Force G-2 Captain Francis Donovan reported 4,506 counted Japanese dead. But many hundreds more had been sealed into caves, and countless numbers had blown themselves to bits in the suicide explosions at Malinta Hill, Monkey Point, and elsewhere. Uncounted corpses had been shoved over Topside cliffs by bulldozers, and perhaps two hundred men had been killed trying to swim to Bataan. Altogether, some six thousand Japanese had died defending Corregidor—a figure dramatically higher than the original six to eight hundred enemy troops Sixth Army had estimated were manning the island fortress.

Even with Corregidor secure, lone Japanese soldiers fought on. On Hooker Point, the tiny rock a hundred yards from the tip of the tadpole's tail, a team of paratrooper flamethrowers cautiously slipped up to a cave and were greeted by a grenade that exploded in their faces. Inside, the last remaining Japanese on Hooker Point breathed defiance until burned to death by a flamethrower.

Paratroop First Sergeant Bernard M. O'Boyle, a former football player and amateur boxer, was a member of a patrol engaged in hunting down enemy stragglers. Suddenly, a shot rang out and a bullet plowed into the arm of Trooper Paul Knapp. O'Boyle, who billed himself as a member of "the Southside Chicago Irish," was bandaging his wounded comrade when the sniper fired again. The bullet detonated a grenade on Knapp's shoulder strap. Knapp was knocked to the ground, badly wounded, and the blast blew off O'Boyle's pack, cut his face, and left him stunned.

Bleeding and dazed, O'Boyle tagged along at the rear of the patrol. Hazily he heard someone call out, "Is O'Boyle still with us?" Just then a Japanese soldier popped up like a gopher from a nearby hole and, screaming *banzai*, pounced on the woozy Sergeant O'Boyle, slashing the American several times about his arms and wrists. Another trooper dispatched the enemy soldier with a bullet through the head.

Violent episodes such as this made Colonel Jones edgy, for Jones had learned that General Douglas MacArthur would soon visit embattled Corregidor. The vision of a die-hard Imperial Marine popping out of a spider hole and shooting the supreme commander left him little peace of mind.

As would be any commander, Colonel Jones was also concerned about the appearance of his troops for General MacArthur's visit. So he was elated on learning that his supply officer, Captain Cracker Atkins, had scrounged up a large number of new field uniforms, which were stacked in large piles outside the roofless barracks that housed the Rock Force CP.

Topside was a very crowded place. In a huge stockpile right in front of the Rock Force barracks, in addition to the new uniforms, were large stacks of artillery and mortar shells, hand grenades, small-arms ammunition, and more than ten tons of dynamite. Parked next to this mountain of explosives was a Japanese jeep. Colonel Jones cared little for war trophies, but he was proud of the jeep and intended to get it home one way or the other after the war.

Just before noon on February 28, Jones was in his office when he heard someone shout, "Smoke's pouring out of the white phosphorous grenades outside!" The WP grenades caught fire, and the blaze spread quickly to other munitions in the stockpile. Grenades began going off and shells exploded. Many on Topside thought the Rock Force CP was under attack by infiltrating Japanese. Colonel Jones was particularly concerned about wounded Americans in the dispensary at the far end of the long building, for the dynamite could ignite at any moment. He began shouting, "Clear the barracks! Clear the barracks!" Those inside needed no urging, and they began scrambling madly out the rear. After everyone had evacuated, Jones started to depart—just as the TNT erupted with an enormous roar. The building shook violently, and three of its concrete walls collapsed. The concussion from the blast knocked Jones out from under his helmet and flat on his face.

Jones, covered with dust, slowly got to his feet and looked out at the blast site. His jaw fell in disbelief. Nearly all of the new uniforms for MacArthur's imminent visit had been burned, and the coveted Japanese jeep—his sole war trophy—had been destroyed. The sun's heat had apparently ignited the stack of white phosphorous shells, causing Colonel Jones, in his frustration, to mutter, "The irritating part about this is that we can't blame it on the Japs."

But there was a bright note. Forewarned that the munitions stockpile was smoking, nearly everyone in the barracks and around it had scattered and taken cover. Only one man was injured in the blast, and that by a flying rock.

While grimy American fighting men were rooting out Japanese stragglers on Corregidor, forty miles to the northeast in Manila, General Douglas MacArthur was preparing to turn over the reins of government in the liberated Philippines to President Sergio Osmeña. Two weeks earlier, on February 12, *Newsweek* magazine had boasted in a screaming headline: PRIZE OF THE PACIFIC, MANILA, FELL TO MACARTHUR LIKE RIPENED PLUM. If indeed it had been a ripened plum, the plum was now saturated with American and Japanese blood.

More than three weeks after Mudge's 1st Cavalry Division had knifed across the northern city limits, on February 3, the savage, no-holds-barred fight for Manila continued to rage. Relentless building-to-building, room-to-room violence, along with constant pounding by artillery and mortars, had turned the Pearl of the Orient into piles of charred rubble. Endless blocks of homes were in ruins. Most buildings were gutted. Everywhere piles of broken glass had spilled out into the streets. Seventy-five percent of the factories and eighty percent of the utilities were razed. Of all the great cities of Europe demolished during the war, only Warsaw suffered more extensively.

In a vain effort to spare civilian lives, General MacArthur had prohibited bombing Manila from the outset. But the only way he could keep American soldiers from being slaughtered and overcome the enemy's fanatical resistance was to blast Japanese positions with tank and artillery fire. Perhaps the most vicious hand-to-hand fighting occurred in the Commonwealth Government structures and in the once-ornate apartments, private clubs, and hotels along Dewey Boulevard.

Few civilian populations anywhere endured more intense pain and horrors than did Manila's. Some one hundred thousand Filipinos in the capital were already dead, killed by artillery and bullets or murdered by the doomed Japanese garrison. There were verified reports of patients being tied to beds and hospitals set afire, or males having their sexual organs hacked off and women being gang-raped before they were killed. Hysterical Filipina mothers told of their babies being snatched from their arms and then being forced to watch soldiers bash their infants' brains.

Surrounded by this scene of utter destruction and violence, General Douglas MacArthur made his way through the rubble-strewn streets to Malacañan Palace on February 27. The morning air reeked of decomposing bodies. Large, elegant buildings were now little more than charred shells. The once beautiful trees that had lined Manila's magnificent boulevards were only good for kindling. Yet, curiously, Malacañan Palace had been virtually untouched, its beautiful crystal chandeliers, stained windows, and ornate carvings remaining intact.

Escorted by senior officers, MacArthur strode briskly into the state reception room amid the glare of photographers's floodlights. Gathered solemnly before a rostrum were President Osmeña, his cabinet, and top government officials. The atmosphere was charged with suspense; all present knew that one of the war's most dramatic events was about to take place: the return of government to the Filipinos. (A brief ceremony at Tacloban, Leyte, a few months earlier had been but a stopgap measure, mainly for propaganda purposes.)

The supreme commander walked to a battery of microphones that would carry his historic words throughout the Philippines and around the world. For a few moments he stood there silently. Only his confidants knew that he was struggling to maintain his composure. General Courtney Whitney's thoughts harkened back to a remark made to him by MacArthur while inspecting a hospital: "It kills something inside me to see these boys die."[1] And die they had—by the thousands—to make this moment possible. Whitney thought back, too, to the officer who had entered MacArthur's office in Australia the day Bataan had fallen and seen tears streaming down the supreme commander's cheeks.[2]

A hush fell over the sumptuous reception room with its red embroidered draperies and sparkling chandeliers as Douglas MacArthur finally began to speak in an even tone:

"Mr. President, more than three years have elapsed—years of bitterness, struggle, and sacrifice—since I withdrew our forces from this beautiful city that, open and undefended, its churches, monuments, and cultural centers might be spared the violence of military ravage. The enemy would not have it so, and much that I sought to preserve has been unnecessarily destroyed by his desperate action at bay; but by these ashes he has wantonly fixed the future pattern of his own doom."

General MacArthur's voice broke. Tears were flowing down President Osmeña's face and those of other Filipinos in the room. Tough-minded American combat commanders had lumps in their throats. MacArthur regained his composure and resumed speaking. "Then we were but a small force struggling to stem the advances of overwhelming hordes, treacherously hurled against us behind the mask of professed friendship. . . . That struggle was not in vain. God has blessed our arms. The unleashed power of America, supported by our allies, turned the tide of battle in the Pacific, culminating in the redemption of your soil and the liberation of your people. My country has kept the faith. . . ."

MacArthur, on behalf of the United States government, then returned the constitutional power of the Commonwealth to President Osmeña and the Filipino people. "Your capital city, cruelly punished though it be, has regained its rightful place—citadel of democracy in the East."

Early on the morning of March 2, General MacArthur led an entourage of high brass onto four PT boats for the triumphant return to Corregidor. The supreme commander, in a buoyant mood, remarked jovially to Lieutenant Joseph Roberts, skipper of PT-373, "So this is the 373. I left (Corregidor) in John Bulkeley's 41." Going along were General Walter Krueger of Sixth Army, General Chink Hall of XI Corps, Air Corps General George Kenney, a few admirals, and a group of officers who called themselves the "Bataan Gang" (they had been with MacArthur there and had escaped Corregidor with him).

At 10:00 A.M. the four PT boats edged into North Dock on Bottomside. Whatever MacArthur's emotions were on returning to The Rock, he carefully masked them. Corregidor looked different after nearly three years. The heavy bombings and the Japanese dynamite explosions had even altered the contours of the hills and ridges. Pointing with his corncob, MacArthur said, "Gentlemen, Corregidor is living proof that the day of the fixed fortress is over."

Hopping into a jeep driven by paratroop Corporal Sims H. Smith, General MacArthur went first to Malinta Tunnel, his headquarters during the agony at Bataan nearly three years earlier. MacArthur promptly walked into the entrance of the burned-out tunnel. They were anxious moments for Colonel George Jones, the Rock Force commander, who could not be certain that there were no Japanese still inside.[3]

MacArthur's jeep cavalcade rolled on to Battery Wheeler on Topside, where the bloodiest fighting of the operation had raged. From there it was on to the bomb-battered Administration Building, where the supreme commander inspected his old office and noted that there was a gaping hole where his desk had once been. Then the little convoy packed with generals and admirals drove to the parade ground, where an honor guard had been drawn up with representatives from each unit that had fought on The Rock.

MacArthur alighted and glanced around at the white and camouflaged parachutes still dangling from trees and wrecked buildings. Brightly colored equipment canopies flapped in the breeze where they hung, their cargoes of guns and ammunition having been cut from their lines under Japanese fire. Bordering the parade ground stood the old Corregidor flag pole, a slightly bent, bomb-scarred ship's mast with twisted rigging and ladders hanging from its yardarm.

The supreme commander walked briskly to where Colonel Jones stood at the head of the battle-weary honor guard in their soiled and torn uniforms. Many were wearing bandages. Jones saluted and said, "Sir, I present to you Fortress Corregidor."

Speaking under a brilliant blue sky, MacArthur declared that Rock Force had carried out "one of the boldest and most daring feats in military history." He paid tribute to those Americans who had fought and suffered and died three years earlier. "Bataan, with Corregidor the citadel of its integral defense," he said, "made possible all that has happened here. History, I am sure, will record it as one of the decisive battles of the world. Its long protracted struggle enabled the Allies to gather strength. Our triumphs today [in the Philippines] belong equally to that dead army. . . . Let no man henceforth speak of it other than as a magnificent victory."

MacArthur paused briefly, then said, "I see the old flagpole still stands." Looking at Colonel Jones, himself gripped with intense pride, the supreme commander said, "Have your troops hoist the colors to the peak, and let no enemy ever haul them down."

Standing in the front row with company and battery commanders, Captain Henry Gibson felt a lump form in his throat and knew that his eyes were misty. A hundred yards away, Captain Bill Bossert, who had been gravely injured in the Monkey Point suicide blast, was lying outside the surgical hospital on a cot. His eyes, too, filled with tears.

Two weeks after the 503rd Parachute Infantry Regiment and attached units had bailed out of Gooney Birds onto this same parade ground, paratrooper Corporal Donald G. Bauer of Dayton, Ohio, raised the Stars and Stripes to the peak of the warped pole. As hundreds of

American eyes watched Old Glory waving in the breeze, proud were hearts filled with grief over the heavy price paid to repurchase Corregidor: 223 killed, 1,107 wounded or injured—nearly one-third of Rock Force.

On March 8, Colonel George Jones's troopers filed down to the Bottomside beaches, where they boarded LSMs for a return to their base on southern Mindoro. As the vessels pulled away from bloody, war-torn Corregidor, very few of the paratroopers looked back.

Epilogue

The retaking of Corregidor, Manila, and Bataan by no means concluded the savage bloodletting in the Philippines. But General MacArthur's forces had secured the principal strategic prizes—the Central Plains and Manila Bay regions of Luzon, whose airfields, naval bases, and ports could serve as facilities for mounting the forthcoming invasion of Japan.

Hardly had the final shot been fired on Corregidor than MacArthur, without bothering to obtain approval from the Joint Chiefs of Staff, launched invasions of seven Philippine islands: Negros, Cebu, Panay, Zamboanga, Palawan, Tawitawi, and Guimaras. At each of these locales, the Japanese fought bitterly to the death. The Joint Chiefs, in effect, read of these invasions in the newspapers and, faced with a fait accompli, could only give their retroactive approval.

In the meantime, General Tomoyuki Yamashita had pulled back his remaining forces on Luzon into the nearly impenetrable mountains of the north, where for months he resisted American efforts to dig him out. When the war ended in August, the Tiger of Malaya came down from the mountains to surrender. With him were 50,500 fully armed and organized troops who would have held out to the death if ordered to do so.

On December 26, 1944, General MacArthur had enraged the fighting men of General Bob Eichelberger's Eighth Army by announcing that "the Leyte campaign is closed except for mopping up." For four months afterward, Eichelberger's weary, hollow-eyed men would be locked in some of the most bitter and exhausting fighting of the Pacific war, suffering heavy casualties in the course of killing some 27,000 Japanese.

For Douglas MacArthur, the return to the Philippines was the dramatic fulfillment of a sacred pledge; for the Japanese Imperial General Staff, the Philippines was a disaster. In the *sekigahara* (decisive battle) of the Pacific war, Japan lost 100,000 experienced troops and saw another 280,000 scattered and isolated throughout the archipelago, unable to join in the defense of the homeland. The Imperial Navy and Air Force, except for the *kamikazes*, were virtually wiped out. There were millions of Japanese soldiers still under arms, but they had been cut off from supplies of crucial raw materials in the East Indies. (After the war, Japanese Navy Minister Mitsumasa Yonai told American interrogators: "When you took the Philippines, that was the end of our resources.") All the Japanese empire could do now was to delay the inevitable: total defeat.

On April 3, the Joint Chiefs of Staff reorganized the Pacific command for the looming invasion of Japan (code-named Operation Downfall). The previous designations of Southwest Pacific (MacArthur) and Pacific Ocean Areas (Nimitz) were abolished. Instead of a joint operation under one supreme commander (such as Eisenhower was given for the D-Day invasion of France), the Pacific command was split into three parts. MacArthur was put in charge of ground forces, Nimitz in command of naval forces, and they were to cooperate closely with Lieutenant General Curtis LeMay, chief of the B-29 Superfortresses that had been pounding Japan's home islands.

This arrangement apparently pricked the vanities of America's brass in the Pacific. When a mid-April strategy conference was held on Guam, a meeting with all the trappings of an international diplomatic summit, controversy erupted, renewing the Pacific command struggle that had alternately raged and subsided since early 1942. Navy brass declared that MacArthur was trying to seize control of Downfall and relegate the Navy to a supporting role. Admiral Nimitz and Air Corps General George Kenney got into a squabble as to which branch could bomb ships ten miles off the Japanese mainland. MacArthur told General Eichelberger that the Navy wanted to control all Pacific positions after the war and consign the Army to "something of a home guard."

Meanwhile, off the island of Okinawa, a stone's throw by Pacific distances from the mainland, waves of *kamikazes* struck the U.S. fleet relentlessly all through April, May, and June, even as a great slaughter was taking place on shore (where some 120,000 Japanese would die). It was by far the worst pounding an American fleet had ever taken: scores of vessels, from battleships and carriers to landing craft, were sunk or severely damaged. Thousands of American naval personnel were killed or wounded.

Deep concern over this mass-suicide tactic gripped those at the highest levels of the government and the Pentagon. Only on April 12 was the *kamikaze* news blackout lifted and the homefront informed of this frightening new hazard in the Pacific. But what should have been blockbuster news, one of the great stories of World War II, hardly made a public ripple, because on that same day, President Roosevelt died.

In Manila, General MacArthur was informed by an aide, Colonel Bonner Fellers, of the president's death. The general had never forgiven Roosevelt for the signals sent to Corregidor in those black days of early 1942, signals that MacArthur had interpreted as meaning massive military help was on the way to the Battling Bastards of Bataan. "So Roosevelt is dead," the general mused to Colonel Fellers. "Now there's a man who would never tell the truth when a lie would serve just as well."[1]

In late July, the Allies's Big Three (President Harry S. Truman, Prime Minister Winston S. Churchill, and Premier Josef Stalin) issued the Potsdam Declaration, threatening Japan with total destruction if she did not surrender. The ultimatum was ignored by the military clique in control.

As a result, with America's impending invasion of mainland Japan, the world stood on the brink of the greatest massacre since the days of Ghengis Kahn. Set for November 1, 1945, Operation Downfall would begin with an assault on Kyushi by three-quarters of a million American fighting men. The battle would be savage. Douglas MacArthur informed the Joint Chiefs that American forces alone would suffer in excess of one million casualties before Japan was brought to her knees.

Even more Japanese soldiers would lose their lives, along with millions of civilians.

The Nipponese would bitterly contest every foot of their sacred soil. Ten thousand *kamikaze* planes were ready to strike at invading ships; young pilots outdid one another in their zeal to volunteer for the suicide missions. Hundreds of *Shinyo* suicide craft, each armed with a 4,406-pound warhead fused to detonate on impact, were concealed in coves, ready for action. Scores of one-man suicide torpedoes were scattered along the coastlines.

Under arms on the home islands were 2,350,000 soldiers, 250,000 garrison troops, and 32,000,000 men and women of the militia. Males between fifteen and sixty and females between seventeen and forty-five had been drafted and, together with children, instructed on how to tie explosives to their bodies, scramble under American tank treads, and blow up the tanks—and themselves. All over the Japanese home islands caves and building basements had been stocked with ammunition, explosives, and food, and from these hiding places tiny bands would resist the invaders until they were wiped out.

On August 6, a lone B-29 Superfortress, piloted by Colonel Paul Tibbetts, dropped what was later described to an awed world as an atom bomb on the industrial city of Hiroshima. Casualties were enormous: Some 60,000 killed, 20,000 injured, perhaps 160,000 left homeless. Yet these casualties were but a fraction of the number that would have been killed and wounded on both sides had America been forced to invade Japan.

At noon on August 15, diminutive, soft-spoken Emperor Hirohito, the ruler regarded as a god by the Japanese, took to Radio Tokyo to announce that the empire was surrendering. The emperor's declaration stunned the Japanese people and set off a flurry of ceremonial *hara-kiri* suicides by generals and admirals. One was Admiral Takijiro Onishi, "father" of the Special Attack Corps, the *kamikazes*. That night he composed a note: "To the souls of my late subordinates [the suicide pilots] I express the greatest appreciation for their valiant deeds. In death I wish to apologize to these brave men and their families." Then he ripped open his abdomen with a samurai sword.

In the early months after the surrender, 1,128 Japanese were put on trial by the conquerors for "crimes against peace," a charge open to interpretation. "Crimes against peace" was retroactive, a "law" that had not been in existence at the time the defendants were said to have violated it. At trials held in Tokyo, 174 men were sentenced to death, a figure later whittled down to seven, including former Premiers Tojo and Koki Hirota. (Tojo tried, unsuccessfully, to escape the hangman's noose by committing suicide.) The seven went to the gallows shouting "*Banzai!*"

Douglas MacArthur's foes on Luzon, General Masaharu Homma in 1942 and General Tomoyuki Yamashita in 1944–45, were tried by a tribunal of American Army officers in the huge reception hall of the Manila high commissioner's residence. The courtroom was packed with Filipinos furious over the destruction of Manila and the deaths of loved ones.

Second- and even third-hand hearsay was admissible as proof under the rules of evidence. American propaganda films were shown as evidence. Homma had been specifically charged in regard to the infamous Bataan Death March in 1942, and while indisputable savageries had been committed by individuals and groups, there was no hard evidence linking General Homma to the atrocities. Along with other charges, Yamashita was held responsible for brutalities in Manila in September 1944, at which time he was in command of an army in Manchuria, several thousand miles away.

Generals Homma and Yamashita were found guilty on the grounds that they had held command responsibility. Before the verdict came in, twelve American reporters who had sat through the trial held a poll and decided 12 to 0 for the Japanese defendants.

General MacArthur reviewed the evidence against his former Philippine adversaries and approved the verdicts. In the early morning hours of February 23, 1946, Tomoyuki Yamashita was hanged at Los Baños, the town twenty-five miles below Manila near where the 11th Airborne Division raiding party and Filipino guerrillas had rescued over two thousand civilians from an internment camp a year earlier. A week later, Masaharu Homma was executed by gunfire in the same courtyard.

On New Year's Day of 1946, nearly ten months after Colonel George Jones and his 503rd Parachute Infantry Regiment had departed from conquered Corregidor, a soldier in an American Graves Registration Company posted on The Rock looked up and blinked his eyes in disbelief. Coming toward him was a file of Japanese soldiers, eighteen or twenty of them, waving white pieces of cloth in surrender. They appeared to be well fed and healthy, and had been living underground. While venturing outside to get water one night, a soldier had discovered an old newspaper, and for the first time the hold-outs learned of Japan's capitulation.

Today, as it has been for many years, Corregidor is a mecca for tourists from all over the world. Excursion boats leave Mariveles on Bataan and circle The Rock. From Corregidor Inn on Bottomside, tour buses run daily. American veterans of the bitter fighting return to view the scene of their ordeal. Japanese civilians still come, looking in vain for the burial sites of loved ones.

As with many battlefields hallowed by death and disaster, Corregidor today has a haunting, almost eerie quality. At night on dark, silent Topside and Malinta Hill, where American GIs once fought off screaming *banzai* charges, visitors hear the gentle rustling of sea breezes. But on occasion, they swear, out there somewhere in the blackness, can be heard the hoarse voices of the Ghosts of Corregidor, crying out in anguish.

Notes and Sources

Prologue

1. William Manchester, *American Caesar* (Boston: Little Brown, 1978), p. 238.
2. Ibid., p. 239.
3. Ibid., p. 239.
4. John Toland, *The Rising Sun* (New York: Random House, 1970), p. 286.
5. Rear Admiral John D. Bulkeley told the author in late 1985 that the one thing that stands out in his memory forty-three years later was Jean MacArthur's exceptional courage during the dash through the Japanese air and naval blockade around Corregidor. Lieutenant Commander Bulkeley received the Medal of Honor from President Roosevelt for getting MacArthur out, and for other feats in the Philippines.
6. Manchester, *American Caesar*, p. 270.

Chapter 1: Confrontation With "Mr. Big"

1. Manchester, *American Caesar*, p. 364.
2. Robert L. Eichelberger, *Our Jungle Road to Tokyo* (New York: Viking, 1950).
3. Manchester, *American Caesar*, p. 364.
4. *Time* magazine, August 12, 1944.

5. Details of this crucial conference were assembled from many sources, including Admiral William D. Leahy's *I Was There* (New York: McGraw-Hill, 1950).
6. Leahy, *I Was There*.
7. President Roosevelt no doubt was especially conscious of casualties at this point. Worldwide, American dead and wounded were piling up at a rate of ten thousand each week. In addition, four sons of President and Mrs. Roosevelt were combat officers. General George Marshall's stepson, a tank captain, had been killed recently, as had been the sons of former ambassador to Great Britain Joseph P. Kennedy, Sr., presidential confidant Harry Hopkins, and Senator Leverett Saltonstall.
8. Leahy, *I Was There*, p. 251.
9. Manchester, *American Caesar*, p. 256.

Chapter 2: Guerrillas, Spies, and Saboteurs
1. Courtney Whitney, *MacArthur: His Rendezvous With History* (New York: Alfred A. Knopf, 1956), p. 144.
2. Ibid., p. 146. Douglas's father, General Arthur MacArthur (1845–1912), had been a famous soldier, received the Medal of Honor, and once served in the Philippines.
3. Allison Ind, *Allied Intelligence Bureau*.
4. Ibid.
5. Whitney, *MacArthur*, pp. 144–145.
6. Ind, *Allied Intelligence Bureau*.

Chapter 3: American Eagles Soar Over Manila
1. William F. Halsey, *Admiral Halsey's Story* (New York: McGraw-Hill, 1947), p. 199.
2. Harold Stassen was elected governor of Minnesota after the war, and served as Special Assistant for Disarmament to President Eisenhower. In 1948 and 1952 he unsuccessfully sought the Republican presidential nomination.
3. Halsey, *Halsey's Story*, p. 202.
4. This story of the boasting Japanese officer was told to Admiral Halsey when he visited Clark Field nine months later.
5. Halsey, *Halsey's Story*, p. 203.
6. George C. Kenney, *General Kenney Reports* (New York: Duell, Sloan and Pearce, 1949), p. 156.
7. Halsey, *Halsey's Story*, p. 206.
8. *Time* magazine, August 27, 1944.

Chapter 4: "The Empire's Fate Is at Stake"

1. After the war, Ruperto Kangleon became Secretary of National Defense to the Philippine Republic, and later a senator.
2. MacArthur had chosen the term "A-Day" to differentiate it in the public mind from the highly publicized D-Day in Normandy. "Eisenhower monopolized D-Day," MacArthur told his staff. MacArthur and his one-time aide, Eisenhower, now both four-star generals, were not mutual admirers.
3. A Japanese communiqué reported that Admiral Arima had "lit the fuse for the ardent wishes of his men" by intentionally crashing his Zero into the carrier *Franklin*.
4. *Time* magazine, October 26, 1944.
5. Halsey, *Halsey's Story*, p. 206. After the war, Halsey said that when he landed in Tokyo, he intended to call on the zoo keeper and inspect the monkey cage that had been reserved for him, but "I never got around to it."
6. Much of the detail in the capture of the four islands was furnished the author by Colonel Robert W. Garrett (Ret.), of suburban Washington, D.C., who led the 6th Ranger Battalion there, and by Ranger Historian Harry Pearlmutter of New York City.
7. Whitney, *MacArthur*, p. 154.
8. Toland, *The Rising Sun*, p. 573.
9. Manchester, *American Caesar*, p. 382.
10. Captain Rikihei Inoguchi and Commander Tadash Nakajim, *Death on the Wing*.

Chapter 5: "Believe It or Not, We're Back!"

1. Whitney, *MacArthur*, p. 155.
2. Ibid., p. 156.
3. Shortly after the war ended, the 7th Cavalry Regiment was commanded by Lieutenant Colonel Brice C. W. Custer, a great-grand-nephew of George A. Custer of Little Big Horn renown.
4. Manchester, *American Caesar*, p. 386.
5. Toland, *The Rising Sun*, p. 541.
6. Kenney, *Reports*, p. 448.

Chapter 6: Death of the Mighty *Musashi*

1. Kenney, *Reports*, pp. 451, 454–455.
2. Ibid., p. 452.

3. Samuel Eliot Morison, *The Liberation of the Philippines* (Boston: Little, Brown, 1969), pp. 179–193.

3. Samuel Eliot Morison, *The Liberation of the Philippines* (Boston: Little, Brown, 1969), pp. 179–193.
4. Ibid., pp. 169–174.
5. Lou Varrone, Medal of Honor historian, to author. Later President Roosevelt pinned the Medal of Honor on Commander David McCampbell for his feats that day. In late 1985 McCampbell was retired and living in Florida.
6. Halsey, *Halsey's Story*, p. 215. Captain Hoskins was fitted with an artificial foot and requested command of the new *Princeton*. He pointed out that he was "one foot up" on other applicants for the post. Hoskins put the new *Princeton* in commission and was later promoted to rear admiral.

Chapter 7: "Where in Hell Are Their Carriers?"

2. Halsey, *Halsey's Story*, p. 216.
3. Ibid., p. 217.
4. Ibid., p. 217.
5. Sources: Edwin P. Hoyt, *Battle of Leyte Gulf* (New York: Weybright and Talley, 1972). John Costello, *The Pacific War* (New York: Rawson Wade, 1981). Morison, *Liberation*.
6. Whitney, *MacArthur*, p. 162.
7. Morison, *Liberation*.
8. Halsey, *Halsey's Story*, p. 218.
9. Costello, *The Pacific War*, p. 127.
10. Halsey, *Halsey's Story*, p. 220.
11. For many years U.S. Navy brass were uncertain why Admiral Kurita suddenly broke off the fight against Sprague's much lighter force and fled from Leyte Gulf. Admiral John D. Bulkeley in late 1985 told the author: "During the Korean War, a Japanese navy captain named Hara met me [at his request] in Sasebo [Japan]. This officer told me that his was the last Japanese destroyer to get out of the Surigao Strait battle that night, and had managed to get a signal to Kurita that the Southern Force had been virtually wiped out. So Kurita fled because he thought his Central Force would be destroyed also." (Note: two or three warships in the Southern Force had not yet reached Surigao Strait when the remainder of the force was annihilated.)
12. George C. Kenney, *The MacArthur I Knew* (New York: Duell, Sloan and Pearce, 1954), p. 170.

Chapter 8: Bloodbath at Breakneck Ridge

1. Lou Varrone to author. Private Leonard C. Brostram later received the Medal of Honor.
2. Lou Varrone to author. Sergeant Charles E. Mower was posthumously awarded the Medal of Honor.
3. Manchester, *American Caesar*, p. 397.
4. Ibid., p. 398.
5. D. Clayton James, *The Years of MacArthur* (Boston: Houghton Mifflin, 1975), Vol. II, p. 606.
6. Jay Luvaas, *Dear Miss Em* (Westport, CT: Greenwood Press, 1972), p. 119.

Chapter 9: Japanese Paratroopers in Suicide Jump.

1. Manchester, *American Caesar*.
2. Author interview with Colonel Henry A. Burgess (Ret.).
3. Author interview with Colonel Kenneth A. Murphy (Ret.).
4. Author interview with Colonel Henry A. Burgess (Ret.).
5. Colonel Kenneth Murphy saw much action as a battalion commander in the Korean War. He told the author in 1985 that the chaotic night at San Pablo airstrip was "one of the worst times I ever spent."
6. Private Ova A. Kelly was posthumously awarded the Medal of Honor.

Chapter 10: Killer Typhoon.

1. Although General Suzuki no doubt knew that Leyte was lost, he continued to hold out and launch raids against American forces until his death on April 16, 1945. By holding out, Suzuki pinned down several U.S. divisions badly needed elsewhere on the road to Tokyo.
2. Lou Varrone to author. Private First Class Elmer E. Fryar received the Medal of Honor posthumously.
3. Manchester, *American Caesar*, p. 405.
4. *New York Times*, December 18, 1944.

Chapter 11: Rain of Human Bombs

1. Manchester, *American Caesar*, p. 406.
2. William Manchester interview with Roger O. Egeberg.

Chapter 12: On to Manila!

1. Even in the mid-1980s, the memory of Douglas MacArthur evokes reverence among thousands of World War II-era Filipinos.

2. Due to the darkness and mass confusion, no accurate count could be made of the number of suicide boats involved or destroyed that night. After the war, Japanese naval officers said that all seventy boats concealed at Port Saud had attacked, and that most had been destroyed.

3. Many Army officers have maintained that the foremost requirement for an effective chief of staff is that he "be an SOB."

4. Luvaas, *Miss Em.* This private observation was a low blow. No one had ever questioned General Krueger's courage, and he was regularly at the front.

5. Manchester, *American Caesar*, p. 412

6. Long after the war, some MacArthur confidants were still bitter over this decision. They remained convinced that the huge stockpiles of American war materiel piled up at Vladivostok were used to support the North Korean Communists against the Americans a few years later.

Chapter 13: Rescuing the Ghosts of Bataan
1. Author interview with Robert W. Prince.
2. Lieutenant Colonel Henry Mucci and Captain Robert Prince were awarded Distinguished Service Crosses for the rescue. Each other officer got the Silver Star and each enlisted man received the Bronze Star.
3. *Time*, February 12, 1945.
4. Some information in this chapter was furnished to the author by Ranger historian Harry Pearlmutter.

Chapter 14: A Mad Dash for the Capital
1. A "stick" is an arbitrary number of men jumping out of the same airplane, usually numbering fifteen to eighteen troopers in a C-47.
2. *Time*, February 12, 1945.
3. *Life* magazine, February 12, 1945.
4. *Life*, February 19, 1945.

Chapter 15: The Pacific War's Strangest Episode
1. U.S. Army in World War II, *Return to the Philippines* (Washington: Government Printing Office, 1952), pp. 427–432.
2. *Life*, February 19, 1954.
3. Whitney, *MacArthur*, p. 189.

Chapter 16: Assault on the Genko Line

1. It was not until a chance encounter in 1977—thirty-two years after the episode—that Jerard Vlaminck learned the identity of the comrade who had saved his life. For his part, Richard Sibio told the author in 1985, Sibio thought all those years that he had rescued another comrade, not Vlaminck.

2. Private First Class Manuel Perez, Jr., was posthumously awarded the Medal of Honor. The citation credited him with killing eighteen Japanese during his rampage. Nonsense, said his comrades in 1985—the figure should be seventy-five or more. When asked in 1985 how many of the eleven bunkers facing his company did Manny Perez clean out, a platoon comrade who saw it all replied, "Every bleeping one of them!"

3. General Douglas MacArthur, *Reminiscences* (New York: McGraw-Hill, 1964), p. 214.

Chapter 17: Angels From Heaven

1. Henry A. Burgess, an attorney in Sheridan, Wyoming, told the author in 1985 that Peter Miles contributed more to the success of the Los Baños raid than any other single person with regard to providing intelligence.

2. Asked by the author in 1985 if there had *really* been any doubt in his mind over the tiny drop zone, John Ringler replied tersely, "No."

Chapter 18: "We're Jumping on Corregidor!"

1. As only a handful of Japanese defenders survived Corregidor, it has been impossible to determine the amount of damage to guns and installations caused by this enormous rain of explosives. But apparently the bombardment had little physical effect on the Japanese who remained underground in bunkers, caves, and tunnels.

Chapter 19: Onslaught From the Sky

1. Monsignor John Powers, who in late 1985 was living in Palo Alto, California, quipped to the author, "I was far more courageous out of my head than in it."

2. In 1985 Karl H. "Doc" Landes was living in New York City and teaching chemistry daily. He told the author that, at seventy-eight, he was "the oldest living veteran of Corregidor."

3. Brigadier General George Madison Jones (Ret.) lives in Tucson, Ari-

zona. He told the author in 1985, "If the splinter had hit only a few inches farther up, I would be talking to you now a pitch or two higher."

4. Captain Frederick Pope, Jr., battery commander in the 462nd Parachute Field Artillery Battalion, and Emmet Spicer's best friend, recovered the medical tag the parachute doctor had filled out on himself as he was dying. In 1985 the tag is part of a memorial set up for Dr. Spicer years after the war at the University of North Carolina School of Medicine, which Spicer had attended.

5. From 1957–1961 William E. Blake was Adjutant General of the State of West Virginia.

Chapter 20: Ape-like Climb up Malinta Hill

1. After the war, John J. Tolson eventually rose to three-star rank and command of the XVIII Airborne Corps. When he retired in 1973 Tolson was deputy commanding general of the Continental Army Command.

Chapter 21: No Quarter Asked or Given

1. Author interview with John Bartlett.

Chapter 22: "Ban-zai!"

1. Colonel Jones never saw his orderly again. He told the author in 1985 that he still would like to tell him personally what a "big part his 'liberated' Scotch had played in the Corregidor operation."

2. Details of Private Lloyd G. McCarter's heroics were provided the author by Medal of Honor historian Lou Varrone. McCarter, who had attended Gonzaga University on a football scholarship, received America's highest decoration for his exploits on Corregidor. One of his wounds was a bullet imbedded close to his heart that could not be removed. For the remainder of his life this caused McCarter periodic agony. His wife died in 1952 and, despondent over this loss and his increasing physical pain, he took his own life.

Chapter 23: Holocaust at Monkey Point

1. In 1985, Harry Drews was living in Mount Carmel, Illinois. Despite an artificial leg as the result of the Corregidor episode, he has led a productive and active life.

2. In 1956, Andrew Amaty and wife Ginny attended a wedding recep-

tion where a guest, learning that Amaty had been with the 503rd Parachute Infantry, told Ginny that he had been a radio man on an offshore destroyer at Corregidor. The former Navy man told of a conversation he had had one night "with some crazy paratrooper who kept demanding that our destroyer keep firing flares." Ginny Amaty pointed to her husband and said, "This is the 'crazy paratrooper.'"

3. An acetylene torch was borrowed from a destroyer and the Sherman tank was cut open. Only one crew member was alive.

4. In 1985, General George Jones told the author, "The Monkey Point experience was by far the saddest moment of my military career. Just thinking about it brings me grief even today."

Chapter 24: "Sir, I Present Fortress Corregidor."

1. Whitney, *MacArthur*, p. 154.
2. Ibid., p. 154.
3. General George Jones told the author early in 1986 that he had felt "immeasurable relief" when MacArthur strolled back out of Malinta Tunnel.

Epilogue

1. Manchester, *American Caesar*, p. 362.

Principal Participant Interviews and Contacts

Andrew J. Amaty, Colonel Robert M. Atkins (Ret.), John E. Bartlett, Major General William E. Blake (Ret.), Rear Admiral John D. Bulkeley, Colonel Henry A. Burgess (Ret.), James Drewes, Lieutenant General Edward Flanagan (Ret.), Edward T. Flash, David Foster, Jesse B. Gandee, Colonel Robert W. Garrett (Ret.), Colonel Henry W. Gibson (Ret.), Walter Gonko, Johnny Grooms, Rear Admiral John Harllee (Ret.), Park A. Hodak, Roy Hollingsworth, Dr. Logan Hovis, Paul A. Hughart.

Brigadier General George M. Jones (Ret.), Colonel Edward H. Lahti (Ret.), Karl H. Landes, Donald Lundy, Colonel Kenneth Murphy (Ret.), Major Rocco Narcise (Ret.), Bernard M. O'Boyle, Major General George Pearson (Ret.), Father John Powers, Robert W. Prince, Thomas J. Quatro, Major John B. Ringler (Ret.), Richard Sibio, Thomas J. Smith, Lieutenant General John J. Tolson III, Leroy Tolson, James B. Vignola, Jerard Vlaminck.

Selected Bibliography

Barbey, Daniel E. *MacArthur's Amphibious Navy.* Annapolis: Naval Institute Press, 1969.

Brown, Anthony Cave. *The Last Hero.* New York: Times Books, 1982.

Clark, Ronald. *The Man Who Broke Purple.* Boston: Little, Brown, 1977.

Costello, John. *The Pacific War.* New York: Rawson Wade Publishers, 1981.

Craig, William. *The Fall of Japan.* New York: Dial Press, 1967.

Duus, Masago. *Tokyo Rose.* New York: Harper & Row, 1979.

Eichelberger, Robert L. *Our Jungle Road to Tokyo.* New York: Viking, 1950.

Fahey, James J. *Pacific War Diary.* Boston: Houghton Mifflin, 1963.

Falk, Stanley L. *Decision at Leyte.* New York: W. W. Norton, 1966.

Gunther, John. *The Riddle of MacArthur.* Boston: Houghton Mifflin, 1975.

Halsey, Fleet Admiral William F. *Admiral Halsey's Story.* New York: McGraw-Hill, 1947.

Hoyt, Edwin P. *Battle of Leyte Gulf.* New York: Weybright and Talley, 1972.

Ind, Allison. *Allied Intelligence Bureau.* New York: David McKay, 1958.

James, D. Clayton. *The Years of MacArthur.* Boston: Houghton Mifflin, 1975.

Kenney, George C. *General Kenney Reports.* New York: Duell, Sloan and Pearce, 1949.

Krueger, General Walter. *From Down Under to Nippon.* Washington: Combat Forces Press, 1953.

Leahy, Fleet Admiral William D. *I Was There.* New York: McGraw-Hill, 1950.

Lee, Clark, and Richard Henschel. *Douglas MacArthur.* New York: Henry Holt and Co., 1952.

Luvaas, Jay. *Dear Miss Em.* Westport, Connecticut: Greenwood Press, 1972.

MacArthur, General of the Army Douglas. *Reminiscences.* New York: McGraw-Hill, 1964.

Manchester, William R. *American Ceasar.* Boston: Little, Brown, 1978.

Morison, Samuel Eliot. *The Liberation of the Philippines.* Boston: Little, Brown, 1969.

Morton, Louis. *The Fall of the Philippines.* Washington: U.S. Army, 1953.

O'Neill, Richard. *Suicide Squads.* New York: St. Martin's Press, 1981.

Romulo, Carlos P. *I Saw the Fall of the Philippines.* New York: Doubleday, Doran & Co., 1943.

Reel, A. Frank. *The Case of General Yamashita.* Chicago: University of Chicago Press, 1949.

Schultz, Duane. *Hero of Bataan.* New York: St. Martin's Press, 1981.

Smith, Robert Ross. *Triumph in the Philippines.* Washington: U.S. Army, 1963.

Toland, John. *The Rising Sun.* New York: Random House, 1970.

Valtin, Jan. *Children of Yesterday.* New York: The Readers' Press, 1946.

Volckmann, Col. Russell W. *We Remained.* New York: W. W. Norton, 1954.

Wainwright, General Jonathan M. *General Wainwright's Story.* New York: Doubleday & Co., 1946.

Whitehouse, Arch. *Espionage and Counterespionage.* New York: Doubleday & Co., 1964.

Whitney, General Courtney. *MacArthur: His Rendezvous With History.* New York: Alfred A. Knopf, Inc., 1956.

Willoughby, General Charles A. *MacArthur, 1941–1951.* New York: McGraw-Hill, 1954.

Wolfert, Ira. *American Guerrilla in the Philippines.* New York: Simon & Schuster, 1945.

Unit Histories

Anonymous. *Moresby to Manila via Troop Carrier*. Sydney, Australia: Angus and Robertson Ltd., 1945.

Chandler, Melbourne C. *History of the 7th U.S. Cavalry*. Annandale, Virginia: The Turnpike Press, 1960.

Frankel, Stanley A. *The 37th Division in World War II*. Washington: Infantry Journal Press, 1948.

McCartney, William F. *A History of the 41st Infantry Division*. Washington: Infantry Journal Press, 1948.

6th Division, Public Relations section. *The 6th Infantry Division in World War II*. Washington: Infantry Journal Press, 1947.

33rd Division Historical Committee. *A History of the 33rd Infantry Division in World War II*. Washington: Infantry Journal Press, 1948.

Wright, Bertram C. *The 1st Cavalry Division in World War II*. Tokyo: Toppan Printing Co., 1947.

Zimmer, Joseph E. *The History of the 43rd Infantry Division*. Baton Rouge: Army & Navy Publishing Co., 1947.

Booklets

Templeman, Harold. *The Return to Corregidor*. New York: Strand Press, 1977.

Warren, John C. *Airborne Operations in World War II*. Maxwell Air Force Base: USAF Historical Division, 1956.

Reference book

The Medal of Honor of the United States Army. Washington: U.S. Army, 1948.

Periodicals

Collier's, Saturday Evening Post, Time, Life, Bluebook, Chicago Tribune, New York Times, St. Louis Globe-Democrat.

INDEX

MacArthur, Gen. Douglas: in Australia, xv, xvi, xvii; awarded Medal of Honor, 55; characteristics and descriptions, xv, 1, 3, 5, 30, 39, 54–55, 115, 116, 122, 124–25, 126, 260; earlier Army career of, 1, 3, 39, 47, 178; "I shall return!" and its propaganda value, xv, 14, 21, 51; Japanese attempts to kill, 55, 56, 82–83; Japanese commanders tried and executed, 262; New Guinea landings and headquarters, xvii, 3, 8, 28, 33; Pacific command for invasion of Japan, 259, 260; Philippine command, xii–xiv, xiv–xv, 1–3, 7, 16, 49, 55, 166–167, 255; promoted to General of the Army, 115

MacArthur, Gen. Douglas: retaking the Philippines: avenge fall of Bataan and Corregidor, xv, xvii, 3, 7, 9, 14, 49, 51, 178, 179, 180, 192, 254; Corregidor visited, 243, 251, 255–57; espionage and intelligence, 12–16 *passim*, 19, 20, 21, 33, 34, 35, 36, 43, 44, 100, 110; government returned to Filipinos, 253–55; Japanese defense strategy, 78; joint command with Nimitz, xvi, 23–24; Leyte, 39, 41, 45–58 *passim*, 82–85, 88, 106; replaces Mindanao as invasion site, 22, 26, 27, 28, 29, 36; sets foot on Philippine soil and broadcast, 50–52, 53; Luzon and Manila, 115–16, 120–28; 154–55, 157, 166, 167, 253; Mindoro, 83, 84, 100–01, 103, 105; other islands, 258; strategy, 1–9, 24, 27, 28–29, 83–85, 95, 109, 110, 137

MacArthur, Mrs. Douglas (Jean), xiv, 16, 166

McCain, Rear Adm. John S. ("Slew"), 71, 77

McCampbell, Comm. David, 61–62

McCarter, Pvt. Lloyd G., 234

McClintock, Comm. David H., 60, 61

McDaniel, C. Yates, 82

McKnight, Capt. Robert, 195

McLain, James, 207

McLain, Capt. William C., 247, 248

MacNider, Brig. Gen. Hanford, 123

Magsaysay, Capt. Ramon, 127–28

Makapili, 15

Makino, Maj. Gen. Shiro, 67

Malacañan Palace (Manila), 150, 253

Manchuria: POWs held in, 54, 129

Manila: declared an "open city" by MacArthur, 154; declared an "open city" by Yamashita, 141–142; Japanese occupation, 15–21, 25–26, 27–28, 37, 253; retaking, 14, 58, 121–29, 142, 144–67, 253

Manila Bay, 112

Manila Hotel, 16, 166–67

Marquat, Maj. Gen. William, 243

Marshall, Gen. George, xii, 3, 4, 7, 27, 33–34, 55

Marston, Pfc Roy E., 244

Martha, Col. John T., 101

Maryland, 46, 70, 99

Maya, 61

Merrill, Lt. Col. Gyles, 127

Mesereau, Lt. Tom, 176, 177

Midway, Battle of, 245

Mikawa, Adm. Gizo, 37

Miles, Peter, 170

Mills, S/Sgt. Joseph, 244

Mindanao, xiv, 31; considered as return invasion site, 26, 27, 28, 66

Mindoro, 22; retaking, 83, 84, 100–06, 188

Mississippi, 46, 70, 119

Mitscher, Vice Adm. Marc A. ("Pete"), 64, 75

Miyasaki, Lt. Gen. Shuichi, 31

Monaghan, 104

Montpelier, 99, 119, 191

Ulvert H. Moore, 112–13

Morris, Sgt. C. C., 197

Moses, Lt. Col. Martin, 14–15

Moulton, Lt. H. Douglas, 67

Mount Olympus, 118

Mower, Sgt. Charles E., 80

Mucci, Lt. Col. Henry A., 130–34, 136

Mudge, Maj. Gen. Verne D., 56, 57, 142, 154, 160, 180, 253

Muller, Lt. Col. Henry J. ("Butch"), 170

Mullins, Maj. Gen. Charles L., 124–24

Murphy, Lt. John F., 130, 131, 132

Murphy, Capt. Kenneth A., 91, 92–93

Musashi, 60, 64–65, 69

Mydans, Carl, 115, 143, 149–50